The Waiting Land

A Spell in Nepal

DERVLA MURPHY

ELAND

London

First published in England by John Murray in 1967
First published by Eland Publishing Limited
6 Exmouth Market, London EC1R 4QL in 2011

Text © Dervla Murphy 1967

ISBN 978 1 906011 65 9

Cover Image:
Kathmandu, Nepal, 1980 by Steve McCurry
© Steve McCurry/Magnum Photos
Printed in Spain by Graphycems

Contents

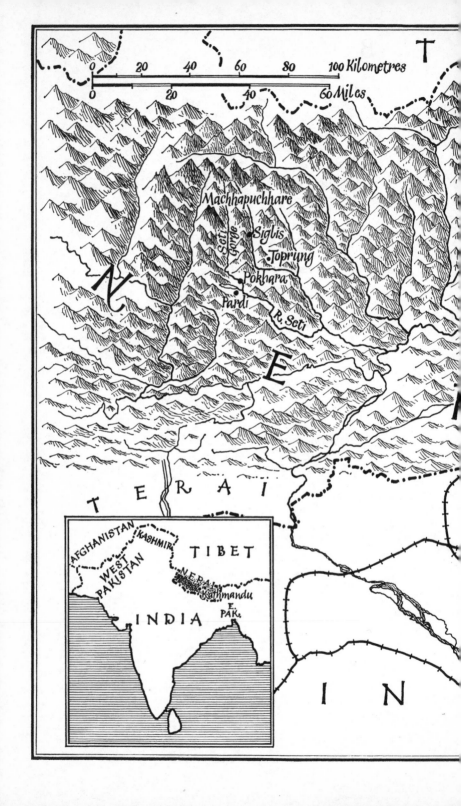

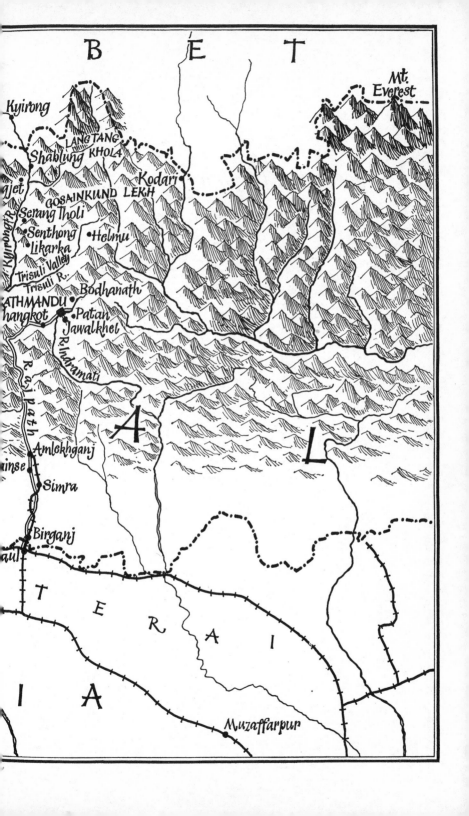

*To Brian, Daphne, Robin
and Peter with love*

Prologue

My six months among the Tibetans in 1963 had shown me that many refugees do not deserve the haloes with which they have been presented by sentimental fund-raisers in Europe or America. But by the time one has been disillusioned by Tibetans one has also been captivated by them; though unpleasant individuals and events may demolish the idealised version there remains an indestructible respect for the courage, humour and good manners that mark most Tibetan communities.

Before leaving India, early in 1964, I had determined to come back to the Tibetans as soon as possible. However, refugee situations can change quickly and by the spring of 1965 conditions in India had improved so much that nothing really useful remained to be done by an untrained volunteer, and I felt that it would be wrong to inflict on the Tibetans yet another aimless 'Tib-worshipper'. But then came an item of news from Nepal concerning a recently-formed refugee camp in the Pokhara Valley, where 500 Tibetans were living as family units in 120 tents with only one Western volunteer to help them. It was considered that here I would at least not be in the way, even if my limitations prevented me from achieving much, so on 5 April 1965 I flew from Dublin to London to prepare for the journey to Nepal.

In contrast with my January 1963 departure from Ireland that flight seemed sadly drained of adventure; but my wanderlust revived next day when I went to the Royal Nepalese Embassy to apply for a visa. There I was presented with a leaflet headed 'A Guide to those who intend to visit Kathmandu, capital of Nepal', and with a booklet – poorly printed in Kathmandu for the Department of Tourism –

entitled *Nepal in a Nutshell*. The leaflet announced with rather touching inaccuracy that, 'The best months to visit the valley are February-April and September-November. The rest of the months are either very wet or too cold'; but the booklet truthfully claimed that 'The cold season is pleasant throughout Nepal with bright sunshine and blue skies' – and at once I warmed to this bewildered country which couldn't make up its mind how best to sell itself to fussy tourists. Then, reading on, I found a still more endearing statement to the effect that 'The fascination of Biratnagar lies in its picturesque spots and industrial areas. Biratnagar has some of the largest industrial undertakings in Nepal'. Somehow it is difficult to believe that those travellers who are fascinated by 'industrial undertakings' would ever go to Nepal to gratify this particular passion.

On the booklet's first page Tibet was referred to as 'the Tibet Region of China' – a politic 'siding with the boss' which would have infuriated me were I not so aware of Nepal's terror lest she should herself soon become 'the Nepal Region of China'. Merely to glance at a map of Asia reveals the uncertainty of the kingdom's future; it is a slender strip of land squeezed between Chinese-controlled Tibet and a decreasingly neutral India, and already a mysteriously-motivated Communist army is arrayed along its northern frontier. Some experts argue that the Central Himalayas are themselves defence enough against any army and that a south-bound Chinese invasion force would always have the good sense to skirt Nepal; but the Nepalese Government has not forgotten how cunningly Tibet was subdued within a decade and at present Nepal's diplomats and politicians are almost dizzy from their efforts to placate simultaneously both East and West.

On 13 April I spent two very interesting and instructive hours at the Nepalese Embassy's New Year party. *Nepal in a Nutshell* had informed me that 'The State was integrated by King Prithvi Narayan Shah the Great in 1769', but now I began to realise that Nepal's nationhood is a very artificial thing. For all the tempering influence of a London social function it was soon clear that the various groups to whom I talked represented a basically tribal society which has only recently acquired the ill-fitting political garments of a modern state. The mistrust, jealousy and dislike of one ethnic and religious group for another showed through repeatedly, and it was interesting to compare the suave, astute Ranas and the ambitious, slightly arrogant Chetris with the inarticulate but gay little Gurungs and the poised, cheerful Sherpas of Tibetan descent. One wonders if there will be time to weld all these dissimilar tribes into a truly united nation before either the Chinese or the Americans annihilate every ancient Nepalese tradition. It seems regrettable that any such welding process should be considered necessary, but perhaps only thus can Nepal hope to preserve her independence.

The flight to Delhi was a mixed experience. We left London Airport at 4.15 p.m. on 21 April and, as always, I resented the slickness of flying and felt too nervous to sleep. As we flew over Erzurum and Tabriz I remembered 'the old days', when I had cycled on Roz through that region, and inevitably I experienced an acute sense of anti-climax.

Then came an uncannily beautiful descent to Teheran. At a height of five miles the engines were suddenly switched off and we began to glide soundlessly down, down, down through the darkness; to look out then and feel the silence and see the gigantic length of wing in a faint shimmer of moonlight gave me the fairy-story illusion of being carried along by some monstrous, softly sailing moth.

Here I disembarked – for Auld Lang Syne – and unmistakably I was back in Asia, where air hostesses mix their passenger lists and then fly off their nests in a delightfully unprofessional way. At European airports hostesses are trim machines who rarely muddle anything and scarcely register on a passenger's mind as fellow-beings: but here they are girls who flush with anxiety and snap angrily at each other because all the passengers bound for New York were very nearly sent to Hong Kong.

When we emerged on to the tarmac two hours later the sky was paling above the mountains and, as we climbed, the stark symmetry of Demavand soared high and proud above hundreds of lesser peaks – a flawless blue cone against a backdrop of orange cloud; and immediately beyond stretched the Caspian, its metallic flatness oddly surprising at the base of the mountains.

One has to admit that just occasionally flying provides beauty of a quality otherwise unattainable. Below us now a scattered school of porpoise-shaped cloudlets lay motionless and colourless in the void; and down on that plain which Roz and I had traversed en route to Meshed several tiny lakes were looking weirdly like pools of blood as they reflected the pre-sunrise flare. We had regained our normal cruising altitude when a crimson ball appeared so suddenly above the horizon that it seemed to have been flung over the earth's rim by an invisible hand – and momentarily I was too taken aback to recognise this object as the sun. Then it climbed – so rapidly that one could *see* it moving – until the sky above the horizon was pale blue, shading off, because of our altitude, to an extraordinary navy blue at the zenith.

We soon turned south, and now the Great Desert below us was covered in cloud so that one looked down on a limitless expanse of grotesque white softness, in which were visible broad 'valleys' and narrow 'gorges' and 'mountains' that threw shadows as real mountains would in early sunshine – the whole 'landscape' exquisitely distorted and eerily immobile, as though all that vapour were frozen solid.

At 5.45 a.m. we touched down at Palam Airport. In a desperate effort to retain some grip on reality I had kept my watch at Greenwich Mean Time, but now I put it on to 10.15 a.m., before staggering out into the dusty glare. Luckily the day was 'cool' (only eighty-five degrees Fahrenheit in the shade) though coming from forty-four degrees in London I can't say it felt particularly cool to me.

As the rickety old airport bus rattled and blared its way along the narrow road to New Delhi I was conscious of an extraordinary sense of peace. When we were approaching Connaught Circus, through the usual tangle of loaded cyclists, ambling buffaloes, sleek cars, lean pedestrians and bouncing, Sikh-driven 'chuff-chuffs', I tried to define what I was feeling – but could only think of it as the peace of poverty. People may jeer at this phrase as romantic nonsense, yet to arrive suddenly in India after a fortnight's immersion in an affluent society does induce a strong sense of liberation from some intangible but threatening power. One is aware of man being free here, at the deepest level, as he cannot possibly be in societies where elaborately contrived pressures daily create new, false 'needs', and wither his delight in small and simple joys.

At Dharamsala, where I had previously worked in the Tibetan Refugee Nursery, it was a joy to see how enormously conditions had improved since my departure. Pema Janzum, the younger sister of His Holiness the Dalai Lama, is now running the camp, and her intelligence, common sense and flair for leadership have transformed the place from a squalid, disease-ridden inferno to a model nursery full of bouncing, rosy-cheeked Tiblets.

Since 1961 the Dalai Lama himself has been living in a heavily guarded bungalow quite close to the Nursery. His residence is usually given the courtesy title of 'Palace', though in fact it is far from being palatial – which no doubt pleases its simple occupant, even if the refugees are saddened to see 'Yishy Norbu' living at such a remove from the splendours of the Potala.

On the morning after my arrival His Holiness generously consented to receive me in audience and I found the change in him scarcely less remarkable than the change in the camp. During my first audience, sixteen months earlier, he had given me the impression of being a little unsure of himself and remaining rather on his guard against foreign observers; but now he seemed much more confident and relaxed, and this meeting felt less like an audience than a discussion between two people with an absorbing mutual interest. Our conversation centred on the problems of the refugees in Nepal, where the political difficulties of the host country create many special complications, and as we talked I realised that it would be impossible for me to enter in my diary and send through the post any detailed accounts of our work at Pokhara Camp. In this sort of situation what may appear to be minutiae can on occasions have the most disconcerting significance.

After two happy days at Dharamsala I went on to Mussoorie – a sixteen-hour journey by bus, train, bus and finally a shared taxi from

Dehra Dun. On leaving the taxi at the edge of the town the first person I saw was Jigme Taring, a Tibetan-Sikkimese prince who runs the co-educational six-hundred-pupil Tibetan school and prefers to be known as a 'Mister'. During my previous visit to Mussoorie he had been away in Sikkim, but though we had never met we simultaneously recognised each other and drove together to Happy Valley, the appropriately-named centre of the local Tibetan community.

For all his illustrious ancestry Jigme Sumchan Wang-po Namgyal Taring is a typical Tibetan – simple and gentle, with a keen intelligence and a tremendous sense of humour. He and Mrs Taring, who runs the Tibetan Homes Foundation, illustrate the best side of feudalism; they feel that the thousands of peasants in exile are partly their responsibility – a logical view, though one that is uncommon among rich Tibetan exiles.

The Tarings' Lhasa residence was near the Potala and during the shelling of the Palace, in March 1959, it too was partially demolished. Their first-hand account of the Lhasa Insurrection interested me greatly because, on reading the Gelders' book, *The Timely Rain*, it had seemed to me that among the authors' few plausible arguments was one supporting the Chinese claim that the Potala had *not* been heavily shelled. Yet Mr Taring, who was then C-in-C of the Tibetan Army, has a cine-film of the actual shelling, taken by himself before he left the capital. As Mrs Taring quietly pointed out, he had obtained this film at the risk of his life, realising how effectively it could counteract Chinese propaganda and foreseeing its future historical value.

When His Holiness left the Summer Palace on 17 March Mr Taring remained behind for two days, to help delude the Chinese into believing that the Dalai Lama was still there. Then he set out on foot for the Indian frontier with one companion – the Tarings' present cook. Meanwhile Mrs Taring had fled on horseback, also with one manservant, and months passed before either knew that the other was safe.

It is significant that both Tarings unquestioningly followed His Holiness into exile, making no attempt to rescue their children and grandchildren. On first hearing their escape story, two years ago, I was privately a little shocked by this 'desertion', since in similar circumstances most Europeans would choose to stand by their nearest and dearest. Yet after several hours' conversation with the Tarings one realises that to them His Holiness *is* their 'nearest and dearest' – not as an individual, but as the living vessel containing the Spirit of Chenrezig. Therefore their sacrifice of family loyalties to his needs was a form of religious martyrdom; they each knew that in exile he would require guidance from those few Tibetans who have received a Western education but who still retain a religious faith as strong as that of the simplest peasant.

The most remarkable characteristic of Tibetan Buddhists is their freedom from bitterness against the Chinese. Despite the emotional scars discernible beneath the Tarings' courageous good humour neither shows the faintest flicker of hatred or anger when discussing the past; indeed they shrink from such reactions on the part of less spiritually disciplined Westerners like myself, who in this context cannot help but utter some impulsive condemnations. The manner in which most Tibetans distinguish between wrong actions and the individuals performing them – with whom they seem to sympathise as fellow-victims of Evil – made me uneasily aware of the immaturity of our susceptibility to petty propaganda.

In Mussoorie the Tarings occupy one large room, partitioned by a curtain into bedroom and living-room, which is rather less comfortable than many of the Homes run by Mrs Taring for Tiblets. The rest of this house accommodates some of the teaching staff, plus seventy-two small children. After we had gone to bed one of the children began to cry and at once Mr Taring hurried to investigate; he and Mrs Taring take it in turns to do 'night duty' in addition to working at least twelve hours a day seven days a week. My own room was a tiny cubbyhole, containing nothing but a charpoy, and it soothed me to observe such unusually austere standards being upheld by workers among the refugees.

The Iron Road to Rexaul

I'm now sitting in the Railway Ladies' Waiting Room being almost asphyxiated by the stench of stale urine and surrounded by recumbent Ladies. Some are on the floor on bedding-rolls, others are lying on lumpy Victorian couches and two are curled up on the table, their saris drawn over their faces. At present I'm conscious only of being in *a* Railway Waiting Room, enduring its unique combination of aesthetic repulsiveness, physical discomfort and powers of suspending mental animation. Notice-boards tell me I'm in Muzaffarpur, but I could as easily believe myself to be in Waterford or Milan.

The twenty-nine-hour journey from Dehra Dun was brief by local standards, yet it was by far the longest train-ride of my life and seemed decidedly penitential. The fare (one pound eight shillings and four-pence all the way to Nepal) covered reservation of a slatted wooden shelf, on which I slept quite well last night, but by morning a gale-force wind was whipping a dust-storm across the endless, arid, grey-yellow plain, and this diabolical torture by Nature continued until dusk. Visibility was down to about a hundred yards, the hot sky was sullen with dust, and dust and sweat formed a mask of mud on my face. All morning I sat in a semi-coma, reflecting that at last I was experiencing *real* hardship; compared with such a journey cycling to India is just too easy.

However, the worst was yet to come. At Lucknow I changed trains and found myself sharing an eight-seater compartment with seventeen Gurkha soldiers going home on leave. Each was carrying a vast amount of kit and initially it seemed a sheer physical impossibility for all of them to enter the compartment; yet it's not for nothing that the Gurkhas have won so many VCs and enter it they did, bravely disregarding the possibility that we would all suffocate to death long before the journey ended. At first they had appeared to be slightly nonplussed by the sight of a dishevelled Memsahib in one corner, but they rapidly decided that I was best ignored and within seconds I found myself nine-tenths buried beneath a pile of bed-rolls, haversacks, wicker baskets and tin trunks. This pyramid was then scaled by two nimble little Gurungs, who expertly inserted themselves into the crevice between the top-most trunk and the roof and immediately began to dice and smoke, dropping unquenched cigarette ends onto my head at regular intervals. I don't doubt that the Gurkhas are a wonderful people, but somehow today I never really managed to appreciate them.

Then, soon after dusk, my luck changed. When we stopped at a junction I strenuously effected an earthquake in the carriage, bringing Gurungs and trunks mildly to grief as I fought my way out through the window. No one had told me where to change trains and as it was now essential to find out I went hobbling anxiously down the platform, every muscle knotted with cramp, in search of some knowledgeable-looking individual. Having questioned three officials, who each indicated that they couldn't care less whether I ended up in Calcutta or Kathmandu, I was enormously relieved to come upon an Englishwoman strolling along the platform beside the first-class carriages. She at once assured me that I did not have to change until Muzaffarpur – and then we began to discuss our respective destinations. When the Englishwoman mentioned that she was returning to Dharan I said, 'Then you must know Brigadier Pulley?' (to whom I had a letter of introduction) and she exclaimed, 'But I'm his wife!' A moment later the Brigadier himself appeared and, when everyone had made the appropriate remarks about the dimensions of the earth, the Pulleys very kindly invited me to continue my journey in their air-conditioned coach. By then my addiction to 'travelling rough' had been so thoroughly – if temporarily – cured that it was difficult for me to refrain from hugging my benefactors.

It is now only 1.45 a.m. and the daily train for Rexaul, on the Nepalese frontier, does not leave until 6 a.m.; but I'm afraid to sleep lest I should fail to wake in time.

30 APRIL – REXAUL RAILWAY STATION RETIRING-ROOM – 9 P.M.

This pedantically-named apartment – no doubt a verbal relic of the era when trains were introduced into India – is equipped with two charpoys, a lukewarm shower and a defunct electric fan; but despite this wealth of refinements I now feel irremediably allergic to everything even remotely associated with railways.

Today's hundred-mile journey on a narrow-gauge track took eight blistering hours. The elderly engine was falling asunder and at each village it stopped, lengthily, to pull itself together before moving at walking speed to the next village. Also it killed a young man; but no one took much notice of this grim sight and we were only delayed ten or fifteen minutes longer than usual. The police did not appear (perhaps there are none in these remote villages) and one gathered that the event was unimportant. My Nepalese neighbour told me that it was probably a case of suicide, as people with family or financial troubles frequently throw themselves under trains; and this seemed a likely explanation, since our snail-paced engine could hardly take anyone unawares.

This morning, on the platform at Muzaffarpur, I met an Irish boy named Niall who was travelling to Kathmandu with a Swiss youth named Jean and an American girl rather disconcertingly known as Loo. Loo had recently arrived in India on a round-the-world air trip, and had been persuaded by the boys, against her own better judgment, to sample life in the raw by going overland to Nepal. She spent most of today pointing out just how much better her own judgment was, and though recriminations seemed futile at that stage one could see her point of view.

Certainly life cannot be much rawer anywhere than it is in these villages of Bihar. Throughout the Punjab one rarely encounters that extremity of poverty traditionally associated with India – but here one does. And, as the hot, squalid hours passed slowly, I began to take a more lenient view of our affluent society. The people all around us seemed inwardly dead, mere mechanically-moving puppets, their expressions dulled by permanent suffering. To look at their bodies – so malformed, starved and diseased – and to sense the stuntedness of their minds and spirits made me feel quite guilty about helping Tibetans when so many Indians are in such need. Yet one doubts if Indians ever can be helped in the sense that Tibetans can. Apart from the vastness of their current material problem the very nature of the people themselves seems stubbornly to defy most outside attempts at alleviation.

Rexaul is a smelly, straggling little border-town, overpopulated by both humans and cattle. It has an incongruous air of importance, since all the Kathmandu truck-traffic passes through its streets, yet its cosmopolitanism is limited. When I went to the Post Office – a dark wooden shack – to airmail the first instalment of this diary to Ireland my request caused unprecedented chaos. To begin with, registration was not permissible after 4 p.m. and it was now 5.30; however, when I had flatteringly explained that I wanted to post from India rather than Nepal the senior clerk consented to make an exception to this rule. But then came the knotty problem of deciding where Ireland was – and the even knottier problem of determining the airmail registration fee for such an outlandish destination. In the end no fewer than seven men spent twenty minutes working it all out, consulting thick, fly-blown volumes, weighing and re-weighing the package on ancient scales of doubtful accuracy, checking and re-checking interminable sums on filthy scraps of paper and finally laboriously copying the address, in triplicate, on to the receipt docket – with hilarious results, since even intelligent Europeans often find my handwriting illegible. I suppose it *is* possible that the package will eventually arrive on the Aran Islands, but one can't help having horrible doubts.

1 MAY – KATHMANDU

The ninety-mile Tribhuvan Rajpath, named after King Mahendra's father, was built by Indian engineers during the 1950s. At present it is Nepal's only completed motor-road – though the Chinese are working hard on an uncomfortably symbolic continuation of it from Kathmandu to Lhasa – and it must be one of the most remarkable engineering feats in the world. Yet the Rajpath's inexplicable narrowness (or is this defect perhaps explicable in strategic terms?) means that trucks are often rammed against cliffsides by other trucks, or go skidding over precipices in successful but unrewarding attempts to avoid head-on collisions. However, the art of truck-driving is only nine years old in Nepal, so perhaps it is not surprising that most drivers apparently long for a rapid reincarnation; doubtless the next generation will have learnt that too much rakshi does not aid the safe negotiation of six hairpin bends per mile.

In view of the Rajpath's reputation it is understandable that trucks are forbidden to carry foreigners. A high mortality rate among visitors might be bad for the tourist trade, so in theory all foreigners use the senile bus that leaves Rexaul daily at 6 a.m. But the bus fare is Rs. 16/- while the truck fare is only Rs. 8/-, and therefore many travellers blithely ignore the illegality of trucks. Fortunately the border police also ignore it, or perhaps are unaware of the law's existence – an anomaly that would be typical of this deliciously topsy-turvy land.

This morning we left the railway station at six o'clock and walked the two miles to the border. The next three hours were spent wandering in and out of tumbledown customs, police and passport offices, where courteous but clueless officials entertained us to innumerable glasses of tea while trying to make up their minds exactly *why* they wanted to interview us. One felt that this profusion of bureaucratic formality was a game, since none of these men seemed to comprehend the nature of his job clearly enough to take it seriously. The whole performance appeared to be part of Nepal's sudden attempt to get 'with it', after centuries of deliberate isolation, and over all those glasses of tea the stiff, alien formalities spontaneously blossomed into flexible, indigenous informalities.

The Nepalese expertly elude the tyranny of Time simply by refusing to allow it to affect any of their actions. We waited endlessly for everything: for glasses of tea to be carried on trays from the bazaar, for a policeman's bunch of keys to be fetched from his home down the road, for an adjustable rubber stamp which would not adjust to be dissected (and finally abandoned in favour of a pen), for a Passport

Officer to track down Ireland (whose existence he seriously questioned) in a dog-eared atlas from which the relevant pages had long since been torn, and for the Chief Customs Officer, who was afflicted by a virulent form of dysentery, to withdraw to a nearby field between inspecting each piece of luggage.

To me all this was enjoyably relaxing and precisely what one expects at a Nepalese border-post – though I suspect that these dilatory methods will twang on my nerves when I am encountering them daily. But unfortunately my companions reacted adversely to this subjugation of Time, and the Nepalese were bewildered to find that neither their conversation nor their tea could begin to compensate for so many 'wasted' hours. In the end I felt thoroughly ashamed of Loo's querulous impatience, Jean's contemptuous sneers and Niall's ill-tempered commands – none of which had the slightest speeding-up effect on the Nepalese. Yet no doubt I myself will behave equally badly on occasion during the next few months.

When at last we were freed we walked another mile or so to the little town of Birganj and there, after much playing-off of drivers one against another, we secured seats in the back of an almost empty truck.

By now the sun's rays were fierce and we had no protection against them as we covered the next twenty miles. This section of the Terai has been spoiled by the railhead and road, and as nothing of interest lay on either side I was all the time eagerly looking north; but the heat haze restricted visibility, and only on approaching the village of Bhainse could one see that gigantic mountain barrier which here rises so suddenly and splendidly from Northern India's eternity of flatness.

At Bhainse we stopped outside an eating-house, and without bothering to replace my boots I hopped out of the truck into the welcome shadow. Loo declined any refreshment, after one shuddering glance around the mud-floored, fly-infested interior, but the rest of us enjoyed piles of rice moistened by dahl and curds – with a very hot curry for the driver. Here the devastating poverty of Bihar was no longer apparent, though otherwise there was little to distinguish these people from their Indian neighbours; only the style of domestic architecture (already some Newari influence was evident) indicated that we had entered Nepal.

When the driver had demolished his Everest of rice he told us to wait in the eating-house, and twenty minutes later I had to walk half a mile, barefooted, to rejoin the truck beyond a tollgate. By now the sun was directly overhead and melting tar on the road forced me to cover this distance by running about ten paces, sitting down to get my agonised feet off the tar, jumping up when my behind became equally agonised – and so on … and on … and on. The locals were vastly amused at this spectacle; but oddly enough the humour of the situation escaped me.

From Bhainse – which is almost at sea level – the road climbed steadily over the Churia and Chandragiri mountains, crossing a pass of more than 8,000 feet. On every side the slopes and crests were heavily wooded and freshly green and this abrupt ascent seemed most dramatic in contrast to the dead plains which stretch from Dehra Dun to Bhainse. At one point we could see below us the *twelve* hairpin bends which we had rounded on our way up that particular mountain, and often the famous cable on which some goods are still brought from India to Kathmandu was visible overhead, its wires spanning the deep valleys from mountain-top to mountain-top. Until we crossed the pass no villages were visible, but at Bhainse the truck had filled up with cheerful, unkempt families who were returning home from marketing trips. These people, bred to walk everywhere, have been very quick to take advantage of the luxury of motor transport.

Even motoring up the Rajpath gives one a sense of achievement, felt on behalf of those Indian engineers and Nepalese coolies – many coolies were killed on the job – who had the brains and the guts to construct a road in direct defiance of the laws of Nature. Most Nepalese believe that the coolies' deaths were caused by enraged mountain-gods and I can sympathise with this view. The Rajpath is a triumphal example of man's ingenuity, but it is also an impertinent defacement and naturally the gods would resent having their mountains so humiliatingly brought to the heel of Progress.

We reached the pass at 3.30 and here the air was tinglingly crisp and keen. To steady our nerves we stopped for tea in a tiny hut near the forest's edge; a few moments earlier, when toiling around the last hairpin bend, we had missed by inches a grossly overloaded jeep taking the corner at top speed.

Our descent to the Palang Valley was more gradual than the upward climb – though hardly less dangerous, for the truck's brakes were not of the best. The two-storey farmhouses scattered around the valley floor looked curiously European, with their curly red tiles and brown brick walls, and they were far more skilfully built than the average dwelling of rural India; I noticed that instead of chimneys square apertures were visible in the gable walls. The people were small, sturdy and gay, and groups of children shouted, waved and laughed as we passed; evidently many of the Nepalese are temperamentally closer to the Tibetans than to the Indians. On all sides this valley was guarded by mountains and, despite the encroachment of 'The Road', it retained an atmosphere of tranquil 'lostness'. Looking at the sunny expanse of cleverly terraced young wheat, and at the high-spirited children and bounding flocks of goats, I was very conscious of being in a new and pleasant country.

When the road began to climb again the nearby mountains became bare walls of reddish clay that reflected the slanting evening light like giant uncut jewels. I felt myself getting more and more excited as we passed the new, neat milestones saying 'Kathmandu 15 miles … 14 miles … 13 miles' – but then suddenly it was dark, and still we were slowly rounding bend after bend, though we had just passed a notice forbidding vehicles to use the Rajpath by night.

At 8.30 p.m. we stopped near the hamlet of Thankot, six miles from Kathmandu, where a tree-trunk on trestles blocks the road outside a Police-Passport-Customs check-post. Now the spice of melodrama filled the air. Our driver – using what can only be described as a hoarse whisper – instructed us to leave the truck quietly, go through the necessary hoops with officialdom, walk on a quarter of a mile and wait for him to retrieve us. We need take only our passports; everything else could safely be left where it was.

At this point my drab European rationality prompted me to wonder what the police would make of four Westerners, equipped only with a passport and two legs apiece, appearing out of pitch darkness on the rim of the Kathmandu Valley and producing visas which declared that they had entered the country a mere ten hours earlier. But at once I reproved my rationality for intruding on this first gay day in Nepal.

The checkpoint was enchanting – a tiny bamboo lean-to, containing an affable character arrayed in pyjamas and armed with a revolver. This officer peered briefly at our visas, by the light of a wick floating in a bowl of grease, and then politely made the required assumption that we had come from Rexaul by magic carpet. However, Loo's native honesty did cause a moment's tension. On being asked if she had cameras, transistors, tape-recorders or binoculars she admitted to one of each and Pyjamas, looking faintly irritated by such candour at so late an hour, dutifully asked her to produce them – whereupon she saw her indiscretion and stared through the low doorway in wild surmise, while the boys and I giggled cruelly. Our driver was in the adjacent tea-house, having something stronger than tea and stolidly feigning not to be acquainted with us, so any attempt to contact him would have been monumentally tactless. But Pyjamas obviously had a quick understanding and a kind heart for now he gestured grandly, saying 'These things are not important' – and immediately we were released, our passports enriched by one more set of convulsed squiggles and solemn seals.

From Thankot the downhill road to Kathmandu was lined with flowering bottle-brush trees, and by the light of the head-lamps their long scarlet blossoms formed glowing curtains of colour on either side. I was a little puzzled not to see, somewhere on the valley floor, that shimmer of light which is to be expected after dark from even the least advanced capital city; but I later discovered that this was one of the not infrequent occasions upon which the urban electricity supply had quietly faded away.

It takes only a few moments to drive through the 'suburbs' of Kathmandu and by half-past nine I was standing in the city centre, beside 'Bhim's Folly' – a cigarette-like white tower erected for no apparent reason by Bhim Sen Thapa, that murderously scheming nineteenth-century ruler of Nepal who instigated the Prime Ministerial reign. The area around the Folly is the General Truck Terminal, and therefore the scene of much haggling, arguing and general commotion at all hours of the day or night; in fact it seems to provide the only sign of life in the city after dark. Already Loo and Niall had been led away by Jean, who is familiar with Kathmandu, and I now discovered that – as pronounced by me – the address to which I was going conveyed nothing whatever to any of the surrounding Nepalese. But eventually I observed two young men, clad in semi-Western fashion, who spoke some English and soon fixed me up with a cycle-rickshaw.

Half an hour later I was installed in this dingy but – by Asian standards – wildly expensive hotel. The charge is £1 per night for a large, filthy room, containing only a plank-bed and a roll of bug-infested bedding – and no breakfast will be provided. In itself the dirt leaves me unmoved, since I have survived even greater extremes of filth elsewhere, but the excessive charge moves me deeply. I only hope that it is not a reliable guide to the general cost of living in Nepal.

2

Kathmandu

3 MAY – KATHMANDU

Yesterday began well when I heard after breakfast that Sigrid Arnd – a Swiss friend first met when we were both working in India – is now living here; and last night she most generously invited me to stay in her Jawalkhel home, near Patan, until I leave for Pokhara on 12 May.

Sigrid prefers to live reasonably close to the local level, and she has proved that in this country one can create a very attractive home through an imaginative adaptation of native materials and customs. She rents a two-roomed wing of this three-storey brick house, and the simple living-room – where I'm now sitting – has a low, black, raftered ceiling, whitewashed walls and pale gold matting. Everything in the room is both beautiful and Nepalese, and Sigrid's four-months-old black and silver mongrel puppy is also both beautiful and Nepalese. His name is Puchare ('Tail' in Nepali) and he has an adorable personality, in addition to being a good deal more ornamental than many an effete thoroughbred I've known. The household is completed by Donbahadur, a Newari daily servant who shops intelligently in the bazaar and cooks like an angel. (Many Westerners in Kathmandu won't even walk through the bazaar, much less eat food that has been bought there.) Donbahadur has a bubbling sense of fun, an almost visible integrity and an awe-inspiring but quite effective method of communicating through the medium of Swiss German-cum-English. One senses that the approves Sigrid's appreciation of things Nepalese, which interests me; in India a Memsahib would almost certainly lose face with the servants if she did not maintain entirely European standards.

A small bathroom (with a cold shower but without a bath) and an even smaller kitchen lead off this living-room, while at the back a narrow wooden staircase, to Sigrid's bedroom, is concealed by a cupboard-like device. Outside, in the large, haphazard garden, twin giant poplars stand handsomely in one corner, and at the moment I can see Donbahadur in another corner, baking delicious bread in that mud-stove which is his contribution to the establishment's excellent system of improvisation. Beyond the ten-foot wall enclosing the garden runs a very wavy, very pot-holed and very dusty track, which unfortunately happens to be one of the valley's main roads, linking Kathmandu, Jawalkhel and Patan. At this season the frequent passage of buses envelops the garden in a veil of yellow, suffocating dust; only the tops of these vehicles are visible as they lurch slowly by, so one has the curious illusion of watching ships on a stormy sea.

Tonight, with Sigrid's blessing, Puchare and I will curl up together on a Tibetan carpet; I don't often encounter the perfect hostess who refrains from registering horror at the prospect of a guest sleeping on the floor.

5 MAY

What a lovable little city this is! Each day I enjoy it more, though before coming here I had thought of the place as no more than a stepping-stone to Pokhara. But my vision of the Kathmandu Valley as being only slightly less dire than India was quite false. Of course there are the obvious resemblances – dust, stench, flies, ubiquitous sacred cows and mangy dogs in gutters. Also many of the women now wear either the sari or the *shalwar* and chemise, though the majority of men have retained their distinctive dress of jodhpur-type loose-seated trousers, high-necked tunics flaring out above the knees and jaunty little caps – a reversal of the common pattern in the East, where men are usually the first to abandon the national costume. However, the obvious differences between the two countries are far more important. The ordinary Nepalese seem to be without a trace of the Indians' servility, or their touchiness, or that excruciating national inferiority complex which masquerades so pathetically as a superiority complex. In the past the Nepalese suffered more injustice and cruelty under their own corrupt and unscrupulous rulers than the Indians ever did under the British; but at least they were spared that lethal blow to a country's pride which can be given only by foreign conquerors. All the other Westerners to whom I have spoken during the past few days agree with me that on most levels the Nepalese are far easier to get along with than the Indians – which alone would make the atmosphere of Kathmandu much pleasanter than that of New Delhi.

Another of my misconceptions concerned the influence of tourism on the valley. I had pictured it as having been already spoiled by and for tourists, but despite the fact that 'everyone' now comes here, in much the same way as 'everyone' leaves London during the summer, it would be ridiculous, at present, to describe Kathmandu as a Tourist Centre. However, in its outward aspect it is already far less 'exotic and romantic' than one has been led to believe; there are almost as many petrol-pumps as temples, and ugly new buildings are going up everywhere. No one could call it a lovely city, yet there is an abundance of beauty to be found here, and the friendly gaiety and inconsequential craziness of the atmosphere have completely captivated me. This craziness is repeatedly manifested in various Gilbertian ways. When I moved from the hotel to the labyrinthine Youth Hostel at Jawalkhel – one of the many tasteless ex-Rana palaces that litter the valley – I found a multitude of h. and c. taps and some very imposing Western flushes above Eastern latrines; but the nearest water was in the nearest well. Also there is an intriguing urban telephone system, installed by the Americans a few years ago in the fond hope that local activities might thus be speeded up, and to date this innovation has made several quite important contributions to the national muddle. On some days it works only in some areas and on other days it works only in other areas, so the consequent alarms and excursions create far more tension than would ever have to be endured if life were philosophically geared to an absence of telephonic communication. Then there are the foibles of the electricity system. These include switches that have been humorously hidden in the most unlikely corners – at floor or ceiling level, or behind window shutters – and that function, if at all, only after prolonged and highly dangerous manipulation. Because of the current's 'erraticism' everyone keeps a supply of candles at the ready, and this evening, at a meeting of Father Moran's Tibetan Refugee Committee in The Royal Hotel, I noted with joy that amidst so much ornate splendour our conference was being illuminated by two candles stuck on saucers.

Since Nepal was opened to foreigners in 1951 The Royal Hotel has been the centre of what passes for social life in Kathmandu. Officially it is a 'luxury hotel' and as such not at all my line of country; but one soon discovers that here even 'luxury hotels' are purged of their uniformity, and in fact The Royal is as outrageously individual as all other local phenomena. Partly this is due to a ludicrous magnificence, both in the building itself (another ex-Rana palace) and in the Grand Opera décor, which is so gorgeously 'un-with-it' that one is immediately charmed into forgiving its excesses. But mainly the uniqueness of The Royal is due to the personality of Boris, that legendary Russian whom I had already met with delight in so many books and whom I met today, with even greater delight, in person. Undoubtedly Boris belongs to that corps of larger-than-life cosmopolitan eccentrics who have been born to redeem this conforming age, yet to me the most impressive thing about him is his simple kindness. He seems essentially a benevolent rural inn-keeper, rather than the owner-manager of an international hotel, and on his account I fear the more ruthless and practical hoteliers who are now beginning to invade Kathmandu.

At The Royal I was also introduced to Peter Aufschneider and Sir Edmund Hillary. Sir Edmund looks and behaves exactly as one would expect a conqueror of Everest to look and behave, and on shaking hands with him I got a positively schoolgirlish thrill – though it is to be hoped that this was not apparent, since the unfortunate man must be bored almost to extinction by thrilled females. Peter Aufschneider (Heinrich Harrer's companion in Tibet) lives permanently in Kathmandu and now works for the Nepalese Government. He is very shy, modest and likeable – but unfortunately I'm invariably struck dumb on first meeting people who have long been admired from afar, so as a conversational unit we never really got off the ground.

Inevitably The Royal forms a hollow into which all Kathmandu gossip finally trickles and, as much of this gossip concerns the sex-life of various Nepalese royal personages, or of prominent foreign residents, the resulting pond is depressingly murky. But more interesting subjects are occasionally discussed, and here I heard that it is now very difficult to obtain a trekking permit for Northern Nepal. Apparently a certain writer recently took unfair advantage of having been granted such a permit, went to or beyond the Tibetan frontier, took a film of various odd happenings there, wrote about his exploits in European newspapers and generally so upset the Nepalese that they are now thwarting innocent travellers who wish to explore Nepal from no motive other than wanderlust. Personally I know only too well how forbidden frontiers tempt one's juvenile devilry and I have once been guilty of succumbing to their lure; yet out of common politeness to the Governments concerned and for the sake of other travellers one should surely refrain from writing up such incidents – especially in a justifiably jittery country like Nepal. No doubt these regrettable activities near the Tibetan frontier are also partly responsible for the Nepalese Government's ban on further Himalayan expeditions.

Another news item concerned the voluntary return to Tibet, within recent months, of an unspecified number of refugees who had been squatting in Eastern Nepal for the last two years. My informant on this matter was as reliable – within the limitations of the subject – as anyone could be, so I was greatly interested to hear that the uncommitted traders who still travel between Lhasa and Namche Bazaar are bringing reassuring verbal messages from those who returned to their friends in Nepal. The messages say that these ex-refugees find themselves a lot better off in present-day Tibet than they ever were in Nepal and that the Chinese, having secured a firm grip on the country, are now relaxing their first savage pressure. Possibly this news simply represents another victory for Chinese propaganda. The Communists badly need more labourers and I remember hearing, about eighteen months ago, of the Lhasa-printed leaflets then being circulated in India and Nepal, urging the refugees to return to Tibet and guaranteeing them a 'pardon' for their flight into exile. Yet it does seem psychologically probable that the Chinese regime is now evolving from its initial fiercely repressive stage, and I can't help wondering if a return home might not be the happiest solution for many of the Tibetans in Nepal. Whether they are living under the Chinese or in exile it is going to be impossible for them to preserve their ancient religious and social traditions, and in Tibet they would at least enjoy a suitable climate and altitude. I suspect that many Westerners, being unprepared to concede that the Chinese are human beings, would be enraged by this suggestion; yet it does seem a pity to let ideological biases confuse humanitarian issues.

Bicycles are among the main ingredients of Kathmandu traffic, and now I must confess that yesterday I was unfaithful to Roz. I had been advised to buy a bicycle for use in Pokhara (it would of course have to be flown there, as not even a mule-track connects the two valleys), but at first I wasn't very enthusiastic about the idea, having only seen Indian models here and knowing from previous experience how difficult it is to come to terms with these parodies. Then yesterday morning, while wandering through the bazaar, I spotted a likely-looking second-hand Russian cycle, tried it, found it congenial and bought it for £10.16s.8d. (Leo, a brother for Roz). Leo is sky-blue and at least twice as heavy as Roz, but he is beautifully balanced and very comfortable on rough tracks, with his huge, well-sprung saddle and broad tyres. He has a bewildering multiplicity of accessories. None of my previous cycles sported a mirror, foot-brake, milometer, tool-case, carrier, front-wheel dynamo, automatic stand and built-in lock with two keys – in addition to the statutory bell and pump. At present the foot-brake is a menace as I am in the habit of casually back-pedalling when going downhill – but I'll soon get adjusted; and this is only one of the many hazards of cycling in Kathmandu.

The traffic here is predictably unpredictable; trucks suddenly begin to back on top of you without warning, buses simply pretend you aren't there, taxis shave your elbow just for the hell of it, brakeless fellow-cyclists charge you at right angles and jogging porters, carrying pairs of laden baskets on yokes, enjoy abruptly changing course to send their loads swinging into your front wheel. All things considered it seems reasonable to deduce that the Nepalese are a people not yet 'switched on' to wheeled traffic; when I ring my bell before overtaking pedestrians, as likely as not they respond to the warning by joyously bounding across the road without looking left or right. Yet another hazard is the umbrella, which at this season is used as a sunshade. Your Nepalese pedestrian, strolling along with a friend, tends to gesture extravagantly with his umbrella just as one is pedalling past and so far these antics have twice unseated me – indeed, were I not wearing sunglasses I'd probably have lost an eye by now.

Today I realised that for cycling very slowly through crowded bazaars a heavy cycle is undoubtedly best. Roz was not built to move at the pace of meandering cattle, and on her slim tyres one has to dismount repeatedly or fall off; but one can sit on Leo when he's almost stationary, while waiting for the sacred cow and her sacred calf to deign to move out of the way – it's the difference between taking a cart-horse and a thoroughbred through city streets. Naturally I wouldn't exchange Roz for half-a-dozen Leos, but in his way he's sound enough and will keep me happy in Pokhara.

This evening I have a lump like a football on the top of my head; the height of the average Nepalese is five foot three, and local doorways are made accordingly.

7 MAY

There are many things one 'should see' in this valley, but I secretly resent being bossed by guidebooks and am therefore a slipshod tourist. To me the little statue that one unexpectedly discovers down an alleyway, and impulsively responds to, means much more than the temple one had been instructed to admire for erudite and probably incomprehensible reasons; so I just go wandering vaguely around on Leo, finding enough incidental entertainment in the three ancient capitals of Kathmandu, Patan and Bhatgaon.

These 'cities' (by our standards market-towns) were for many centuries the seats of the rival Newari dynasties who ruled and fought over this valley before it was conquered by the Gurkhas in 1769. As a race the Newari had an exceptionally developed aesthetic sense and the ordinary people of the valley seem to have attained an almost freakishly high level of craftmanship, most notably displayed in the bronze or stone temple sculptures and in those intricate weather-worn wood-carvings which adorn so many of the older buildings. If any European city had produced in the past such a concentration of artistic achievement it would long since have been demolished, bombed or self-consciously preserved – and whatever its fate the spirit of its craftsmen would have been well and truly exorcised. But here all this beauty is taken for granted, and its survival has been entirely a matter of chance. Some corners of the cities, where nothing has visibly intruded from another age or civilisation, seem quite powerfully haunted by the force and fervour of those nameless men whose work still lives on every side; and in such corners Time can occasionally slip into reverse, so that one is no longer deliberately reaching back into the past with one's imagination but actually *experiencing* it for a few brief, bewildering moments.

By now these Newari arts and crafts have all declined and the majority of the valley's original inhabitants are petty traders or minor clerks. Some people argue that this is a consequence of Gurkha domination, yet it seems probable that Newari inspiration was already flagging by the eighteenth century and that apathy must in any case have succeeded those rich centuries of enthusiasm.

In many parts of the valley elegance and crudity clash violently – especially where the graceful Newari houses emphasise the ostentatiousness of the Rana palaces. These ugly edifices proliferated during the last century, when the avaricious ruling family were breeding like rabbits and building like beavers, and against any other background they would remain for ever intolerable; yet so strangely does Kathmandu affect one that a certain bizarre charm can be found even in such monstrous mistakes.

Another aspect of Kathmandu's crudity is referred to in *A Winter in Nepal*, where John Morris quotes Dr David Wright, who spent some years here as surgeon to the British Residency and wrote, in 1877, 'From a sanitary point of view Kathmandu may be said to be built on a dunghill in the middle of latrines.' Mr Morris himself found this description still accurate in 1960, and I feel that he was being charitable when he stated that 'this is *one* of the filthiest cities in the world'. (My italics.) In some quarters reeking water lies stagnant in square stone public baths, and I doubted the evidence of my eyes when I first saw people drinking this brew. After the scum has been pushed aside and the liquid – one can hardly describe it as water – has been collected in earthenware or brass pitchers it looks like strong tea; what immunity (or what dysentery) these people must have! Yet despite all this squalor most of the children seem reasonably healthy, though many of their elders have been prematurely aged by a lifetime of carrying unbelievably heavy loads.

There are surprisingly few beggars about, and today I was approached only once – by a small, Murillo-faced boy with whom I became on very good terms *after* I had made it clear that no baksheesh would be forthcoming. Indeed everywhere I went I was greeted with laughter and gestures of friendship, and for me the effervescent happiness of the Kathmandu Valley more than counterbalances its filth.

Today I went to the ramshackle GPO to register some letters, since unregistered mail from Kathmandu rarely reaches its destination. At present a new post office is being built, as part of Indian Aid to Nepal, but I'm glad to have had the singular experience of patronising the old one. The Nepalese have no conception of queuing so one is at once caught up in a loose maul of sturdy little bodies, each with an arm thrust out towards the clerk, in whose face envelopes, money and forms are waved vigorously while requirements are shouted as though by the rules of the game the loudest demands must win. I felt a bully when using my superior height to achieve the necessary victory; but clearly there was no future here in being ladylike.

When the clerk had scrutinised my envelopes he politely asked if London was in Germany. I equally politely said 'No, as a matter of fact it's in England,' and – still thirsting for geographical information – he next enquired if Ireland were one of the United States of America. Having sorted that one out with some difficulty, since neither islands nor oceans meant anything in his young life, I asked him how long he had been a post office employee. (By now the scrum had subsided, as everyone was absorbed in our unintelligible conversation.) He grinned at this question, admitted to having started work only this morning and explained – superfluously – that he had not yet invented a formula for controlling his customers.

Before leaving the building I went into the courtyard to watch the mail being sorted. Here some dozen men were squatting on the ground surrounded by hillocks of envelopes, the majority to or from foreign countries. Between the hillocks the 'plain' was littered with stray envelopes, across which coolies and chickens and dogs and a buffalo-calf wandered casually; I deduced that these were the ill-fated epistles – addressed to obscure places like London – for which no suitable hillock could readily be found. And all the time I was looking wistfully for a few Irish envelopes with green and orange around the edges – but none appeared. Maybe the buffalo-calf had eaten them.

The weather here is much more pleasant than I had expected, with an average midday temperature of only about seventy-five degrees Fahrenheit and a cool breeze blowing almost constantly from the near though invisible snows. Every day since I arrived the sky has suddenly clouded over during the afternoon and an hour or so later we get a magnificent thunderstorm, with bigger hailstones and heavier rain than I've ever seen before: even in India during the monsoon we had nothing quite like it. This is a very satisfactory arrangement, as the rain lays the dust – if only briefly – and slightly lessens the stink by washing away some of the excrement and rotting garbage that accumulates on the streets. Half an hour ago I stopped writing to revel in a truly classic thunderstorm. The first crash made my ashtray leap off the table and literally deafened me, so I blew out the candles and sat at the open window to enjoy the display. Overhead it was as though some mischievous god were switching on and off a brilliant blue electric light which revealed every detail of the garden and neighbouring house. Then the sheet lightning stopped and instead the sky seemed alive with writhing dragons of flame flashing from horizon to horizon, while the thunder roared continuously from mountain to mountain like a million lions – and then the rain came and gradually the storm subsided. I must be getting more and more animistic: this is the sort of thing that now awakens my religious fervour.

8 MAY

At this season a permanent heat-haze veils the Himalayas, and for me one of the most unexpected things about the Kathmandu Valley is its lack of a 'mountain atmosphere'. Nor, I feel, is this merely a temporary effect of climatic conditions for Kathmandu has long been a place apart, isolated from, ignorant of and indifferent to both the outside world and the rest of Nepal. Now the outside world has enthusiastically invaded it, either for pleasure or profit, and it has been forced reluctantly to consider itself in relation to other countries – but it still ignores the mountains.

It is remarkable how the fact of coming to a country to work rather than to explore completely alters one's approach. The always exciting discovery of an unknown land takes on an entirely new texture when one is planning to settle, for however brief a period, and since it is essential to learn to live with local idiosyncrasies the tendency to criticise is blunted. Also, instead of eagerly pursuing knowledge and understanding from the moment of arrival, one waits for them to come, how and when they will. Yet I have to admit that something is missing too – the incomparable thrill of wandering for wandering's sake.

It has been calculated that Nepal has approximately a hundred and twenty national holidays per annum (apart from the fifty-two Saturdays, which are the weekly day of rest) and all these – including the King's birthday, as he is popularly believed to be a reincarnation of Vishnu – are religious festivals. So far I have failed to comprehend even dimly the religion of Nepal, where Hinduism and both schools of Buddhism mingle and subtly interact on each other; but I am consoled by the knowledge that even distinguished scholars go astray in this theological maze and have to end their expositions with a flurry of generalities. However, it *is* clear that the Nepalese are devout adherents to something and their many and much-feared gods are immeasurably more important to them than their politicians – and very likely more useful too. Almost everyone believes implicitly in charms, and astrology determines each important decision, including affairs of state. I often wonder what happens when events belie the astrologers: but no doubt there are well-established formulae to cover up for the stars' mistakes. To us, all this is ignorant superstition in its most extreme form, and the payment of fees to miserly Brahmin priests does keep many families in perpetual debt; yet to the Nepalese these payments are a sensible insurance against disaster.

During the past week the important Machendranath Rath Jatra Festival has been in progress at Patan – about ten minutes' walk from Jawalkhel – and this morning Donbahadur informed us that the astrologers had pronounced six o'clock this evening to be the most auspicious time for drawing the god's two chariots through the streets of the town; so, having arranged to meet Sigrid beside the wooden floats at 5.30 p.m., I went early to Patan to get the feel of the occasion.

On the way I passed through the 'Street of the Pigs', a low-caste quarter where an inconceivable number of tiny black sows lie all over the place suckling an equally inconceivable number of piglets whose size, colour and shape make them indistinguishable from rats. Here, also, dozens of naked children, manure-smeared buffalo-calves, congenitally mangy puppies and grubby chicks are to be seen tumbling around together in filth-blocked gutters, half-filled with inky, glutinous liquid. Most of the higher-caste Nepalese avoid this street – not through any fastidiousness, for their own home area could well be equally unsavoury, but simply because the proximity of pigs would make them ritually unclean. Yet the inhabitants do not seem to be in the least cowed by their inferior social status; they are now used to seeing me passing by, and today quite a few of them leaned from their first-floor windows and shouted greetings, which gave me a warm 'accepted' feeling.

In the small square where the god's chariots were parked a

considerable crowd had already gathered – including many hill-people, some of whom had walked for more than a week to attend the festival. During my first few days at Jawalkhel I had often stopped to watch these chariots being assembled and decorated; each float is surmounted by an unwieldy fifty-foot tower of wood, bamboo and bast, festooned with greenery and long strips of coloured cloth. At the summits fly scarlet flags, and in a shrine at the base of the leading chariot's tower sits Machendranath, one of the 'Grand Magicians' of Buddhist tantrism, who normally lives in the Bungmati Temple, south of Kathmandu. On the night of the full moon preceding this festival he is washed in milk to prepare him for his slow, week-long journey through the city streets – a journey during which he is believed to bestow greater fertility on humans, animals and crops. If either of the towers collapses – as one did in 1953 – this is interpreted as a prediction of bad luck for the coming year, and to lessen the chances of any such collapse all overhead cable wires are cut along the god's route – which perhaps explains why the electric current has been so very erratic during the past week. Within the shrine a Brahmin priest sits in constant attendance on Machendranath, and as the crowd drifts to and fro people pause to bow to the god, and pray for a moment with joined hands, before throwing a fistful of rice or a small coin into the shrine. Each of the floats has two unsteady-looking, giant wooden wheels, on which three big eyes have been awkwardly painted, and a twelve-foot shaft made from a curved tree-trunk. To the outward ends of these shafts, where they curve upward, are tied huge, carved, painted masks – grotesque and gaudy – that grin at the populace with ambiguous expressions in which threats and promises seem intermingled.

When I arrived beside the chariots scores of small boys were doing acrobatic tricks on the shafts, sitting astride the masks, climbing the towers and generally behaving as though this were a funfair rather than a solemn occasion. To the Nepalese Machendranath Rath Jatra is one of their most important religious festivals and this deity is very sacred, very powerful and very easily angered; yet here that subdued sense of reverence which we cultivate towards things sacred is quite unknown, and fear, worship and gaiety flow together as inseparable parts of daily life. Only for a brief, solemn moment, while they show homage, pray and make offerings, do people withdraw from the joyous tumult around them – and when they rejoin it they appear even happier after 'making *puja*'.

Sometimes a strolling musician would pause beside the chariots and play to Machendranath, and when two adolescents spontaneously started a dance near the chariots I hurried to join the circle that was forming around them. These were village lads from the hills, clad in homespun grey tunics, yet they gave an extraordinarily good performance of one of those stately temple-dances that long ago were imported into Nepal from South India. To an initiate every turn of the boys' wrists and flicker of their eyelashes would have been eloquently symbolic; but even uninitiated spectators can enjoy the grace of these slow, formal movements, and I found myself being also very much moved by that strange beauty which so transformed the faces of two quite ordinary boys, as they became more and more absorbed in their chosen way of worshipping the god.

Afterwards I went to sit among a group of Newari women halfway up a flight of temple steps. Within this ancient square were only mellow brick dwellings, semi-ruined pagoda-style temples, their roofs grass-grown, time-damaged shrines of obscure significance, and ornate, sunken baths, where water came gushing from the mouths of brass serpents into the pitchers of local housewives, who then pushed home through the crowd balancing their gleaming pitchers on their hips. By now the sun was just above the curly-tiled roofs, the golden light was soft and one could sense an increasing excitement. With every moment the crowd grew denser and more colourful, and as the women thronged to Machendranath with their handfuls of rice they seemed to create a splendid tidal wave that was tinted red and black, and green and blue, and gold and white.

When at last the auspicious moment came for the chariots to be drawn forward, and their uneven wheels began to roll slowly over the bumpy ground, I was horrified to see the towers' incrustations of small boys remaining defiantly in position. Fortunately others shared my horror, and after a few moments the boys obediently detached themselves and leaped into the crowd.

It now looked as though all the men, women and children of the valley were cramming the narrow streets, filling the overhanging balconies and straddling the roof-tops. Yet as Sigrid and I were directly behind the chariots we could see every detail, including the creamy-coloured, bushy yaks' tails with which Machendranath's Brahmin attendant was being fanned by his acolytes. The extraordinary technique of moving these colossal contraptions through narrow laneways is to attach to each shaft two steel ropes about one hundred feet long, at which scores of men pull and pull, as in a tug-of-war – though facing away from the god – while a drum and cymbal band plays encouragingly beside them, accompanying that curious chant which the men shout in unison before each straining heave on the rope. When at last the chariot has been induced to progress some twenty or thirty yards (it never gets further without a pause) the whole crowd cheers wildly, and Sigrid and I had by now become so involved that we too yelled triumphantly as the cumbersome float groaningly moved forward. Then, as the floats proceeded on their crazy but curiously dignified way, some hundred yards apart, we noticed with alarm that the front 'tower' was becoming more and more unsteady, until it seemed quite likely to go toppling homicidally forward into the crowd. But apparently this threat was familiar, as four men now climbed halfway up the swaying superstructure, from where they released two more ropes, throwing them out behind the float. Another army of men at once manned these and, by hanging on desperately, managed to keep the tower on a comparatively even keel, though the braking effect of this precaution made progress even more difficult.

Now we looked back towards the other chariot and saw that it too was in trouble, of a different sort. One of the gigantic wheels had stuck in a pond of that gluey black mud which is among Kathmandu's specialities and all the efforts of its team of draught-humans were being of no avail. We began to force our way back to see how this problem would be dealt with, but then our attention was violently recalled to the first chariot, and now we really were alarmed. Here the ground sloped slightly downwards for some fifty yards, and the chariot, suddenly becoming unnaturally frisky, was pulling the men on the brake-ropes so strongly that they had to run, while the men in front had panicked a little and were plunging into the crowd on either side. A few people fell and were trampled on slightly, but happily the slope levelled out – or Machendranath relented – before this panic spread. I hate to think what a real panic would have meant; as it was we were being pushed around fairly roughly – not out of any discourtesy, but through sheer necessity – and I felt truly *in* Nepal as I was carried along by that compact mass of sweaty little bodies, all shouting and laughing and pushing and shoving and praying and enjoying.

The god's tour, begun in warm, golden sunlight, ended by the cloud-filtered light of a half-moon. Now tiny lamps were being hung outside each unglazed window to honour the passing god, and we could see into first-floor living-rooms where lanterns, hanging from low rafters, illuminated the little shrine-niches set into the walls. Each finely carved balcony was crammed with exuberant family groups, looking down in comfort on the seething gaiety and fervour in the street and throwing their offerings of rice towards the chariot as it drew level.

When Machendranath had reached his resting place for the night – another temple-filled square – the crowd thinned out, and Sigrid and I returned to investigate the second chariot's situation. We saw at once that it was hopeless: no amount of heaving was going to dislodge the float from its mud-trap, and Donbahadur told us that the astrologers were being severely criticised for having miscalculated the most auspicious moment to begin the procession. He added that perhaps tomorrow a lorry would come to tow the chariot to its companion – a possibility which saddened me, as it seemed to foreshadow the day when the gods would succumb to motor transport.

9 MAY

This morning I paid my third visit to the Swiss-run Tibetan camp here at Jawalkhel, where about four hundred refugees live in one-roomed mud huts roofed with straw. Most of the adults are employed in the Self-Help Handicraft Centre where they make – mainly for export to the West – carpets, coats, sweaters and boots in modified versions of the traditional Tibetan style. Both adults and children appear to be in reasonably good health, despite this relatively low altitude of 4,500 feet, and it does one good to see the families still united, instead of being split up as so often happens in India.

Yet it is becoming obvious to me that all is not well in this Nepalese province of Tibland. Since my arrival I have repeatedly noticed how uneasy is the relationship between helpers and helped – and indeed I had some forewarning of this last month in Dharamsala, where I met hundreds of Tibetans who had recently, and illegally, crossed the frontier from Nepal because of extreme dissatisfaction with conditions here. It seems clear enough that some of their grievances are genuine and that the various relief agencies operating in Nepal have not always avoided those pitfalls which everywhere await workers among the Tibetans. But unfortunately it is equally clear that a 'taking-help-for-granted' attitude is now being developed by many Tibetan leaders, in direct opposition to His Holiness's strongly-expressed wish that the refugees should strive increasingly for independence. One finds among these leaders a spoiled-child petulance if they don't always get what they want – though often their demands are quite unreasonable – and this development is something I foresaw and dreaded more than a year ago. Such an attitude was no part of the Tibland scene as I knew it in India, yet it did seem likely to evolve as a result of the pampering policies adopted by so many relief agencies, and of the deep affection and admiration which the ordinary refugee inspires in his Western helpers – including myself. It was inevitable that the totally unsophisticated Tibetans would eventually be to some extent demoralised by our well-meant but ill-judged mixture of lavishness and adulation; so now we are finding it necessary to use clumsily harsh methods in an attempt to remedy our own mistakes, much as a badly brought-up child might be sent by despairing parents to an extra-strict school. And – understandably – the Tibetans don't quite know what this is all about.

At the Handicraft Centre I met an English-speaking Tibetan youth whom I'd known in India, and after lunch he borrowed a bicycle to accompany me to Bodhanath as my interpreter on an official visit to the Tibetan monastery there. Bodhanath is four miles east of Kathmandu and we stopped for a few moments *en route*, on finding ourselves outside the Pashupatinath Temple – a site which rivals Benares as a place of Hindu pilgrimage. My copy of *Nepal in a Nutshell* had informed me that 'only Hindus are allowed to go inside the courtyard of the Temple', so we stood and stared from the arched entrance at the giant statue of the Golden Bull, who naturally has his back turned on non-Hindus, giving them a splendid view of his world-famous behind – which displays such disproportionately massive testicles that one is tempted irreverently to diagnose mumps. Just to test Pasang's reaction I innocently asked if Christians were allowed to enter Buddhist temples, and looking deeply shocked he said, 'Of course! *Anyone* can enter our temples!' He then asked the man who sat outside the gate, in charge of worshippers' shoes, if Buddhists could enter this Temple: and in defiance of my little guidebook, but in harmony with the liberal traditions of Nepal, the reply was, 'Yes, but only Tibetan Buddhists. Not Chinese' – which seemed to me a very revealing confusion of politics with theology. I rather like the idea that we Westerners, so often condescending, should occasionally be slapped down by Hindu prejudices; yet there seems to be a flat contradiction between the Hindu philosophers' teaching on the Oneness of the Universe and this priestly ban on non-Hindus entering certain temples.

The Bodhanath stupa – on which are painted four pairs of enormous eyes, gazing gravely in the four cardinal directions – is one of the highest Buddhist stupas in the world; one sees it first from afar, across the flat fields, and unlike most religious buildings here it is freshly painted and in good repair. Pasang told me that it is more than 2,000 years old;

but one keeps an open mind on the dates, measurements and general statistics quoted by either Tibetans or Nepalese – though this date may well be accurate enough, since Professor Tucci thinks it possible that Nepal formed part of Asoka's empire in the third century BC.

Bodhanath is now chiefly associated in foreign minds with the rich and influential Chine Lama, a prominent character who is sometimes erroneously described as the Dalai Lama's representative in Nepal – a position that in fact is held at present by a Khampa layman named Sergay. I can think of no two men who are less alike than the Dalai and Chine Lamas; yet foreigners accept him as a bona fide example of a Tibetan lama – which error might be funny were it not so unfair to many thousands of genuine lamas. As Pasang and I cycled towards the monastery around the base of the stupa, past scores of giant copper prayer-wheels set in the circular wall, we saw a Tourist Office mini-bus decanting some dozen wide-eyed visitors outside the Chine Lama's house. Pasang then asked me if I too would like to meet him; but I declined with thanks.

The Bodhanath Tibetan monastery was built about thirty years ago and now houses some forty monks and lamas, ranging in age from a charming sixty-five-year-old Rimpoche to several Incarnate Lamas of eight or nine, who when we arrived were happily scampering around the courtyard in their long, ragged maroon robes. I visited the temple first, with some excitement, being conscious that it was the nearest I'm ever likely to get to a genuine Tibetan temple of the traditional style. And indeed it was as genuinely Tibetan as could be – filthy and magnificent and untidy and awe-inspiring, with gross, ferocious effigies of gods and goddesses lurking in the gloom, swathed in ceremonial white scarves and presiding over the hundreds of *tormas* and wispily luminous butterlamps that had been laid before them. The monks' praying-seats lined the aisle in front of the 'High Altar', facing each other. Some had incongruous tins labelled Farex Baby Food or Andrews' Liver Salts beside them, containing roasted flour for making that *tsampa* on which the monks somehow survive during their long chantings from the scriptures – and when there are a hundred and eight thick tomes to be chanted aloud quite a lot of flour must be required.

Each member of this community has his own cell, and from the temple Pasang and I were conducted to the Rimpoche's quarters – a tiny cupboard of a room, some ten feet by four, with a plank bed, one thin blanket and a miniature shrine where eleven butter-lamps burned before a picture of the Lord Buddha. Here we each consumed five cups of heavily buttered tea – a smiling young lama stood beside us throughout with poised kettle – and reluctantly ate the damp but very expensive Indian biscuits which, despite this monastery's evident poverty, were produced from a tin trunk under the bed.

Here one soon sensed a concentration of all that is best in Tibetan Buddhism – simple, ardent piety, cheerful courage, gentleness, instinctive courtesy and a quick sense of fun. Then, as we talked with the Rimpoche and the four other lamas who had squeezed into his cell, I became painfully aware that now I was glimpsing part of the last act in the drama of a civilisation's history. By the time the young Incarnate Lamas of this community have grown to manhood only a shell will be left of that unique tradition which bred them.

11 MAY

Among the friends I've made here during the past ten days is a nine-year-old schoolboy with one of those beautiful young faces that misleadingly denote an extreme degree of virtue. He is a pupil at St Xavier's College, the big boys' school run by American Jesuits for Nepalese students, and he speaks quite fluent English – as do an astonishing number of middle-class youths in the valley. I first met Rambahadur outside the GPO, where he loiters daily to contact his clients – those foreigners who wish to change money or travellers' cheques on the black market. He came sauntering up to me and said – naturally out of the corner of his mouth – 'Want to change?' and when I replied 'Yes, but not today', he took my hand in his, showing a touching childishness rather at variance with his spare-time profession, and off we went to have a cup of tea together and make mutually convenient arrangements. At his age the ability to conduct shrewd financial transactions has a certain charm, and the necessity to do so a certain poignancy; we quickly became friends when I noticed that he was not a scrounger, but simply worked to earn honest, if illegal, commission, and I arranged to meet him this morning to cash a £50 cheque. However, when I arrived at our New Road rendezvous I found not only Rambahadur but *four* others – two men and two youths – all waiting to capture my custom. Rambahadur looked small, forlorn and scared; but he was evidently going to stand his ground like a good little Gurkha and secretly I had no intention of deserting him. Yet this was my chance to hold an auction and secure a better rate, so I played the five off against each other until, in desperation, Rambahadur promised me Rs. 32/-N.C. to the pound. One of the men (a nasty-looking character) said that he too could get me Rs. 32/- and when I shook my head and held out my hand to Rambahadur the boy was at once knocked into the gutter by a savage blow from his rival. At this I lost my temper and gave the bully a box on the ear, whereupon all four vanished, leaving me to retrieve a sobbing Rambahadur from the gutter. And before my business could be transacted the negotiator had to be consoled and cuddled and mopped up. This incident struck me as typically Eastern: at one moment Rambahadur was a tough man-of-the-underworld, all set to do nefarious deeds down a back-alley, and the next moment he was sobbing in my arms, a big baby with a painful shoulder.

We then turned off New Road, with its would-be Western-style shops, and immediately were amidst that dank maze of narrow laneways which still forms the main part of Nepal's capital. When we came to a small square Rambahadur glanced furtively around, though no one was in sight, before darting through a very low doorway and beckoning me to follow him. The domestic courtyard we now crossed was scattered with stone gods and phallic symbols, but I had no time to study these before being quickly hustled into a pitch-dark interior and led up a steep, shaky wooden stair to a squalid 'bed-sitter', where Rambahadur instructed me to await developments. He then disappeared, locking me in the little room – presumably as a precaution against inquisitive neighbours.

For the next twenty minutes there were no developments. The small window overlooked the courtyard, where a wrinkled, much-bejewelled woman was now scouring brass pots and platters with handfuls of black mud, afterwards rinsing them in sour-looking water. A dejected pi-dog, which had accompanied her, was nosing unhappily at a heap of refuse, and then a tiny naked boy toddled out to make his contribution to the excrement already in evidence – being afterwards called by granny to have his bottom cleaned, also with black mud and water. In general this scene was not uplifting and I soon turned away to observe the interior of the room.

In one corner stood a large, padlocked tin trunk, which I rightly assumed to be the 'safe', and on top of it were piled a number of poorly-printed paperbacks in Nepali, indicating that the money-changer – who of course would also be a trader – had had some education. Several garish Hindu oleographs were pinned to the walls between a large photograph of King Mahendra with Queen Elizabeth II and a TWA picture calendar for 1952. And, presumably as a demonstration of strict neutrality, small photographs of Nehru, Gandhi, Chou-en-lai, President Kennedy and Khrushchev were huddled companionably in a corner by the door.

I had become thoroughly bored by these gentlemen when at last Rambahadur returned with our fellow-conspirator – a lean little Chetri who looked sharp-eyed but honest. Having scrutinised my cheque, passport and various signatures very closely he requested me to write both my local and home addresses in his 'register' – a scruffy exercise book. Then he took the key of the trunk from round his neck, walked to the corner almost ceremoniously and finally, after much muttered counting and recounting, handed me the cash in brand new notes. I couldn't help wondering what practical purpose my credentials could serve in these circumstances; if my cheque were a dud there was no method of legal redress open to him and equally, if his notes were duds, I was debarred from protesting officially. In fact this was the most pleasing part of the transaction: it demanded a high degree of mutual trust – and so far his notes have not been questioned. I also wonder, being conspicuously ignorant about financial matters, how and where such cheques are eventually cashed. It is said that in many countries with an unstable currency they are never cashed, but are passed from hand to hand as legal tender; yet this seems unlikely, for the simple reason that they would disintegrate comparatively quickly. Even now in parts of Nepal the country's own paper currency is unacceptable for the same reason.

This afternoon I spent four and a half hours buying medical supplies for the refugees in Pokhara – a fascinating experience, unlikely ever to be repeated elsewhere. To begin with most of the stocks – imported from India – have passed or are rapidly approaching expiry date and the anxious salesmen look at you pathetically when you point out that this terramycin or that sulphaguanidine has been useless since last March. They then explain hopefully that local doctors unquestioningly use these drugs every day (which doesn't surprise you in the least) and having declined to follow the doctors' example you resignedly move on to the next chemist. Naturally everything takes ten times as long as it would at home – finding the articles, searching for the semi-illegible invoices, painfully and not always accurately pin-pointing the relevant articles on the invoices, typing the account with one finger on a machine that looks like the first of its kind, checking, packing, *un*packing because that box was too small, repacking, finding straw because the other box was too large ... If one were new to the Asian business scene (of which Nepal is admittedly an extreme example) one would go mad within an hour; even though reasonably adjusted I very nearly did go mad after four and a half hours. But mercifully the petty dishonesty so common in India seems to be much less evident here; every night I leave Leo in Sigrid's garden – an act of faith which no one but a lunatic would make in India.

It will sadden me to leave this warm-hearted little household, which has recently been augmented by two domineering hens, bought by Donbahadur to provide Sigrid with *really* fresh eggs. At dusk they come strutting into the living-room, watched by a disapproving but discreetly unprotesting Puchare, and demand to be put to bed in the kitchen under the standard Nepalese wicker coop. Now Donbahadur is murmuring ambitiously about the advantages of owning a buffalo heifer – to provide Sigrid with *really* fresh milk. But I suspect that his stockpiling enthusiasm will be checked at this point, to avert the occupation of the bathroom by cattle.

3

Descent on Pokhara

This morning, when delayed by a series of typical Kathmandu hitches, I foolishly allowed myself to fizz slightly; all passengers for Pokhara were due at the Royal Nepalese Airways Corporation Terminal at twelve noon, but it was 11.58 a.m. before I had got myself, my knapsack and assorted boxes of medical supplies, dried milk and old clothes assembled at the appointed spot. (Leo cannot travel until a day when the plane is less loaded with freight for Pokhara.) Yet I needn't have fizzed; minutes passed, and more minutes, and half an hour, and three-quarters of an hour – and then an impatient-voiced young man told us to hurry out to the bus, his tone implying that the delay was all our fault. We next had to walk some three hundred yards up a side-street and with so many bits and pieces in my charge I was the last to reach the smart, blue airport bus (donated by the USA). Disconcertingly, it was quite empty, but an exceedingly decrepit Afghan-type bus stood a little further on, packed to the roof (part of which was missing), and now someone beckoned to me and shouted 'Pokhara? *This* Pokhara bus.' So I squeezed in, having paused to pick up from the ground under the bus a British Embassy mailbag, gravely but not very effectively labelled 'On Her Majesty's Service'. My luggage was then insecurely attached to what remained of the roof and I engaged a small boy to ride with it and scream loudly if anything fell off. Now all we needed was a bus-driver; and one did appear after about ten minutes. He took a pair of sandals from beneath the driving-seat, slipped them on to mark the resumption of his official duties, climbed leisurely into the cab, lit a foul-smelling cigarette and started the engine. Giving a roar like a wounded tiger the bus at once leapt convulsively across the rough street and I trembled for my small boy on the roof; but curiously enough both he and my luggage were still there when we arrived at Gaucher Airport forty minutes later.

There are eight landing-strips in Nepal, all but two – Pokhara and Gorkha – being in the Terai, and RNAC runs daily flights (weather permitting) to each of these favoured points. This means that as fares are relatively low (about £3 for a hundred-mile flight) many Nepalese villagers have graduated within a decade from the earliest-known method of transport to the most modern. At first I was astonished to see so many poverty-stricken peasants queuing for planes, but I soon realised that if one can arrive in thirty-five minutes instead of walking for ten days, spending money on food and lodging *en route*, it is undoubtedly more economical to fly.

At Gaucher Airport a wind-stock is not necessary during this season when the wind rhythmically blows columns of yellow dust across the field – a sight both horrible and fascinating. Even more fascinating is the airport's indescribable turmoil; it is entirely beyond my under-standing how anyone ever gets to their prearranged destination – or ever finds their luggage on the same plane as themselves.

The Pokhara flight was scheduled to depart at 2.30 p.m., and at 2.15 I went into the small airport restaurant for a cup of tea. At 2.25 the loudspeaker made a rapid crackling noise, so indistinct that it could have meant anything in any language, and I optimistically deduced that the Pokhara flight was being called. But looking out of the window I saw our huge handcart of luggage still standing near the verandah where it had been loaded; so I relaxed again, aware that this was no reliable indication of the flight's postponement, but determined to stand by those hard-won medical supplies.

After another cup of tea I moved out to the verandah, where an ocean of humanity and luggage was ebbing and flowing amidst a despairing babel of sound as everyone pleaded with everyone else to tell them when *their* flight was departing and which plane was going where. At this stage four Dakotas (two of them venerable machines bought long ago from Aer Lingus) were enigmatically lined up on the airfield and one simply had to watch to see which plane one's luggage was put into – and go on from there. The luggage itself was a classic Asian array – tin trunks, bed-rolls, padlocked wooden boxes, bundles tied up in filthy clothes, bulging sacks, plastic baths filled with miscellaneous objects, cardboard cartons uncertainly roped together, canvas satchels, cloth bags, biscuit tins, and wicker *dokars* (porters' baskets) shaped like overgrown weaver-birds' nests. When at last our cart was pushed and pulled to a plane by four coolies I somewhat cynically followed to supervise the loading, for here the public are allowed to wander at will among arriving and departing aircraft.

Half an hour later the loudspeaker made another of its rude noises, people began to move towards our plane – and now it seemed we really were on the way to Pokhara. Then suddenly everyone stopped moving and started to gesticulate and protest, and a young Nepalese teacher beside me announced in English that our flight had been postponed until seven o'clock tomorrow morning. To me this seemed so true to form that I wasn't even slightly surprised – nor was I half as annoyed as my Nepalese fellow-passengers. Strolling back to the verandah I sat awaiting the unloading of the plane and a reunion with my medical supplies, for which I was by now developing an almost maternal affection, having guided them through so many dangers. The young teacher came to sit beside me, his pale-skinned, fine-featured face puckered with frustration. When I asked him if he knew why the flight had been cancelled he sighed and said, 'The crew never came – this often happens after a party that is late to end. And in Kathmandu we have many parties.' He added, 'For you our country is full of difficulties – I'm sorry.' To which I sincerely replied that for me his country was a joy, and not half as full of difficulties as the West; but I'm afraid my sincerity failed to convince him.

By now our handcart had arrived back at the verandah and was being rapidly unloaded; my companion explained that the next flight, to Simra, had just been postponed as this cart was needed to load the relevant plane. Then, when half our luggage had been flung to the ground, a rumour started that our flight *might* be going after all – and instantly the confusion became unbearable, as the Simra coolies had been impatiently loading the cart with *their* luggage before *our* luggage was all unloaded and now the piles on ground and cart were inextricably muddled. As no definite statement had been made regarding the Pokhara flight it had become a matter of opinion whether our luggage or the Simra luggage should be unloaded or reloaded and on this point the coolies were disagreeing violently – so after some moments I decided to rescue the medical supplies before they were whisked off to the Terai.

Time passed and the coolies squabbled and bits of luggage went flying around like shuttlecocks. But then there came a new flurry and fuss, followed by joyous exclamations from my fellow would-be passengers, and it was confirmed that we had indeed been reprieved – because, as I later discovered, the American Ambassador and his wife were booked to Pokhara on our flight, which circumstance had inspired someone to filch the crew from another unfortunate plane.

When we finally took off at 2.45 p.m. I was not as nervous as I might have been, because RNAC's multiracial team of pilots and engineers has established during the past eight years a safety record that many more experienced and disciplined airlines might envy – and this in a country where high peaks, treacherous valleys, swiftly changing weather and scanty technical equipment increase the normal hazards of flying.

At this season cloud hides the Himalayas, and our thirty-five-minute flight to Pokhara was quite tame. As I gazed down at the 4,000- to 8,000-foot hills below us I longed to trek through them instead of merely having a quick, teasing glimpse. Yet this would be a gruelling trek in May, for now the broad, stony riverbeds are mere thirsty trickles and the terraced hillsides a series of dry, brownish undulations, only relieved by the thick green forests that cover the higher ridges. Few villages were visible, for their mud-walled houses blend perfectly with the surrounding earth: but on the highest hills we could see straggling little hamlets set amidst strips of maize, and it was possible to follow for miles the thin connecting thread of porters' paths, endlessly winding around the mountains.

We made a perfect landing in this broad valley and stepped down from the plane into a chaos of Nepalese, through which could be glimpsed five conspicuously tall Peace Corps volunteers, struggling through the mob towards their Ambassador and his wife. In every direction swarmed dirty, inquisitive, laughing children, and vigorously-elbowing, barefooted passengers eager to embark for the onward flight to Bhairawa before our cargo had even begun to be unloaded. We were at once surrounded by predatory, dictatorial porters – mainly women, wearing tattered, vivid clothes and heavy, noisy jewels – and by a vast number of interested locals, few of whom have ever flown anywhere or will ever fly anywhere and most of whom have nothing whatever to do with passengers or cargoes. Having disentangled myself from this throng I was at once pursued by a young policeman in creased khaki, armed with a cumbersome ledger in which all arriving foreigners are requested to write down 'particulars'. For political reasons the country north of Pokhara has recently been made a Restricted Area and one gets the impression that the Government, which only opened its frontiers to foreigners in 1951, would be quite pleased to have an excuse to re-impose restrictions on all tourist travel outside the Kathmandu and Pokhara valleys.

While I was doing my duty by the ledger a tall, thin Tibetan in European dress came towards us, welcomed me warmly and introduced himself in a mixture of Tibetan and English as Amdo Kessang, the proprietor of The Annapurna Hotel – a new, one-storey, Tibetan-style building which overlooks the airfield from a rise of ground about one hundred yards away. Prayer-flags flutter happily beside the arched gateway and though this establishment is hardly a hotel in our sense of the word, its easy Tibetan friendliness more than compensates for the disadvantages that may strike the passing visitor.

Kessang next introduced his cousin Chimba, a Lhasa-born trader who has spent some years in India and speaks fluent Chinese, Hindi and Nepali – and adequate English. Chimba is now the Pokhara Refugee Camp interpreter and general dogsbody and it was a relief to have someone to take responsibility for the medical supplies while I went to drink tea with Kessang.

Twenty minutes later Chimba reappeared and offered to introduce me to Mrs Kay Webb, the infinitely resilient and resourceful English grandmother who has been in sole charge of this camp's health since last December. For three years Kay worked as doctor-cum-nurse among the thousands of Tibetans in the Mysore settlement and, though she has never had any medical training, apart from a Red Cross course, in certain respects she is the more effective for being untrained; too much conventional knowledge would inhibit one from practising those unorthodox improvisations which are often the only way to achieve results in places like Pokhara.

It was no more than a ten-minute walk over level common-grazing land to the village of Pardi – a strung-out collection of wood, brick and mud houses situated at the western end of the airstrip. Here Kay lives, on the outskirts of the village, in a two-roomed house with a rickety wooden 'staircase', a rat-infested thatched roof and uneven mud floors. She uses the downstairs room as the camp dispensary and upstairs is her bed-sitting-room, where she cooks what little food is available on a tiny oil-stove.

Kay and I had been talking for less than fifteen minutes when Chimba came rushing back to inform us that the American Ambassador and his wife would like to tour the camp – so we all hurried off down the rough village 'street' to that other stretch of level common land where some 500 Tibetans of all ages have been camping since their trek last winter from the northermost part of the Dholpo region of Nepal. Most of these Tibetans belong to the independent nomad tribes who tend flocks of sheep and yak in the Nepalese– Tibetan frontier areas, and they have never been accustomed to discipline or control from any quarter; they do acknowledge some tenuous link with His Holiness as their religious leader, yet they were never within the political sphere of influence of the Lhasa Government or the spiritual sphere of influence of the Potala. In Kathmandu one hears many different versions of the same stories about the intractability of Tibetans in Nepal – depending on the teller's racial, religious, political, social or personal biases – and it is almost impossible to sift out the truth. But I suspect it *is* fair to say that in general the Tibetan refugee in Nepal differs considerably from his compatriot in India and is much more difficult to cope with.

At present these Tibetans are being issued with a weekly ration of US Surplus Food – Bulgar wheat, cotton-seed oil and dried skimmed milk – and they are living in 120 ragged cotton tents; but we hope to provide better shelter for them before the monsoon breaks in mid-June.

During our tour of the camp I made an impulsive purchase. As we walked between the tents my attention was distracted from what His Excellency had to say by an object lying on the palm of a Tibetan's hand. The object in question was very small, very black and very vocal; its piercing squeaks fatally attracted me to Ngawang Pema's side and a moment later I had done a deal and one twelve-day-old Tibetan mongrel bitch was promised to me for all of ten-and-sixpence. I wonder what the astrologers would make of the fact that this pup and I entered Nepal on the same date – the first of May.

Penjung, the camp leader, had just invited us all to drink tea in his tent when a rainstorm broke and the Ambassador's Peace Corps escort decided that he and Mrs Stebbins had better be transported at once to the comparatively luxurious Peace Corps house some four miles away in Pokhara Bazaar. So Penjung hurriedly produced a pair of white scarves and draped them around the Stebbinses' necks before the rattling Tourist Department jeep arrived to rescue the visitors.

Kay and I then had tea with Penjung and his wife and four daughters. The rain was cascading down both outside and inside their flimsy tent, where we sat cross-legged on filthy bamboo matting while chickens pecked around us, and Penjung's wife coughed incessantly, and a baby with dysentery whimpered in one corner; yet Tibetans are never as gloomy as their conditions might warrant and my happiness at being back among these people was undiminished by the surrounding squalor.

When the downpour temporarily ceased we slopped our way back to the village through slippery, ankle-deep mud – and there we found a broken-down jeep, with which two mortified Peace Corps boys were frantically fiddling while the Stebbinses sat on wooden benches in a bazaar-stall, looking blissfully happy. (At the time this happiness seemed to be a brilliant exercise in diplomacy, but later I discovered that both are quite capable of enjoying such misadventures.) Kay immediately invited them to her room, where we talked – above the roar of the wind, the crash of thunder and the rattle of hail – until seven o'clock, by which time it had become evident that the jeep was very severely incapacitated. However, the Stebbinses are unusually adaptable Americans who genuinely love Nepal, having now been here seven years, and they adjusted without difficulty to the prospect of dining and sleeping in The Annapurna. When we had been joined there by four sheepishly apologetic PC boys, Kessang produced a quite elaborate Tibetan banquet – which astonished everyone, for food is scarce at this season and most things have to be imported from India. In the end we had quite a party, enlivened by ambassadorial gin, Nepalese *rakshi*, Tibetan *chang* and Irish whiskey – a combination which may reasonably be expected to produce some rather interesting variations on the hangover theme.

Apart from these PC boys the only other Westerners in the valley are the three medical missionaries in the Leper Colony beyond the airfield, the eight medical missionaries in the Shining Hospital north of the main bazaar and the MacWilliamses, a young New Zealand couple (he is a sheep-breeding expert with FAO) who live on the outskirts of Pokhara Bazaar.

Before retiring I went out to the field and from there saw a vision of such supreme beauty that momentarily I wondered if it could be real. To the north, under a clear sky and a high-sailing moon, the whole Annapurna range stretched in one massive white tumult and, dominating the range – seemingly dominating the world – was the sharp-peaked, austere and infinitely lovely Machhapuchhare, home of Pokhara's tutelary deity. One should not try to trap such splendour in mere words, but beneath the moon, in the utter stillness of the valley, all those silver snows burned coldly with an overwhelming, undeniable life and spirit of their own. This silent, vital grandeur almost compelled me to kneel down and worship; and perhaps if no inbred self-consciousness intervened and it were possible to do so I would be all the better for it.

13 MAY

I awoke at 5.30 to hear the familiar, soothing hum of Tibetans saying their morning prayers, and when I went to wash at the tap in the field the eastern sky was orange and the sun's first rays were firing the tip of Machhapuchhare. Then the new light spread rapidly over the entire range, tingeing the snows with nameless colours – to gaze on these mountains almost lifts one off the ground with joy.

This valley, which lies only 2,500 feet above sea-level, is considerably hotter than Kathmandu. Its population is estimated to be between 12,000 and 15,000, and apart from Kathmandu it is the only level stretch of land north of the Terai. Being at the converging point of most routes from central and west Nepal to India it has a certain importance as a trading centre, yet it does not seem nearly as prosperous as the more fertile Kathmandu Valley.

From Pardi the valley opens out to the south-east and low foothills are visible in the distance; to the south-west the hills are near and covered with dense green forests, and at their base – a few moments' walk from Pardi – lies the long, emerald-green lake which gives this valley its name. (*Pokhara* is the Nepali for lake.) The beauty of the place is incomparable, with sub-tropical vegetation flourishing on every side directly beneath the cold white lines of the snow-peaks, and it is not surprising that the Nepalese hope eventually to develop it into another Kashmir.

However, on a more practical plane Pokhara does have its disadvantages at present. The prices of obtainable essential commodities are astronomical, and as most supposedly essential commodities are unobtainable at any price one soon learns to regard them as inessential, which is very good for one's pampered Western soul. Sugar is half-a-crown per pound, tiny eggs are sixpence each (it takes three of them to make what looks like one scrambled Irish egg), small potatoes and onions are fourpence each and no other vegetables or fruit are to be had at this season. Fresh milk, butter, cheese, meat, bread and flour are all unobtainable, so rice, dahl, dried beans and eggs must therefore be our staple diet – and for luxuries we can import from Kathmandu

Indian instant coffee of a peculiarly vile variety and stale Indian Cadbury's chocolate at one-and-sixpence per very small bar. Just now excellent Russian sweetened condensed milk is available in the local bazaar at four shillings per pound tin, and recently good quality Chinese tinned jam was also available; but the supply of these 'propaganda-type' goods is very uncertain. Occasionally Kay treats herself to Indian cream-crackers at seven-and-sixpence per pound – a good example of 'give them cake . . . ' One feels that the Nepal Tourist Bureau could use this situation as a new advertising gimmick aimed at overweight Westerners – 'Enjoy the Breathtaking Beauty of Pokhara Valley and Regain Your Figure!'

Today Chimba told me that I could soon move into a room at the lower end of Pardi Bazaar – for a rent of fifteen shillings per month – so this afternoon I went marketing in the main Pokhara Bazaar. From Pardi the rough track climbs all the way, past neat two- or three-storey Brahmin, Chetri and Gurung homesteads, their ochre walls warm against a freshly-washed background of maize-fields, bamboo-clumps, banana-trees, orange-groves and many other trees and shrubs unknown to me. Everywhere smug black cattle roam free, blatantly conscious of their sacred status and looking a lot healthier than their Indian cousins. It seems lunatic that we have to buy tinned milk from Russia in a valley overrun by herds of healthy cows; but I can see that these cattle are not bred as milkers: their udders are completely undeveloped, so the little fresh milk that is used by the locals must come from buffaloes.

An hour's unhurried walking took me to the centre of Pokhara Bazaar, and at once I fell hopelessly in love with the place. Its attraction is not easy to define: one cannot claim that it is especially beautiful, or colourful, or gay, or exotic – but as yet it is utterly *itself*, a small Nepalese town (or Nepal's second city, if you wish) where one feels immediately and intimately in touch with an ancient, strong tradition that still determines every action, thought and emotion of the local people. One may be aware that in the course of many centuries much of this tradition has become distorted, and therefore socially damaging; yet the basic stability and tranquillity inherent in such communities – despite the perennial anxieties of debt, disease and political unrest –

appeal most powerfully and significantly to our tradition-bereft Western hearts.

On either side of Pokhara's 'Main Street' stand dignified, three- or four-storey tiled houses, their ground floors open-fronted shops, and from any given point on any of the town's streets or alleyways at least one dilapidated but much-frequented Hindu shrine is visible. At various corners squat ragged hawkers, with their pathetic stock-in-trade of gaudy Indian glass bracelets, small religious oleographs, bunches of safety-pins, flimsy combs, heavy bead necklaces and sundry other trinkets spread on the dust at their feet; it is to be hoped that they are not dependent on their sales for a living. Then, halfway up the Main Street, one is startled to see the carcass of a large motor-truck. There are now six or seven small Willys jeeps in the valley, but as all vehicles have to be flown in I was fascinated by this remnant of someone's over-optimism; considering the nature of local tracks and the absence of local mechanics it is not surprising that the truck died young.

Even by Nepalese standards the surface of the Main Street is incredibly rough: it looks as though it had been torn up by some enraged god who was determined that no one should ever again be able to walk in comfort through the bazaar. And sure enough I was told this evening that it had indeed been deliberately torn up a few years ago, when the local authorities were afflicted by delusions of grandeur and yearned for a 'with-it' paved road. However, by the time the previously tolerable track had been turned into this present inferno of boulders and chasms the authorities had recovered from their delusions and lost all interest in paved roads – so the inferno remains.

At first sight Pokhara Bazaar appears to be quite an impressive shopping centre: but a brief scrutiny reveals that its stock is virtually limited to cloth, cigarettes, matches, pens, electric torches, lanterns, saddlery, kerosene oil, rice, dahl, dried beans, dust-tea, rock-salt, sugar, biscuits and Bournvita at fifteen shillings per quarter pound. I tried to buy a small oil-stove for cooking but none was available so I returned with only two enamel mugs, three little aluminium bowls in lieu of plates, a tiny kettle, a slightly larger saucepan and three teaspoons – all of the most inferior material though they cost me thirty-five shillings.

Almost everything in the bazaar has come from India (though the rock-salt still comes from Tibet), which perhaps explains why I paid for my purchases by *weight*. The system by which they were weighed was most intriguing – even foreigners who have lived for years in Nepal can't begin to comprehend it, though the Nepalese themselves take these proceedings quite seriously. To begin with little shapeless lumps of metal are thrown onto the scales by the handful – and then, if these prove unequal to the occasion, the merchant casually leans forward, without bothering even to uncross his legs, and picking a few stones off the ground throws them, too, on to the scales. But I feel that somewhere there is method in this madness and I have no suspicion of being diddled. Indeed, I was very gratified today when on two occasions merchants handed me back excess rupee notes which I had given them in error because of my ignorance of Nepali. Such gestures do a lot to make one feel at ease in a new environment.

This evening, at sunset, I went for a swim-cum-wash in the lake, which was too hot to be refreshing, though with the aid of carbolic soap it served to remove sweat and dust. Even by strictly controlling one's imagination it is impossible to believe this lake to be clean; yet at present it is our only source of drinking-water, so quite a lot of expensive kerosene will be needed to boil the brew before use. It is rather annoying that so many Nepalese favour the edge of the lake as a latrine – obviously because they can then jump straight into the water and combine a swim with the ritual washing enjoined upon Hindus after defecation. But the abundant consequences of this habit diminish even my enthusiasm for swimming. Incidentally, one good result of nomadism is that the camp here has always been kept spotless – providing quite a contrast to the many Tibetan camps in India, which tend soon to become revolting manure-heaps. These Tibetans are so used to the hygiene of camping that even the hobbling grandparents and toddling infants go far over the fields each morning, and every day the whole camp is cleared of litter and swept as clean as a Mayfair street.

4

Under Machhapuchhare

It is a (long) month today since I left London and I've just now moved into my new home, after a week of inexplicable but not unexpected delays. (I reckon that at least half one's time in Nepal is spent waiting for something to happen that probably won't happen until tomorrow, or the day after – if ever.) This unfurnished apartment is in a fairly recently-built semi-detached house and it measures some twelve by fifteen feet – very nice too, apart from an excess of rats. Just now a glitter caught my eye, and looking up towards the crude wooden beams that support the flat corrugated-iron roof I thought at first that I was seeing fireflies or glowworms: but then I realised that three monster rats were peering speculatively down at me – no doubt wondering how securely the new tenant would lock away her food supplies.

The mud-floored lower room, where Leo lives, is designed as a 'shop', with a few rough shelves facing that double-door which one bolts when coming in for the night and padlocks when going out for the day – though this latter precaution is ludicrous, as almost every padlock in Pokhara answers to the same key. From the lower room an unpredictable bamboo ladder gives access to my wood-floored bed-sitter, through a trap-door without a door. A thin partition separates this room from its twin over my landlord's shop and there are such wide spaces between the planks of the partition that all my sounds and movements are audible and visible to Thupten Tashi, the young Tibetan teacher who is my neighbour. As I write Thupten is holding a night-class in English grammar for some of the more studious older children and a moment ago they were all solemnly chanting 'Where *did* you *went*? Where *did* you *went*? Where *did* you *went*?' But one can't stand this sort of thing for long so I interrupted with a cry of anguish – 'Please, Thupten – Where did you *go*!' Not that I blame Thupten; the other day I saw a Nepali-English primer full of 'quotable quotes' – e.g., 'He is a girl,' 'This is a pictures on the walls.'

My unglazed, wooden-shuttered window is large by local standards – four feet by three – and it looks south across level farmland to a green curve of wooded hills. Two little niches at eye-level in the outer wall (designed for religious emblems) hold my kitchen utensils and toilet articles (i.e. toothbrush and paste), and I'll sleep in a corner on a bamboo mat; at this season bedding is unnecessary, and before the cool weather comes I hope to have bought a flea-bag from one of the homeward bound mountaineering expeditions. My furniture consists of a new table and stool which were very promptly and quite skilfully made for me by a carpenter in Pokhara. I also have a wooden box as food-cupboard and an empty four-gallon kerosene tin to hold my drinking-water. (These square tins are sold at two shillings apiece in the bazaar, and because they are easily carried on the back they have become the most popular local water-containers.)

Tonight I feel very well-adjusted to the world around me: the camp is almost opposite and I can now hear the Tibetans enlivening their evening with some communal singing, while next door Thupten's pupils are giggling wildly – obviously they have too much horse-sense to take his English lesson very seriously. It would be hypocritical to pretend that I could live happily ever after in this state of Noble Savagery; yet at the moment I am more than content to have so decisively Got Away From It All.

23 MAY

I find it extremely difficult to keep track of days and dates here – not that they matter very much. Yet for official purposes one does sometimes need to know the date and this aspect of life in Nepal is chronically confused by the fact that the Nepalese month begins in the middle of our month and that both calendars are used indiscriminately by English-speaking Nepalese, who rarely explain which system they happen to be using on any given occasion. This can – and does – lead to unspeakable mix-ups: yet it also provides an excellent excuse when Nepalese officials break their appointments, which they do rather more often than they keep them. Then they can say, with an air of indignant innocence, 'Oh, but *I* meant *our* twenty-third – and that isn't till next Friday week!'

Recently I have been negotiating for the employment of some of the Tibetans on the Indian Aid Hydro-Electric Project and today, on visiting the work-site, I made a wonderful discovery. This site is about 300 feet below the average level of Pokhara plain, in a very hot gorge through which a small river flows from the lake, and after my discussion with the Indian foreman I went hopefully to investigate the river. What I found far exceeded my hopes – a perfect swimming-pool, about 150 yards long, 10 yards wide and 20 feet deep. The pool is only five minutes' walk from the work-site, where my duties will often take me during the weeks ahead, yet comparative privacy is ensured by a high, grey cliff on one side and a sheer, forested mountain on the other. The water is a clear green and less warm than the lake; also one can persuade oneself that it is less filthy, because of its movement – and certainly it feels much more refreshing. I spent the lunch-hour swimming happily up and down the length of the pool, since it is now far too hot to eat anything at midday; but unfortunately the very steep climb up from this gorge leaves one again pouring sweat by the time one reaches level ground.

Today, near the river, I saw my first Nepalese snake. Here there is a wide stretch of rock-slabs, glittering with the distinctive local deposit of mica, and while I was walking over this my concentrated thinking on labour-relations was suddenly interrupted by a most curious noise as a snake at least six feet long swished away over the rocks from under my very toes. It travelled fast, its dry scales sounding like a distant swarm of bees, and I just had time to observe that it was olive-green, with brown markings, before it poured itself into a crevice between two boulders. When I came out of the river I looked – cautiously – into the crevice and it was still there, doubtless saying to itself that it didn't know what the world was coming to, with all these dangerous humans clumping about, disturbing an innocent reptile's sunbathe.

This afternoon I cycled up to Pokhara Bazaar to attempt to sort out three different accounts at the local bank. The building is guarded by two heavily-armed, sloppily-uniformed and chain-smoking soldiers of the Nepalese Army, and one penetrates to the office by crossing a dim, derelict ground-floor shop premises and climbing a dark, trembling staircase. Some ten individuals staff the low-ceilinged, dingy cavern which one assumes to be the office – but only one of them, so far as I could judge, is literate in any language. If it is accurate to say that banking is in its infancy in Nepal, then this establishment is very decidedly a cradle. Yet as a person inside a glasshouse I shouldn't throw stones: my own ignorance of the financial world is total, which made the afternoon's transactions very trying indeed. I had to fill in countless forms to send to Dublin and London, but as they were all printed in Nepali it is difficult to imagine them achieving the desired effect at the other end, and I have a nasty suspicion that since neither I nor the young manager really knew what we were trying to do they were probably the wrong forms to begin with.

This evening Kay lent me her table-thermometer to enable me to see the worst, and now, at 9.30 p.m., my room temperature is eighty-eight degrees Fahrenheit and all the time I am mopping sweat off my face, neck and arms. Yet one shouldn't complain – this is moderation compared with current temperatures down on the Indian plains.

28 MAY

Like most Asian peoples the Nepalese are very curious about any foreigner's way of life and their respect for privacy is nil. During this past week they have been coming in droves to inspect my room and their dismay at what they see vaults all language barriers. After one quick look they intimate that it is altogether wrong for me to sleep on the floor, to do my own cooking on a tiny temperamental stove and to wash myself and my clothes in the river. They point out severely that I should have at least one servant and a bigger room with a more tractable stair, a mud floor and a cool grass thatch. So far my Nepali vocabulary consists of one word, meaning 'good', and gesturing widely I repeat this adjective – at first cheerfully, then firmly and at last, as their indignation grows, almost aggressively, in self-defence. But my enthusiasm fails to quell their disgust, and when they finally withdraw I can hear their condemnations being repeated to passers-by in the street below.

European adaptability might be expected to promote harmonious race-relations, but I can see that in this country it does nothing of the sort. Instead the Nepalese suspect the integrity – or perhaps the sanity – of a European who fails to maintain European standards, either through preference for the simple life or through lack of cash. They cannot conceive of any European *choosing* to live on their level – or below it, as all but the very poorest Nepalese families have servants of a sort about the house – and obviously they are embarrassed by a memsahib 'going native'. So now I am realising sadly that in such a class-conscious and conservative society 'going native' is the longest way round to integration.

Our local mail system is thrilling. A Nepalese postal service does exist in theory, but as no one cares to test it in practice the British Embassy very nobly sends a mail bag by plane on Fridays, for the benefit of the missionaries, Kay and myself. Both hospitals are some distance from the airfield, so Kay and I have permission to break the seal when the bag arrives and sort out our own mail before Joseph, the wiry little Magar servant, trots away with the sack over his shoulder. Undoubtedly this ritual is the highlight of our week; it is most exciting to squat on the dusty airfield, beside a large pile of envelopes and packages, and eventually to discover the few familiar and precious envelopes addressed to oneself – a much more gratifying system than the dull process of having letters pushed through one's letter-box. But naturally there is no certainty about which flight The Bag will come on, and at 10.30 a.m. today, when I saw a speck in the eastern sky, I went hurtling off to the airfield on Leo only to find that The Bag had not been put aboard this plane. Nor did it come on the next flight, which landed at 1.40 – but two hours later we saw with joyous relief our beloved canvas sack being tossed into Joseph's arms, from the last plane of the day.

For a variety of reasons I find myself having to spend a prodigious number of hours each week simply awaiting the arrival of planes. Luckily one cannot tire of a place where horsemen on richly caparisoned steeds may frequently be seen galloping across the airfield – briefly framed by the wing of a Dakota – with bells ringing a wild harmony and hoofs pounding an exultant reply; or where, under blue skies, a dozen women in swirling crimson skirts gracefully pace the length of the field, half-hidden by their baskets of sweet green grass and their enormous golden wickerwork sunshades.

Another diversion is provided by the Gurkha soldiers. Sometimes one sees scared, barefooted youths from remote hill villages coming to the airfield, carrying battered little tin boxes of meagre possessions, on their way to join those elder brothers, cousins and uncles who are 'doing well' with the British Army in Hong Kong, Borneo or Malaya. Then one often sees Gurkhas returning on six months' leave, after three years' service, and invariably they look sensationally spruce among their welcoming family. The grimy stay-at-homes wear unwashed, fraying garments, while the well-scrubbed soldiers are attired in starched, neatly-creased khaki shorts, flowered bush-shirts and broad-brimmed straw hats. And instead of the modest little tin box with which they departed from home they now possess at least four huge padlocked trunks. These, of course, are left for their wives, mothers or sisters to carry – one on each bent back, supported by a broad canvas band across the forehead – while the Returned Hero strides importantly ahead, an expensive camera slung over his shoulder and a raucous transistor screaming in his hand as he chats with those male relatives who trot respectfully beside him, carrying light pieces of hand-luggage. Usually at this stage the hero's pocket is full of newly-acquired rupees, for he will have paused long enough on the airfield to sell a selection of excellent Swiss watches and Japanese pocket-transistors at incredibly low prices.

At first one is appalled by the apparently lethal degree of chaos which prevails on every side at the airfield. The least timid Westerner recoils with incredulous horror from a landing-ground on which, ten minutes before a plane is due, children are flying kites, babies and dogs are romping together, cattle are grazing placidly, mule-trains are plodding stolidly and trans-country porters are carrying loads as big as themselves.

When the plane has landed one frequently sees members of the general public standing in the welcome shade of its wings, nonchalantly smoking. Then, when it eventually taxies away, creating a gale-force wind in which the children dance joyously, no one bothers to move and from the booking-office doorway newcomers are subjected to the harrowing optical illusion that at least twenty people are about to be decapitated by a wing. Incidentally, for the village mongrels this is the climax to their day's fun. Yelping hysterically they pursue each departing plane with a verve undiminished by the proven futility of the exercise – and just occasionally one of them is rewarded by *almost* getting his teeth into the rear wheel. Yet appearances are in this case deceptive, and though the situation seems to be so irrevocably out of control none of the accidents which should happen do happen. When a speck appears in the sky at the end of the long valley a man blows a quavering blast on what sounds like a referee's worn-out whistle and immediately frenzied herdsmen leap onto the field, hurling stones and imprecations at their cattle who, disgruntled but resigned, file off through a gap in the sagging barbed-wire fence. Meanwhile the dogs have also temporarily dispersed, the children have pounced on the babies and removed them, the mule-trains have broken into a canter and the porters into a trot and, as the plane roars low over the camp at the end of the runway, nothing or no-one remains to be killed – which by my reckoning constitutes a daily miracle.

Recently I have been chiefly occupied in supervising the building of bamboo huts, into which we hope to move most of the Tibetans before the monsoon breaks. However, at this season it is not easy to obtain the necessary matting and poles, and today we suffered yet another setback when a local farmer, who had agreed to sell us forty bamboos, announced that his astrologer had advised against the sale as it would be most inauspicious to cut bamboos on his land before the rains came. A practical streak was perceptible in this edict, since

May is the least suitable month for felling bamboos; but obviously it simplifies life if one can refuse to honour one's promise on the advice of an omniscient astrologer. Everybody knows that this sort of argument is incontrovertible in Nepal, where the hour at which King Mahendra begins an air-journey is still determined by astrology as well as meteorology.

It was 5 p.m. when Chimba informed me of this development and at once we set off on our bicycles to hunt for a more amenable farmer, cycling through one of the many beautiful corners of the valley that I haven't yet had time to explore. By now the level land south of Pardi is grey, arid and harsh to the eyes – but half-a-mile north of the village one is in a new, cool green world where the narrow laneways are shaded by towering, leafy trees and where clumps of powerfully curving bamboos, more than one hundred feet tall, bend their feathered tops over fields of shoulder-high maize. At about 6.30 a strangely muted light began to come from the west and soon this suppressed sunshine, slanting through torn copper clouds, was casting a red-gold glow over the whole landscape until the circular, ochre farmsteads seemed like giant lanterns against their dark green background.

For over an hour we toiled from farm to farm along stony tracks ankle-deep in fawn, powdery dust and often blocked by droves of obtuse buffaloes who panicked at the unfamiliar sight of bicycles. At the first farm we negotiated with a timid boy of eight or nine and his great-grandad – an ancient whose skin was so wrinkled that his legs looked as though he were wearing brown nylon stockings several sizes too large. Not surprisingly these negotiations came to an unsatisfactory conclusion; and at the next two farms the owners, having discovered that we were not going to pay a fancy price, brusquely claimed to need all their bamboo for themselves. I was very aware that these Brahmins were hostile to us non-Hindus – less, I should think, because of our ritual uncleanness than because they see the infiltration of foreign ideas into the valley as a threat to their present profitable influence over the villagers. However, we were eventually promised twenty-two bamboos, of varying sizes and qualities; but tomorrow being Saturday (when it is inauspicious to fell bamboos) we can't send the Tibetans to collect until Sunday morning – by which time there may have been further astrological intervention.

We cycled home along the lakeside, past the hideous new pseudo-European Royal Palace, and the very sacred Hindu temple that rises out of the water some two hundred yards offshore. When we were out of sight of the Palace I dismounted and asked Chimba to go ahead; then I sat for a little time by the lake. Rarely have I seen anything more lovely than that still, vast expanse of emerald water, beneath a tremendous arch of bronzed cloud, through which a few nearby peaks and crags were just discernible.

29 MAY

At five-thirty this morning a jubilant Chimba came scrambling up my ladder (fortunately Tibetans are not at all embarrassed when confronted with semi-nude females) to tell me that the German Annapurna Expedition want forty-two porters for twelve days at Rs. 12/- per day – and are willing to employ our Tibetans. When you remember that Rs. 3/ – is the average daily coolie wage Chimba's elation is understandable, and together we rushed off to the camp to choose twenty-one men and twenty-one women – a list of whose names and registration numbers would have to be presented to the Anchiladis when we applied to him for permission for the refugees temporarily to leave his district.

By nine o'clock we had made our selection of those most suitable and I had written out the list for Kay to type; but then we received a message that, for a very odd reason, only men would be acceptable. Apparently one of the Hindu hamlets *en route* to the base camp is fanatically orthodox, and recently the inhabitants have been experiencing great difficulties with their local god because some passing travellers killed a chicken in the village. Therefore it would be extremely dangerous further to provoke this god by admitting into his territory outcaste women who might happen to be menstruating at the time without heeding any of the very strict Hindu taboos that apply to the occasion. As we returned to the camp to revise our list I noticed that even Chimba, who has his full share of Buddhist tolerance, was finding this hitch hard to stomach – perhaps because it had followed so soon on yesterday's astrological débâcle!

Lately I've observed that among Nepali diseases there is an affliction, peculiar to resident Americans, known as 'Cultural Shock'. In older English this means not liking local smells and being disturbed by the national habit of flinging garbage into the streets; nor does any consolation derive from the fact that in villages all such garbage is instantly disposed of by battalions of cattle, pigs, dogs, horses, goats, hens and ducks. Fortunately Europeans are immune to this disease and, though Kay and I were both quite nicely brought up, we have long since adjusted to flinging through our windows eggshells, potato-peelings, onion-skins and basins of filthy water, with never a thought for the passers-by – who anyway are usually protected by umbrellas at this season, which I am not when I cycle past *their* windows at dumping-time. We must take great care to break this habit before returning to countries where it might culturally shock the natives.

At noon today there was a marathon row in the street below my window. It began when one young woman accused another of having an affair with her husband – accompanying the accusation with a blow across the face. Then, within moments, an excited crowd of about a hundred and fifty mysteriously assembled, and I was looking down on a sea of bobbing black umbrellas, beneath which men and women were furiously arguing and gesticulating, each trying to shout or scream more harshly than the rest. Personally I should have thought this an exclusively family matter – but possibly these hundred and fifty protagonists did all belong to the three families involved. The argument continued for some forty minutes, and then the husband vigorously whacked both women on the back with his rolled umbrella and told them (if one may judge by his tone and expression) to go to the Hindu equivalent of Hell – or, perhaps, to become worms in their next incarnation. In Nepal a man is not expected to pretend to be faithful to his wife (though she is required to be very discreet about her own infidelities), so this should have concluded the argument. But instead of accepting their chastisement with womanly humility these two shrews promptly declared a truce and united to attack the husband with their hastily rolled umbrellas – at which point they were seized by several men, on whom they lavished kicks and scratches before being partially subdued and frogmarched away out of sight. Now I noticed that the original dispute had sparked off a variety of subsidiary quarrels among the crowd, all of whom were enjoying themselves enormously. Clearly this sort of ding-dong battle is the Nepalese peasant's favourite recreation, and one can't help wondering if the apparent lack of civilisation revealed by such scenes is not in some respects healthier than our repressive over-civilisation, in which sedatives and tranquillisers are necessary to so many.

After watching one of these not uncommon mass-arguments, or even after spending a few hours dawdling around the bazaar, waiting for someone or something, a return to the camp provides the most extraordinary contrast. Tibetans rarely raise their voices, however heatedly they may be disputing, and instead of the Nepalis' cheerfully shouted 'Namaste' one is welcomed by a silent bow or a tongue stuck out respectfully to its full length. It is curiously moving to find the distinctive Tibetan gentleness showing through so often among these uncouth and at times unruly nomads; and in their case one cannot reasonably associate this gentleness with the practice of Buddhism, since it is obvious that they have been chiefly influenced by the cruder and more ancient Bön-po religion.

The weather is really grim now; there has been no rain for eight days and the temperature of my room, under this low tin roof, reaches 102° or 103° Fahrenheit by 2 p.m. At bedtime it's down to about 88° and I lie naked on my bamboo mat, tormented by a heat-rash, while the rats provide background music by upsetting dishes and spoons and squealing angrily at each other. At first I found it rather disquieting to lie on the floor with these brutes scampering around me – there seemed no guarantee that they wouldn't nibble at the edges of recumbent bodies – but now I've become adjusted, though I'm still afraid to chase them as they are reputed to turn savage if treated rudely; recently Kay was bitten on the finger when she tried to push one off her pillow in the small hours. But in a way the millions of tiny, red-brown ants are even more troublesome than the rats: they get into all the food and swarm over one at night in tickling (but not biting) hordes. Initially I tried to pick them out of the rice, dahl, sugar and tinned milk, but I soon gave up – life's too short – so now I suppose cooked ant is my chief source of protein. All things considered I don't especially look forward to night-time at the moment. Yet on the whole I'm very happy and one can't have perfection.

3 JUNE

Today I distinguished myself by getting hopelessly lost for eight hours. Kay had asked me to go up to the Shining Hospital for some medical reports and then to collect an X-ray result from the Indian Military Hospital on the other side of the Seti Gorge; but at the Shining Hospital one of the missionaries very kindly, though rather vaguely, directed me to a short cut and by 2 p.m. I realised that I was probably halfway to India. However, as there has been no opportunity to take a day off since my arrival I decided to make the most of this involuntary expedition, without feeling too conscience-stricken.

On the whole my sense of direction is quite reliable, yet soon it was clear that I was becoming 'loster and loster' – and my compass was in my knapsack at Pardi. The sort of reasoning which can usually be applied to such situations seems to count for nothing in Nepal, and I'm seriously tempted to believe that here even the sun flouts the natural laws. One complication is that those low, wooded hills which rise at intervals from the valley floor look identical to the newcomer, so one is wildly misled and lured over the plain for two or three miles in the conviction that Pardi lies just *there* – only to find oneself on the verge of a magnificent 1,000-foot river-gorge one has never seen before and which is certainly not negotiable; and so it goes on … and on … and on.

Though Pardi and Pokhara have now been put on the tourist map by the airfield one only has to travel a few miles beyond them to reach, within the valley itself, villages so untouched by outside influence that a white woman on a bicycle creates a veritable sensation; and this unblemished picturesqueness has its snags, for whenever I asked for directions the villagers were too astonished, too scared or too amused even to attempt any helpful response or gesture. Once a man did point down a track that appeared to be leading direct to the middle of nowhere, and optimistically I followed it to its terminus on the brink of yet another gorge – or perhaps at a different point along the same gorge.

All day the heat had been intense and by 3 p.m. I was feeling quite dehydrated, having covered over forty miles according to Leo's milometer. Partly for this reason, and partly because I despaired of ever disentangling the inconsequential tracks of the plain, I now attempted to descend to river-level and follow the course of the Seti – an idiotic move which involved Leo and me in a series of gymnastic feats and stamina-tests such as even Roz and I have never had to endure. And Leo is twice the weight of Roz ... Eventually I discovered that one could descend to within about one hundred feet of the water, but no further – something which would have been obvious from the start to any moderately intelligent person. So I sat down in the shade of a tree by the cliff-edge to smoke a cigarette while reflecting on the sad fact that soon we would have to ascend somehow to plain-level and resume our war of nerves with those tracks.

However, it was impossible to remain glum for long in such surroundings. Below me the Seti (its name means 'white') was a swift, seething torrent, narrow at this season but still violently strong amidst a desert of pale, rounded stones. From the opposite cliff rose smooth-browed, forested hills enclosing the gorge in a wide, gentle curve, while behind, rising in layers to the plain, lay the rough, silent, sun-beaten countryside that we had just traversed. I hadn't expected to find such solitude within this valley; yet for hours past people had appeared only in the vicinity of the few hamlets and from here not a trace of humanity was visible. But then, when my almost pathological aversion to 'turning back' drove me on up the gorge – I was able to cycle for about a mile over the short, burnt grass and pungent herbage – a lone farmhouse appeared on the very edge of the cliff. This building, clumsily constructed of timber and stone, was a mere loft over an open-sided shelter for cattle, crops and firewood – yet in it lived an old grandmother, her son and daughter-in-law and their five children, of whom the younger three were stark naked and pot-bellied. Around this pathetic dwelling (the most impoverished I've seen outside of Gilgit) stood a few acres of poorly maize and three feeble banana trees, beneath which a starved-looking buffalo lay chewing the cud. (Though what that cud consisted of I can't imagine.) The usual Nepali 'ladder' – a notched tree-trunk – led up to the entirely unfurnished living-room, where the family were sitting idly, sharing a local version of the hookah. When they saw Leo and me at the foot of the ladder their astonishment was considerable, but they responded to my urgent plea for '*pani*' by beckoning me 'upstairs' and handing me a brass pint-measure of river-water which tasted faintly of human excrement (or was I imagining things?) yet which at that moment seemed an ineffably delicious drink. With wild disregard for the probable consequences I emptied three of these measures, while the family tried to question me and registered incredulity at my ignorance of Nepali. They were a remarkably cheerful group, though not one of them looked healthy, and after their first shock of surprise they treated me as though we were old friends.

I longed to be able to find out how they came to be living in such isolation; it seems likely that they belong to the Siva Bhakti tribe, which was formed of ex-slaves after the abolition of slavery in Nepal on 28 November 1924, and which now constitutes an almost untouchable caste of people who are allowed to marry only among themselves. It is estimated that about 50,000 slaves were freed at that time, their 16,000 owners receiving a cash compensation from the state. The majority of those freed became apprenticed to their previous owners for a seven-year period, eventually settling down as labourers, and this 'improvement' in their status often left them worse off than before, since employers were no longer bound to provide food, clothing and shelter. An enterprising minority, however, set up as independent coolies and in time had saved enough money to settle on just such scraps of wasteland as my friends of this afternoon are farming.

Before saying goodbye I made a determined effort to obtain some idea of where Pardi might be and at last the eldest child, a boy of about fourteen, volunteered to show me the track for a fee of one rupee. I had already paid these unfortunates for their water (as requested) and I certainly didn't grudge the boy a rupee: yet I couldn't help contrasting this profiteering attitude towards a stranger in difficulties with the boundless generosity of those equally poor Muslims and Tibetans whom I've met elsewhere on my travels.

Leaving the shack we walked away from the river for some half a mile, through dense, knee-high, prickly bushes which tore deep scratches in my legs, to the base of a 500-foot cliff. There the boy pointed towards the sky, said 'Pardi', smiled a farewell and briskly trotted off.

Surveying the cliff it seemed to me that I had had a very poor rupee's worth of guidance; this precipice was completely overgrown with tangled shrubs and looked like a monkey's playground rather than a route to anywhere. But then, hidden beneath the bushes, I saw what might possibly be described as a track, though it more closely resembled a dried-up watercourse. This ascent would have been strenuous without a bicycle and only by a savage combination of obstinacy and brute force did I finally get Leo over the top and on to the plain. By then every muscle in my body was throbbing from the fearsome contortions involved in heaving both of us over five-foot-high boulders, across four-foot-wide crevices and through thick patches of scrub, so I sat down to recover while studying our new horizons – which unfortunately did not look very new. I saw the same identical hills, rising on three sides, and the same gorge – from a different angle – and the same brand of little-used track that tends to expire at a moment's notice. In fact the only change was overhead, where the sky had suddenly become black with welcome storm-clouds. But as progress in some direction seemed advisable I mounted Leo and bumped off hopefully towards the north-west, which seemed just as good a bet as the south-east.

Twenty minutes later I rounded a hill and saw a village ahead and another river-gorge on my left; and providentially the storm broke only as we reached the outskirts of this village. Normally being exposed to a storm delights me, but now I raced for the nearest shelter – a small Gurung farmhouse – with head bent to protect my face from being lacerated by the hail which a 110 m.p.h. gale was driving horizontally across the valley. (Later this evening a stranded air-pilot gave me details of the wind's force and told me that during such storms cattle are occasionally beaten to death by the hail.) Of course this is not what we think of as hail; I measured many of the jagged pieces of ice that came shooting like bullets through the open doorway and several of them were three inches by two and at least an inch thick – extremely effective ammunition for the use of angry mountain-gods!

Certainly some god was very angry today; never have I witnessed anything approaching the ferocity of this storm, either during my previous monsoon among the Himalayas or during my winter months on a North Atlantic island. As I crouched just inside the doorway among an assortment of frightened villagers, for whom this house had been the nearest shelter, I could see my host's little field of six-foot maize being plastered to the ground within moments – then his one stack of hay was swept off its high platform and went sailing out of sight, twenty feet above the ground, creating a curiously Mary Poppins-like effect. I could sense that my companions' fear was not merely for the safety of their families, dwellings or crops: they were responding also to the spiritual malevolence which was being conveyed to them through the devastating fury of the elements. My normal reaction to any demonstration of Nature's power is a simple awe, yet I found it easy today to sympathise with these peasants' taut perception of some sinister force behind this onslaught.

Within moments of the storm breaking the temperature had dropped so abruptly that soon everyone was shivering. Forty minutes passed before the gale suddenly died and allowed us all to proceed, through almost solid sheets of rain, to our respective destinations. For the duration of the gale rain had been as continuous as hail and now all tracks were rivers, flowing between piles of greyish, unmelted ice-bullets. Then, cycling against the current through a foot of water, I realised that we had passed this village quite early in the day, which meant that though I still had no idea how to find Pardi I could at least try to retrace our original route from Pokhara Bazaar.

The whole valley – this morning parched and quivering silently in the heat – was now an ocean of noisy brown water, rapidly moving on every side as the fields are so designed that the rains pour from one to another before finally reaching river-level. Very soon cycling became impossible; I simply walked through a sort of submarine world in which the cold rain falling around me seemed no less in volume than the knee-deep, earth-warmed torrent through which Leo was being dragged. At one point we had to re-cross a river – for all I know the ubiquitous Seti again – that earlier had been ankle-deep but was now breast-high and positively dangerous. Then, incredibly, from a slight hill I saw through the curtain of falling water an aeroplane parked under a tree; and that vision could only mean that I had – as might have been predicted – lost the Pokhara track and inadvertently found Pardi. But between us and the airfield lay wide, flooded paddy-fields of such soft mud that I sank in to my knees at every step and could not possibly get Leo through. I was determined to make for that aeroplane in a straight line, lest we might find ourselves behind one more low, green hill, so I painfully carried Leo along half a mile of the narrow, slippery ditches that intersect paddy-fields, frequently falling into three feet of muddy water and feeling rather like a drunken tightrope walker. Then, as we crossed the airfield at 6.15 p.m., the rain stopped and a startling gleam of sunshine lightened the valley.

I went direct to the camp, dreading what I might find. Inevitably it is in a shambles: most of the tents have been torn to shreds and four have been blown away, including the chief lama's. From the airfield sheets of water raced across the whole site, and to enter the camp one had to wade across a twenty-foot wide, four-foot deep torrent in which one of the children had nearly been drowned a few minutes before my arrival. All clothing, bedding and firewood are saturated and the little cooking-holes in the ground will be unusable for the next twelve hours; so these unfortunates cannot even console themselves with a hot drink, much less change into dry clothes as I have now done. When I arrived some of the torn tents were already being moved to less flooded spots, and piles of drenched possessions were stacked on the high firewood heaps all over the camp. Many families had begun frantically to dig drains, using spoons, knives, hands and feet in an attempt to get the water away more quickly. The sodden remains of those prized cardboard US milk cartons, which are used as domestic altars, were floating off rapidly in every direction and most families' weekly grain ration was soaked through. Tiny children stood shivering beside their collapsed tents, and stiff-jointed grandparents searched in vain for a dry spot on which to sit.

The whole heart-rending picture would have made a real tearjerker had it been filmed, but for one detail which ruined it all – the unconquerable good humour of the Tibetans. Wherever I looked I saw people roaring with laughter as they waded around through the flood, and it was plain that the majority regarded this whole performance as the funniest thing to have happened in years. So I gave up feeling guilty about my own good fortune in having a roof over my head and came back here to enjoy it.

I had often wondered why all the local lanes and streets look like dried-up riverbeds and now I know – they *are* dried-up riverbeds. On the way to my house a knee-deep torrent was swirling furiously between the buildings – which, as in Kathmandu, are almost all raised some three or four feet above the ground – and three dead hens and a dead puppy were swept past me as I waded home.

As usual I had left my window open and the room had been thoroughly blitzed: on the floor lay rice and onions and smashed eggs, sodden papers and books, and a broken lantern and spilled kerosene. I swept up the rice, which is in any case filthy when one buys it, and lifted a neighbour's dog up the ladder to dispose of the eggs, and now I'm writing by torchlight, pending the replacement of the lantern. Luckily my 'cellar' escaped so I'm not deprived of spiritual consolation. At the moment this consolation consists of a brew distilled in Kathmandu, sold at seven shillings per pint bottle and imaginatively described on the label as 'Pineapple Wine'. Somehow such a description conjures up pictures of elderly ladies (retired missionary type) daringly sipping a beverage made from great-grand-mamma's recipe and containing .001% alcohol: yet here this coy name disguises a spirit that would make hair grow on an egg. (A recent visitor of mine went so far as to claim that the stuff could propel a steamroller up Mount Everest, but I feel this may be a slight exaggeration.) Most certainly 'Pineapple

Wine' is *not* wine and I doubt if pineapples play any part in its production – at a guess I'd say that it's pure poteen, coloured green. For even the best heads two tablespoonfuls produce the desired effect, and it is probable that three tablespoonfuls would result in macabre hallucinations, quickly followed by death. What it does to one's inside, when taken regularly, I hate to think – but time will tell.

4 JUNE

As from today I'm living with a lama – the untented one, who presented himself on my doorstep this morning and said, 'Please may I come and live with you?' or words to that effect. At first I had some misgivings, not for the conventional reasons that might operate in Europe, but because it is against the rules for any refugee living outside the camp to draw rations. However, a lama is a lama, so after a moment's hesitation I said, 'Very well, come right in – but you must give me your ration-card and every Friday morning I'll bring you your supplies.' A big grin then spread over his face, and after many expressions of gratitude he hurried off to collect his possessions.

Half an hour later I beheld a brigade of twenty-two small boys marching towards my door, each child carrying five enormous cloth-bound volumes – except the last, who was carrying only three. I then did some simple mental arithmetic and realised that this was the full Buddhist Canon – all one hundred and eight volumes of it – arriving as item number one of the lama's luggage. Mercifully the other items were less impressive – an incense burner, a prayer-wheel, a prayer-drum, a *dorje*, a prayer-bell, a small photograph of His Holiness, eleven tiny silver butter-lamps to burn before it and (as non-religious goods) a dented kettle, a wooden, silver-rimmed bowl to drink from and an uncured, stinking yak-skin to sleep on. The little room downstairs (or down-ladder) has now been transformed into a miniature temple, from which the exquisite scent of incense comes wafting up, and my life is further brightened by ecclesiastical music; I find the sweet melody of drum and bell so absolutely enchanting that when it starts I simply drop everything and listen.

This afternoon we had another violent storm – not as devastating as yesterday's cyclone, but a passable imitation of it. These storms are not to be confused with the monsoon, which isn't due for another week or ten days, but I'm told that they herald it annually in this region. Tonight the room temperature is down to a blissful seventy-five degrees Fahrenheit and, as my body is now free of heat-rash for the first time in weeks, I'm looking forward to a good night's sleep.

5 JUNE

Famous Last Words! I've discovered that living with a lama has its limitations, the chief of which is His Reverence's predilection for praying – with full instrumental support – from 3 a.m. onwards. Unhappily this is an hour at which the very sweetest of melodies leaves me quite unmoved so perhaps I'd be justified in asking him to postpone his Matins until 5.30 a.m. But somehow this seems slightly disrespectful, though as he doesn't conclude his devotions until 11 p.m. it might be good for his health to force him to sleep a little longer. The unfortunate thing is that these advanced lamas seem to have long since transcended our frail needs for regular meals and eight hours' sleep, and His Reverence is capable of praying non-stop for six hours without moving a muscle.

6 JUNE

This evening I learned quite a lot about my exalted guest, when he invited Thupten Tashi and me to supper. Armed with our own dishes, spoons and salt, we joined him downstairs at seven o'clock – by which time I am always ravenously hungry, having eaten very little since breakfast-time – but the meal did not start until half-past nine. However, it was preceded by much interesting conversation and nine or ten cups of buttered tea (about five cups too many for the average Western stomach) so I'm not really complaining.

Thupten Tashi is by far the best Tibetan interpreter I've ever known, and with his assistance the lama briefly recounted his own life-story. Though he had always wanted to enter a Gelugpa monastery as the only son of a rich farming family he was forced into marriage with a neighbouring farmer's daughter at the age of eighteen; but bringing a horse to the water doesn't necessarily make him drink and bringing Lama Ongyal to his bride's bed did not make him consummate the marriage. Then, after two years of domestic celibacy, he renounced his inheritance and ran away to a monastery in Kham – no doubt to the considerable relief of his still virgin bride, who was now considered free to seek a more practical mate. In Kham he studied for sixteen years under a very learned Rimpoche, before spending three years as a hermit in a Himalayan cave at an altitude of 18,000 feet. Next he returned to his monastery, did his final examinations and moved on to be a tutor or *guru* at Drepung Monastery – from which he fled to Dholpo in 1959.

Encouraged by my revelation of a very rudimentary knowledge of Tibetan Buddhism he followed this potted autobiography with a lecture on the importance of accepting the impermanence of all matter and acting accordingly. But at this stage my concentration began to be seriously impaired by most inappropriate pangs of hunger and, though the spirit was willing, I can now remember few of his profound remarks. He asked me if I believed in God, nodded approvingly when I said, 'Yes', and observed that he had heard rumours to the effect that many modern Europeans were atheists, which seemed to him a pity, as they had a very good way to God in their Christianity. Whereupon I felt compelled to admit that I wasn't exactly an orthodox Christian and on hearing this the lama looked slightly worried, and said he hoped I wasn't a Buddhist, as the Western Buddhists he'd met in Kathmandu were very unhappy people and in fact only imagined themselves to be Buddhists – which is as good an analysis of the breed as I've yet heard.

Meanwhile our supper was being cooked, on a wood fire between stones, by the twelve-year-old boy who is Lama Ongyal's personal servant, and when it at last appeared I noted that our host was not eating with us. I longed to ask if he ever ate *anything* – since as far as my observation goes he exists on buttered tea only – but fearing that the question might sound impertinent I restrained myself. The meal consisted of rice, green dahl and potatoes – a true banquet by Tibetan standards, and it tasted none the worse for the fact that I knew it to have been cooked outside the backdoor almost exactly where I (and not a few Nepalese) habitually answer Nature's calls.

Incidentally, I have had the undeserved good luck to escape unscathed after my reckless water-drinking of a few days ago.

10 JUNE

This morning two Dakotas took off from the airfield loaded with the remains of the German Expedition's equipment – and this was apart from the masses of food given away today because it's not worth the freight-charges back to Kathmandu. What looked like the whole Nepalese and Tibetan population of Pardi and exactly half the European population (that's me) were at The Annapurna for the share-out, and in due course I came away shamelessly bearing a tin of chocolate biscuits and two jars of meat extract – a month in Pokhara makes you put your pride in your pocket when such delicacies are going gratis. As for the Tibetans – this evening the camp is full of the most exotic things in tubes, tins, packets and plastic bags, and the people are as thrilled by these colourful luxury containers as they are by the mysterious contents. Walking around the camp at supper-time I saw pâté de foie gras being tentatively mixed with *tsampa*, salad cream being added to tea and soup cubes being chewed as toffees and then suddenly spat out. Terrifying howls of agony were coming from one tent, where some unfortunate little girl had just been given a spoonful of neat mustard by her loving mamma.

Trade is also brisk this evening; at the conclusion of an expedition the Sherpa guides receive as 'perks' sleeping-bags, anoraks, boots, transistors, boxes of electric batteries, nylon rope and many other locally rare objects, most of which they auction in the courtyard of The Annapurna before returning home. Tomorrow the 1965 Japanese Dhauligiri Expedition is due back here – in a rather depressed state, as their two senior Sherpas were killed by an avalanche. They are reported to have even more fabulous equipment than the Germans, both in quality and quantity, so we're all agog for the morning!

Tomorrow, too, is King Mahendra's birthday, a national holiday and in theory an enormously important occasion of universal rejoicing. During the past week all the local Government officials of every grade have been busy organising the celebrations to the detriment of far more urgent practical matters. It's rather obvious that in Pokhara Valley at least the general public have no great desire to demonstrate their loyalty to the King, and for this reason it is essential to *organise* these festivities, though the innumerable complicated religious festivals seem just to *happen*, powered by tremendous popular support.

Going on my own very limited knowledge of the Nepalese political scene I would say that the King is certainly doing his best to impose some sort of order on the indescribable mess bequeathed him by the Rana rulers. Also I have tremendous admiration for the moral courage he displayed in 1960, when he admitted that feigning to operate a democratic government in Nepal was a piece of pernicious nonsense. In the nine years since the overthrow of the Ranas in 1951 Nepal had had ten different governments, each more corrupt and cynical than the other, but now at least there is some degree of stability, though few of the needed improvements have yet taken place.

One of those improvements concerns land redistribution, about which there is at present a great deal of talk, but very little action. Here the King is up against problems similar to those of the Shah of Persia: the rich Brahmin landowners, with their superstition-based influence over the people, are analogous to the Persian mullahs – and apparently even more powerful – and the King's position is not secure enough for him to defy these Brahmins effectively. In the Kathmandu Valley he seems to have the affectionate support of a majority of his subjects, but to the average person in Pokhara both the King and Kathmandu are remote and unimportant. I have met many ex-Gurkha soldiers who have been to Delhi, Hong Kong, Singapore, Cairo and even to London – but who have never been to Kathmandu. And when I ask them, 'But don't you want to see your own capital?' they stare at me and say, 'For what?' In theory Kathmandu is their capital, but in practice they feel that they owe allegiance only to their tribe – and one can see the justice and logic of this attitude. For centuries no ruling power in Kathmandu knew or cared anything about the hill-people, and even now the King is an exception in his concern for the welfare of *all* his subjects; the majority of Government officials are still completely ignorant of and indifferent to what happens outside the valley and for them 'national improvements' mean the shoddy modernisation of Kathmandu and the installation of refrigerators in their own homes.

Today I have had quite the most gruesome experience of a lifetime. Dolma, a forty-two-year-old Tibetan woman, died last night of debilitation (following prolonged dysentery) at the Military Hospital, where I went this morning to enquire about three other patients from the camp. On my way, while walking by the river, I rounded an outcrop of rock and found Dolma's severed head at my feet. I must confess that to come on such a sight unexpectedly, when less than twenty-four hours earlier this woman had been sitting with her head on my shoulder, receiving cheering-up treatment, gave me rather a shock. Nearby the four camp chiefs were dismembering the trunk with blunt little wood-axes, before throwing it into the water, and I left the scene as quickly as possible.

Here the Tibetans choose this method of corpse-disposal in preference to the chopping up of bodies on a 'cemetery-rock' for birds of prey to eat – the more popular method in Tibet itself. Some Nepalese tribes, who live at high altitudes where wood is scarce, also use the rivers as graves, and I should think the bones are picked clean very soon after the dismembered body enters the water; at the moment I have a few open sores on my legs, and when I'm swimming these attract swarms of savage little fishes. In Tibet the office of undertaker – or chopper-upper – belonged to a special caste who were shunned by the average Tibetan; but the camp has no member of this caste and the task is so unpopular that the chiefs are forced to do it themselves. However, it would be wrong to imagine that these nomads are averse to such a job out of our sort of squeamishness; they decline to do it for superstitious reasons, not because the actual chopping up of a human body is repugnant to them.

11 JUNE

Our Royal Birthday Celebrations had been scheduled to begin in the camp at 12.30 p.m., when the Anchiladis and local Panchayat officials were due to assemble and make speeches and listen to the Tibetans praying for the King and expressing their non-existent gratitude for Nepal's reluctantly extended hospitality. A large piece of tarpaulin had been borrowed from the Indian Army Pension-paying Post and under this were arrayed a table (as altar), chairs and pictures of His Holiness and His Majesty (all borrowed from The Annapurna Hotel), while scarves and garlands of paper flowers were laid in readiness to be draped over the pictures. My worry was that the mailbag plane would arrive when Kay and I were shackled by courtesy to the camp – and sure enough in it came at 12.20 p.m., its wheels seeming almost to touch the tops of the tents. I then calculated that Nepalese officials due to appear at twelve-thirty would never present themselves before one o'clock at the earliest: so I leaped on Leo, dashed through the village to collect those precious envelopes, was back in camp by a quarter to one – and found that I had ample time to read ten letters before the Anchiladis' party arrived.

The heat was intense today and all the officials looked exceedingly bad-tempered and unfestive, having already attended several ceremonies in various places – and with many more to come. I gathered that they had only consented to attend the camp 'celebrations' because of pressure from certain quarters in Kathmandu, where a demonstration of 'solidarity' between the people of Pokhara and the refugees was considered very desirable. The whole thing felt extremely phony; of solidarity there is none and our celebrations here were incredibly bogus. Amdo Kessang, Penjung and Chimba had all vigorously exhorted the people to smarten up and produce appropriate symptoms of loyal rejoicing – yet when the officials arrived no one was paying the slightest attention to the Occasion. On every side Tibetans were going about their ordinary tasks or sitting in their tents digesting lunch – and I have to admit that I was glad of this. Contrived demonstrations of insincere feelings may be good diplomacy, but they are anathema to me.

The arrival of the Anchiladis' jeep presented an extraordinary spectacle; in Asia overloaded vehicles are a common sight, but this really was the ultimate in overloading. Though the jeep in question is the tiniest possible model it brought eleven men to the camp, and as the last three emerged one began to feel that one was watching a conjuring trick. The Anchiladis immediately announced – with comically un-Nepalese time-consciousness – that they could stay for only fifteen minutes; but ten minutes had passed before Penjung's wife and daughters produced the ritual tea and expensive, repulsive Indian biscuits and toffees; and a further twenty minutes passed before a sufficient number of Tibetans could be persuaded to assemble around the shelter to watch scarves and garlands being draped on the pictures and to hear the various speeches. At the conclusion of the speechifying everyone unenthusiastically chanted a prayer for the King, and finally the schoolchildren – if they can be so described – sang the Tibetan National Anthem, recently taught them by Chimba; and that was that. I particularly liked this last touch, which could easily be interpreted as showing a certain *lack* of solidarity on the King of Nepal's birthday; but the attendant press-photographer took countless shots with his archaic camera, and as facial expressions do not reproduce well on Nepalese paper the desired effect will doubtless be obtained in Kathmandu.

Then, when the jeep conjuring trick had been repeated in reverse and the vehicle had swayed away – invisible under its festoon of men – a demonstration of a different kind started spontaneously.

Suddenly the camp realised that a picture of His Holiness was hanging beneath the tarpaulin and their reaction astonished me. Normally these nomads don't seem nearly as devout as the Tibetans one meets in India but now everyone, including great tough men with shaggy hair and knives in their belts, came rushing to prostrate themselves before the simple black and white photograph, and then proceeded to pray lengthily with clasped hands and a look of near-ecstasy on their sun-plus-dirt-blackened faces. I couldn't help reflecting that if Tibet went under so comparatively easily to the Chinese, despite the unifying force of this tenacious loyalty to His Holiness, Nepal could go under even more easily with its lack of any such leadership.

15 JUNE

This morning I awoke to what looked like heaven – a world mistily draped in gentle clouds that completely hid the great mountains and almost concealed the nearer hills. It's impossible to describe the relief of seeing and feeling this grey dampness; of course the temperature was still about seventy-five degrees Fahrenheit – but what a joy, after the glare of the past weeks, to experience such cool dimness and to find clouds still shielding us as the morning progressed! Then at midday the sun reasserted itself and shone until about five o'clock when (cheers!) the monsoon started – not with any spectacular storm but just as a steady downpour, accompanied by incessant rumblings of thunder and frequent glares of blue sheet-lightning. On my way home from supper at Kay's house I fell repeatedly on the slippery, flooded road, in the coal-black intervals between lightning flashes that clearly and beautifully illuminated the whole width of the valley; and now the din of heavy rain on the tin roof is so deafening that I can hardly hear myself think.

I've refrained from giving details of the trials and tribulations involved in erecting monsoon huts for the camp – but the number and variety of these trials and tribulations would drive Job to drink. Between Nepalese procrastination and Tibetan laziness the whole operation is taking ten times as long as it should and today it was possible to move only half the camp from badly leaking tents into less badly leaking bamboo shelters. I suspect that in this case the Tibetans' laziness is a form of passive resistance; these nomads obviously prefer the seclusion of their traditional tent life, however inadequate the available tents may be, to the sort of communal existence they will have to endure in the new shelters – and as someone who values privacy far more than comfort I secretly sympathise with them. Having never experienced the persistent damp of a monsoon season they don't yet realise that their removal to less unsuitable accommodation is literally a matter of life or death – especially as many of them are already in a weakened condition because of the debilitating heat of this valley and an ill-balanced diet.

16 JUNE

Rain was still step-dancing on the roof when I awoke and the room temperature was down to seventy-two degrees Fahrenheit. Today Pardi seemed strangely hushed without the intermittent roar of planes landing and taking-off – life in this remote Central Nepalese village has at least one feature in common with life in Hounslow or Southall! However, as Nepal has a very mild version of the true Indian monsoon it is unlikely that we'll ever be cut off from Kathmandu for more than a week at a stretch. This morning the rain stopped at about ten o'clock and until it started again this evening the damp heat was rather exhausting – though luckily the sky remained overcast.

For the past four days I've been enjoying two pairs of fish-hawks who have come to live on the wooded precipice over-hanging my swimming-pool. They are falcon-sized, with glorious red-gold plumage, and it is wonderful to watch them swiftly swooping down to skim the surface of the green water, and then rising triumphantly against the blue sky with a silver fish in their talons. Here too I have twice seen a giant blue and silver kingfisher, looking like a tremendous sapphire as he flashes in and out of the water. The valley also has many other types of hawk and a great variety of unfamiliar sweet song-birds, as well as jays, tits, crows, finches, swallows and of course the very important, very ugly scavenging vulture, with its brilliant hooked yellow beak, ungainly walk and unpleasantly avid expression.

Last week two unusual patients were presented to me in camp – a pair of fledglings whose mother had been killed in the forest by Nepalese hunters and who were then rescued by Dawa, a firewood-gathering Tibetan. There was a certain pleasing incongruity about this great hulking fellow – looking as tough as Tibetans come – when he advanced towards me tenderly carrying these two tiny objects wrapped in a filthy rag. His trouble was that they wouldn't eat the Bulgar wheat he offered them, so what to do? When I advised insects Dawa carefully put his charges inside his *chuba*-pouch and hurried off on an entomological expedition – instead of getting on with his shelter-building work. And rather to my surprise the fledglings have survived and are now happily hopping around Dawa's tent to the delight of his three-year-old son.

Already I can see that the worst side-effect of the monsoon is going to be a nightly insect-plague. Nepalese shutters have little square ventilation holes near the top and through these fly an inconceivable number of insects, attracted by my lamp. At present the table and everything on it are literally being made to move by the creatures; I have just stopped writing to count eighteen different varieties, from enormous, exquisite moths, bright green two-inch grasshoppers and horny russet beetles, to mosquitoes and winged ants and half-a-dozen weird objects that I can't even attempt to identify. The combination of buzzes and bangs and whizzes and whines and bumps and drones adds up to quite a din. What is worse, the floor is swarming with big black ants – in addition to my permanent army of tiny red ones – and with cockroaches. I must admit that when sleeping on the floor cockroaches seem to me expendable, though I'm not neurotic about them as I am about spiders. Luckily – almost miraculously – spiders seem to be the only form of insect life *not* represented in the room at the moment.

Incidentally, my rats are becoming impossibly truculent – and obviously their mothers brought them up not to eat poison. Last night one of them knocked a zinc bucket off a tea-chest on to my head, so today I have a big lump above my ear; on moonlit nights it is positively depressing to see so many grey shapes scurrying around the room.

5

Tibetans on Trek

About a hundred and fifty more bamboo mats are desperately needed to complete the new shelter, but we have already bought all those available in the valley. However, I heard today that it should still be possible to buy some in Siglis, a village two days' walk from here, so I instructed Chimba to leave at dawn tomorrow morning with twenty-five Tibetans and to bring back as many mats as could be wheedled out of the villagers. I had expected him to rejoice at the prospect of even so short a trek for, like most Tibetans, he has an inborn inclination both to wander and to trade; but he showed an odd reluctance to go to Siglis and on being questioned as to the reason he declared that the track was exceptionally difficult at the best of times and would be downright dangerous now that the rivers were rising. This seemed a fair enough argument, yet it did not entirely convince me. When I enquired further he admitted that there was also a possibility of trouble with the Nepalese in Siglis, where the raiding exploits of Khamba brigands have made Tibetans so unpopular that the villagers would be more likely to attack our party than to trade with them; at which point I suddenly and delightedly saw that here was a perfect opportunity for me to combine duty and pleasure by accompanying the party as a pacifying agent, while getting my first experience of travel in the hills. Chimba at once agreed to organise the expedition if I came too, so tomorrow morning at six o'clock we will all set off together.

Today I found that the river had risen about five feet during the past twenty-four hours, transforming my placid pool into a frothing swirl of water. I got myself wet by cautiously going in at the edge of the torrent and hanging on to a rock while the water raced powerfully over me; then I pulled myself out, soaped all over and re-immersed for a rinsing-off session. All the time the river was rising fast; while rinsing and dressing I left my soap on a little ledge of rock some six inches above the water and within those few moments it was swept away and the ledge completely covered.

19 JUNE – TOPRUNG

This seems a very appropriate name for a hamlet near the summit of a 6,000-foot hill overlooking a deep, narrow valley; but my spelling is purely phonetic and it may be that Anglo-Nepali experts have an entirely different way of writing the word.

Our early start didn't come off today, because of persistent heavy rain, and it was seven o'clock before we marched out of camp in a pleasant grey coolness. Then there was another delay, caused by several men disappearing into The Annapurna on some obscure business connected with the private trading they hope to do in Siglis, so it was almost eight o'clock by the time we crossed the airfield.

Siglis is due north of Pokhara, according to my Swiss map of Nepal, yet because of the terrain's intractability we began our journey by walking more than five miles due south along the valley floor, before turning east for two miles up a broad side-valley. Here flowed an erratic river which we had to ford often, but in spite of a very fast current this was not difficult as the water never came above thigh-level and the bed was of firm gravel. Though this valley is about half-a-mile wide it is not cultivable, being merely a dried-up river-course which later in the season will be entirely submerged, and its stony surface was not appreciated by the barefooted Tibetans. Many of them had started out proudly wearing formidable mountaineering boots, acquired from various expeditions, but soon these unbearably unfamiliar prestige symbols had been transferred from feet to shoulders. Now the sight of so many bare feet on such cruel stones caused me considerable vicarious pain, so I urged a temporary resumption of boots; but this idea was at once rejected and in consequence we made slow progress during the next ninety minutes.

On either side of the valley rose steep, heavily-forested hills and occasionally we came to hillocks of grass on which a few handsome black cattle were grazing under the care of inquisitive, skinny children. By now the sky was almost cloudless and the heat considerable, so I often lay in the river for a moment without bothering to remove my shirt and shorts – a sensible idiosyncrasy which provoked uncontrollable mirth among the Tibetans. The fact that none of us had ever been to Siglis was giving the trek a faint tinge of adventure. Chimba had spent the previous evening searching for locals who knew the track and discussing it with them – but the Nepalese are not very precise in their directions and now he wasn't even pretending to be sure of where we went next.

Near the head of this valley we forded the river for the fourth time and then began to follow one of its tributaries up a steep side-valley, which was cultivated here though later it narrowed to a ravine. At the confluence of the rivers stood three solid Gurung farmhouses and all their occupants, of every age group, were now working at full pressure in the flooded paddy-fields, ploughing them with bullocks in preparation for the replanting of rice seedlings.

To me such evidence of harmony between Nature and man is wonderfully soothing. During the long hot days preceding the monsoon little work can be done and the people sit about idly enjoying themselves; then suddenly the rains come and overnight the landscape is utterly changed and the whole tempo of life altered to a most urgent activity. Here man, to survive, must co-operate fully with Nature, and it is impossible to see this severe yet dignified work-pattern as inferior to that of an industrial community in which men labour as dully in November as in May, obsessionally conscious of their individual 'rights' while remaining stuntedly unaware of themselves as part of a whole. Increasingly one senses a threat to racial sanity in this artificial sealing off of ourselves in a solitary compartment where pride in technological ingenuity replaces the old, instinctive recognition of our links with the rest of creation and our dependence on 'the gods'. Yet, even if it were possible to go back, any such denial of the good in our civilisation would be still more destructive than the present indiscriminate worship of both good and evil.

I had lingered to watch the ploughing and now, hurrying to catch up with the rest, I tried to imagine the unimaginable – life in 2065. Probably the most we can hope for is a gradual growth beyond this current adolescent idolatry of man's omnipotence towards a new, deliberate recognition of the necessity to worship *something* other than ourselves.

The paddy-fields all lay on one side of the river – by now I was too foxed up to know whether it was the north, south, east or west bank – and the only path was along the top of a narrow irrigation ditch, now sealed to retain the rain. As we advanced in single file the soft clay often crumbled, sending some unfortunate toppling into knee-deep liquid mud, and every one of the workers and animals was covered from head to foot in this thick dark liquid – which was all very well for the men, who wore only loincloths, but can't have been too pleasant for the women in their voluminous skirts. The men of our party are wearing ragged gift-parcel slacks or shorts – they reserve their *chubas* for festive occasions – but the women have not yet discarded the traditional Tibetan clothes. However, six out of the ten girls are dressed in the unusual Dholpo divided skirt, which neither Kay nor I had ever seen among the Tibetans in India; at first glance these garments look like ankle-length gowns, but they are in fact very loose pantaloons which allow great freedom of movement when walking or climbing.

As we ascended this valley the incline became much steeper and the river swifter and noisier among its tumble of rounded rocks. When the paddy-fields had been left behind I overtook the Tibetans, whose walking pace was apparently geared to that of laden yaks, and soon they were all behind me and I was happily alone in a fresh and lovely world of high, forested cliffs, glinting water and herb-sweet air. Occasionally fifty-foot waterfalls came leaping strongly off the cliffs, and in places the valley broadened enough for the path to wander briefly away from the river's edge across new green grass between silvery rocks. After about forty minutes I came to another fording place – and now I saw why Chimba had been apprehensive. Here the current was so powerful and the water so discoloured that it was impossible to judge depth and one had to feel with a stick before taking each step, all the time bracing oneself against the force of the water. But this river was no more than fifteen yards wide and I was soon across; the most disconcerting thing during such fordings is the shifting of stones on the river-bed beneath one's feet.

I sat on the bank to smoke a cigarette and de-leech my legs while waiting for the Tibetans. Surprisingly, most of the girls made quite a fuss about the fording and it was comical to see those tough nomad youngsters giving an excellent imitation of nervously giggling mid-Victorian ladies whose carriage has broken down on the way to a dinner party. Possibly this display was being put on mainly to attract the men's attention – though one can see that for non-swimmers such a crossing could be rather frightening. The ability to swim would almost certainly prove irrelevant if one were swept away by a mountain torrent but it does illogically give one an extra degree of confidence.

Chimba decided to call a halt here as many of the party were already 'creating' about being leech infested; this was the Tibetans' first monsoon so these pests were unfamiliar to them. Foreseeing several septic legs by the time we got home I hastened to explain that never must a leech be forcibly detached from the skin; either salt or a lighted cigarette are the only answers. As we have nothing but rock salt with us – and salt is in any case too expensive to waste on leeches – I went around from leg to leg with my cigarette, assuring the Tibetans that contrary to appearances they were not going to bleed to death within half-an-hour. Pasang, one of the more argumentative men, pointed out that he had already pulled his leech off and that his leg was *not* bleeding – nor did he appear convinced when I explained that this was exactly the point, and that bleeding was essential after the wretched creature had been removed. I didn't even attempt to explain that the bleeding was so copious only because leeches inject an anti-coagulant before beginning their meal.

Soon after this rest-halt we left the river and began the toughest part of today's walk – a climb to the crest of a 6,200-foot hill. (My natural impulse is to call this obstacle 'a mountain'; but by local standards it is of course a mere molehill.) For much of the way up – through dense forest – the track was not a track but a stone stairway; so if you can imagine ascending a two-mile stairway with very deep steps you will have some idea of how we felt on the crest.

By now it was apparent that these Tibetans have become seriously debilitated after six months in an unsuitable climate on an inadequate diet. Though travelling light and bred to walk far in rough country they made very slow progress at this stage, and for their sakes I'm thankful that on the way home, when they will (we hope) be carrying heavy loads, the journey will be mostly downhill. I waited for them at each porter's-rest – those stone squares, usually built around the base of a large tree, where a man can sit on one ledge and rest his load on the ledge above. The comfortable fixing of heavy and often unwieldy loads can be quite complicated so these rests are designed to take the weight off the body without the removal of the load. Many of them must be centuries old, for on the shiny stone seats one can see where the impress of countless buttocks has worn into the surface.

On the crest of the hill I again walked briskly ahead – and then suddenly came to one of the eeriest spots I have ever known. Here the path overhung a deep ravine, and where it turned right to climb the next ridge a tiny Hindu shrine, covered with stale bloodstains, had been built in the shadow of a gigantic, fantastic tree. The weird distortion of this tree gave it such an unnerving personality that spontaneously one thought of it as a demon in disguise; and to add to the unreality of the scene the monster roots were growing around a colossal black rock, about a hundred feet high and thirty feet wide, that had become detached from the mountainside and was poised unnaturally above a sheer, thousand-foot drop. These complex roots were as thick as a man's body and they clasped the rock with a nightmarish, writhing ferocity that produced an extraordinary effect of repellent beauty. Even on this brilliantly sunny afternoon the place was merely twilit and in the absolute silence of the forest the steady, quiet dripping of water off the rock sounded ridiculously, but definitely, sinister. I am not given to psychic reactions and perhaps, had I been forewarned, I would have had my shield of scepticism in place and felt no more than interest at observing a curious natural phenomenon. But as it was this corner of the forest frankly scared me and I'm not surprised at the erection of a shrine to propitiate the spirits of the tree and rock, who obviously have extremely unpleasant dispositions. I rang their heavy iron bell three times as a precautionary salutation and its curiously amplified echoes were still resounding as I climbed towards the crest of the next ridge.

Such encounters with the mysterious can be at once stimulating, chastening and annoying. It is always exhilarating to glimpse regions that can't be mapped, and it is healthily humbling to be challenged by subtleties against which rationality is no defence. Yet it is irritating, too, to be proved still vulnerable to influences which one is supposed to have long outgrown; and in the end one is left with just another big question mark. After firmly deciding that rocks and trees do not have spirits the only alternative explanation for such 'atmospherics' is that over many centuries enough people have come to this place with enough awe for its visible peculiarities and enough terrified belief in the power of its spirits to leave an enduring deposit of fear and unease in the shadow of that root-gripped rock. But this leads on to speculation as to *why* certain natural phenomena should so overwhelm the minds and imagination of men – and if one doesn't then think quickly about something else one is back where one started.

Now the track was climbing through maize-fields to a little village built on a series of narrow shelves just below the top of the ridge. There appears to be a vast amount of marble available locally, and this has been used here to create a uniquely beautiful village. For the final quarter of a mile the track was very steep and as I ascended a stairway of smooth marble slabs I had the illusion of approaching a royal palace rather than a primitive hill settlement. This marble is of many soft colours – pink, white, green, yellow, fawn – and discovered amidst the glory of the surrounding heights and depths it is intoxicatingly lovely. Then I found myself walking between the houses on shiny marble paving-stones, instead of the usual rough paths, and – most striking of all – I saw, on the ledge below, roofs of multicoloured thin marble slates, glowing with a gentle lustre in the clear air.

I waited for the Tibetans in the centre of the village and when they had joined me Chimba explained that the local people were Gurungs, who would be less unhelpful than the orthodox Hindu Chetris in the next settlement; so we agreed to eat here. He and I then sat on the verge of a minor precipice and ate our hard-boiled eggs and raw onions, while the rest of the party dispersed throughout the village to beg for the use of fireplaces on which to prepare *tsampa*.

Rarely have I picnicked amidst such enchantment. In addition to the marbled splendour of their roofs these houses had smooth walls of handsome stone slabs, so cleverly cut that no mud was needed to stop up cracks, and each separate stone seemed to be tinged a different shade of brown, cream or grey. Yet it was the texture of the stones and the apparent simplicity of the well-proportioned structures – which in fact must require considerable skill – that pleased me most. It is interesting that the availability of such unusual building materials has inspired local craftsmen to attain a much higher level of artistry than is evident in any of the neighbouring villages; and Chimba tells me that in all his Nepalese travels he has never seen anything comparable with this little settlement.

No milk was to be had here, but when we had finished our meal Chimba proudly produced tins of powdered milk and Swiss drinking chocolate (both scrounged from the German expedition of happy memory) and while we were drinking this delicacy one of the many eagles that float continuously over these valleys swooped down with talons outstretched and seized a hen which was pecking nearby at our eggshells. What fierce-looking birds these are, seen close to and in action!

When we continued after an hour's break the path first went downhill through terraced maize-fields, then crossed a river before climbing steeply through more forest, and finally levelled out to swing around the shoulder of another mountain and bring us to this small village of grass-thatched ochre-washed Chetri houses.

My crossing of the above-mentioned river made the day for the Tibetans. The 'bridge' was a single, narrow, slippery tree-trunk, about thirty feet long and some fifty feet above a flooded river-bed crowded with hideous-looking boulders. A single slip could mean nothing but death and after one horrified look I said, 'No, thanks – perhaps in my reckless youth but certainly not now'. The Tibetans were tickled pink by such cowardice and several of them at once volunteered to carry me across on their backs; but I emphatically declined this terrifying though noble offer and while they all trooped over without a second thought I investigated alternatives. There were none. So I despairingly sat astride the damn thing and cautiously propelled myself across, which device had the Tibetans literally rolling on the ground with mirth. But it did get me safely, if slowly, to the other side.

It was only 5.30 p.m. when we arrived here and as two hours of daylight remained we intended walking further; but on enquiring about shelter we learned that none existed between Toprung and Siglis, which is seven hours' walk away. So, as sleeping out without tents isn't very healthy during the monsoon, we are now billeted on the unwelcoming though not overtly hostile villagers. We will sleep on various verandahs at the approximate cost of one penny per sleeping-space and I'm among the honoured few who are to be accommodated on the verandah of the village store, which sells nothing but cigarettes, matches and cloth, plus kerosene at certain seasons. The weary Tibetans were jubilant at this unexpectedly early halt and it suited me too. While wood was being collected to boil big saucepans of tea for our *tsampa* supper I set off on an exploratory walk to the top of this mountain, revelling in the cool evening air and in the dramatic splendour all around me.

The steep track of slippery yellow-red mud led me past several farmsteads set amidst fields of seven-feet-high maize. There were many goats about, and the usual Nepalese proliferation of undersized poultry, and despite the terrain quite a few cattle – mostly working bullocks in excellent condition. Here rice and maize are the chief crops, and even at this altitude there were a few banana trees, though their fruit was small and as yet unripe.

While walking along the mountainside, away from the track, I was often looking down into farmyards on the terrace below and glimpsing vignettes of domestic life – a young father absorbed in play with his two tiny sons, an elderly husband yelling abuse at his cowed wife and menacing her with an axe, or a grandad milking goats while keeping one eye on his toddling granddaughter as she romped ecstatically with a pure white, newborn kid. Watching such scenes unobserved, one can forget the many gulfs that separate race from race and find security in our common humanity; then someone notices the foreigner and the moment of comforting union is gone. Every activity is neglected while curiosity seeks satisfaction and again the gulfs appear – wider and deeper in Nepal than in any other country I have known, because here, outside of the Kathmandu Valley, it is uncommon for people to come halfway to meet the friendly stranger.

It would be futile to try to describe this region, for in exclusively mountainous countries every beauty is too extreme to be conveyed by any words that I might choose. None of the books or photographs studied before leaving home had even slightly prepared me for such majesty. Truly this is something that does have to be seen to be believed, and that once seen must be continually yearned for when left behind, becoming as incurable a fever of the spirit as malaria is of the body.

When I arrived back in Toprung village it was still quite bright at this level – but the immensity of the valley far below was already filled with a solid-seeming, dark-blue dusk and above the opposite mountains towering clouds were gathering fast. Now it is half-past nine and for the past two hours sheets of water have been streaming from a black sky.

20 JUNE – SIGLIS

It was a relief to get up at 4 a.m. and escape from the hordes of bed-bugs that had tormented me all night. Their invincibility made sleep impossible; I merely dozed lightly, woke to swear and scratch furiously, then dozed again, woke again, swore again, scratched again and so on through what felt like a week of nights. But on either side of me Tibetans were sleeping deeply, their total immunity affording thousands of bugs a blissfully undisturbed banquet.

For me one of the advantages of Tibetans as trekking companions is that their conception of essential equipment matches my own; within ten minutes of rising we were on the track again, walking by moonlight for the first quarter of an hour. Then quite suddenly it was light and we could see banks of silvered cloud softly rolling up the valley below us. As the rain had just ceased the whole world was dripping and rushing with water, and for the first half of our long descent to river level the path was in fact a swift stream, calf-deep, through which we scrambled among shifting stones and rough rocks. It is difficult to decide whether these paths are streams converted into 'highways' or vice versa. This area of the mountain was a mere tangle of scrub, neither forested nor cultivated, and once we lost our way and went scrambling down a few hundred feet in the wrong direction before Chimba, using some sixth sense, realised our mistake and led us up again.

Today leeches were much more plentiful than yesterday, and the Tibetans made an absurd fuss about this minor annoyance; to hear their screams and roars one would imagine them to have been attacked by tigers. It was obvious that if I were to burn off every leech immediately its host noticed it we'd never get anywhere so, as the leech's sucking is completely painless, I told the party to ignore the creatures till we had arrived at Siglis, where we could hold a mass de-leeching session.

The latter half of our descent was from paddy-field to paddy-field – a relaxation after the rough track, yet tiring in its own way because for much of the time we were dragging ourselves through knee-deep sticky mud. Each terraced field was about twenty yards long, ten yards wide and three or four feet high; stepping stones were sometimes set in the dykes, and it was only by finding and correlating these that we could follow the route, since our track as such was no longer in existence.

We were still about three hundred feet above river level when we rounded a corner and saw Siglis – a tiny cluster of houses near the summit of the next precipitous mountain. I reckon that the village was then about two miles away as the crow flies – but eight miles as humans walk.

From here the central valley broadened out for some miles to the north and was noisy with the speed of a wide, frothing river – which fortunately did not flow between us and our destination. Now we could also survey the narrow side-valley separating us from the Siglis mountain, and the tributary that here went raging down to the main river looked sufficiently daunting to set the Tibetans muttering prayers. I brightly remarked that when we got down to this torrent we would probably find quite an easy fording spot – but I was wrong. In fact it proved to be far too swollen for any attempt at wading, and there was a long delay while we searched for a spot where we could cross by leaping from boulder to boulder. Eventually Chimba found such a spot, though as the boulders in question were all rounded – and entirely submerged – no one considered this leaping game to be very amusing. I was then tempted to worry in a fussy Western fashion about the state of this river by tomorrow and the safety of the Tibetans when re-crossing it with heavy loads; but happily my temperament is in some respects more Eastern than Western, and as the Tibetans themselves were obviously not looking this far ahead I reminded myself that 'sufficient unto the day . . . '

The sky was now cloudless and clear early sunshine filled this wild world of powerful mountains, racing waters, scattered rocks and new green growth. I longed to be alone here: yet if I had had to choose my companions I would have chosen these Tibetans, who are so attuned to such remoteness that they never come between it and me as even the most congenial of Western companions inevitably would do.

About half-a-mile from the river we came upon an isolated, impoverished Gurung farmhouse which also acts as a 'transport café', and here we stopped (having had no breakfast) to drink glasses of ginger tea before tackling the brutal climb to Siglis. This was my first taste of ginger tea, which is popular among those Nepalese who can't afford the real thing, and I found it most refreshing.

The track, now quite distinct, continued level along the valley floor for another mile or so. Then directly below Siglis, which was no longer visible, it turned left and went up and up and up, and still further up, until it seemed that we were doomed to spend the rest of our lives dragging aching bodies and rumbling bellies up an everlasting incline. Yet there was – at least for me – the reward that always makes such efforts worth while; even non-mountaineers know the ineffable joy of *going higher*. A peculiar triumph tingles in the blood when at each stop one looks down and sees how much farther away is the valley from which one started. Why this triumph should result from perpendicular rather than horizontal progress it is not for me to say; no doubt the psychologists have a word for it – but I don't particularly want to submit the ingredients of this special joy for clinical analysis.

Significantly, Chimba and I – the only adequately nourished members of the party – arrived here soon after eleven o'clock, an hour ahead of the rest. Siglis has a population of about 4,800 Gurungs, and during the past few years it has had a school of sorts, now closed because the teacher left since the government had forgotten to pay him any salary for fifteen months. Nor is this an exceptional case; all over Nepal recently-opened rural schools are folding up for the same reason. There is only one tiny store-cum-tea-shop, doing the usual trade in cloth, cigarettes, matches and, providentially, those nauseating Indian biscuits which are so inexplicably prized by the Nepalese. When we arrived I immediately devoured a whole pound of (literally) mouldy biscuits, while Chimba boiled a saucepan of rice on the storekeeper's fireplace.

I got through my biscuit marathon sitting outside the store on the edge of the terrace (inevitably every laneway here is a terrace) overlooking the valley far below. From this height the river's roar is inaudible, and I savoured with gratitude the uniquely calming stillness of high places. Away to the north, at the head of the valley, gleaming snow peaks soared above the nearer mountains and directly opposite Siglis – beyond the river – I could see another high village; it looked deceptively near, though for the duration of the monsoon no communication will be possible between these two settlements.

I had felt myself being almost weakened by the sun, which at 9,000 feet begins to have an odd sting in its heat, but as we ate our rice a procession of plump grey clouds came floating up the valley in a stately way; and soon long, coiling wisps of vapour had detached themselves from the main mass to send their cold moisture eddying through the village. Then, as we de-leeched the exhausted Tibetans – who came crawling up the laneway in twos and threes, characteristically laughing at their own fatigue – rain began to bucket down in a true monsoon deluge. Luckily, however, the efficient Chimba had already arranged for us to be accommodated in the local Panchayat headquarters, on the terrace below the store, and we hurriedly retreated from the downpour.

This new building is a very unsound erection of wood, stone and mud, with a leaking corrugated iron roof. Such roofs are tremendous prestige symbols here, each iron sheet having been carried on a man's back from India, and their impracticality is equalled only by their ugliness – which is the more distressing for being found in the midst of so much beauty. I cannot help suspecting some political significance in the extraordinarily bad workmanship of this Panchayat head-quarters. The men who built it would certainly have done more skilful jobs on their own homes; but the Panchayat system is a political imposition from Kathmandu and the haphazard construction of its local headquarters reveals indifference to the innovation – and may well be a deliberate, oblique protest against Government interference.

After my buggy night at Toprung, followed by a hard climb and a heavy meal, I was now almost asleep on my feet, so while the Tibetans prepared their well-earned *tsampa* I curled up in a corner on the lumpy mud floor and slept soundly for three hours.

On our arrival here Chimba had tried to circulate the news that we had come to buy mats, but at this season the farmers are so busy that virtually no one – man, woman or child – is to be found in any village between 5 a.m. and 7.30 p.m. (When you have to climb down two or three thousand feet to reach your fields you do *not* come home to lunch!) A small group of us set off to tour the village at 5.30, but we met only tottering, toothless, totally gaga great-great-grandfathers, who had long since forgotten what bamboo mats were, so we soon gave up our futile braving of the savage mastiffs who were chained to stakes in front of every homestead.

Siglis is quite unlike the ochre-washed, straw-thatched villages of the lower slopes. Here the houses are built of enormous stones plastered over with brown mud and the majority are roofed securely with weighted slates. Steep, uneven steps lead up from one row of houses to the next and this evening each of these stairways was a miniature waterfall. At first I had wondered – rather stupidly – why the original settlers, with a whole mountain at their disposal, had chosen to build at this height; but now, studying the village, I realise that it was sited on the rockiest part of the mountain, where cultivation of any crop would have been impossible.

At dusk we borrowed a lantern from the storekeeper and set off again to attempt to trade. For the past half-hour people had been streaming back from the fields, carrying antique wooden ploughs over their shoulders and driving sleek black bullocks before them, and I was fascinated by the agility of these great animals as they climbed the narrow steps between the houses. Our camp had attracted great, though not very friendly, interest from the passers-by and we now found that though many mats were available few of the villagers were willing to sell them to Tibetans. Despite Chimba's warning I was somewhat taken aback by the degree of sullen hostility shown towards us; whether it would have been more active without the restraining presence of Authority, obscurely represented by me, it is impossible to say, but undoubtedly my activities as liaison officer were useful, if not essential, and when I had solicited the aid of the co-operative headman we began to make some progress. Eventually he assured us that all the mats we needed would be brought to us early in the morning – but it remains to be seen how effective his influence is. It's now nearly ten o'clock and the Tibetans are snoring happily around me; I only hope that the bugs in our bedding have been sufficiently atrophied by the cold for me to sleep too.

21 JUNE – TOPRUNG

The headman's influence proved so effective that at 4 a.m. laden villagers began to queue outside the Panchayat building and by 8 a.m. we had purchased eighty mats (heavy rain meant that no one was going early to the fields). Then the supply dried up abruptly – doubtless because the weather did likewise – but we were promised forty more mats this evening. I then decided that fifteen of us, including all the girls, should return today, leaving ten to follow tomorrow. It would have been fun to wait and explore further, but

Chimba had to stay as interpreter, and one of us two had to shepherd
the fifteen, so I led the party off at 10.30 after a hearty 'brunch' of
tsampa.

Each Tibetan was carrying a roll of five or six heavy mats – supported
by a broad band around the forehead – which made me feel dreadfully
guilty about carrying nothing: but it's no use pretending that I could
carry even one mat (they measure eight feet by three) on any of these
tracks. It was agony merely to watch the Tibetans struggling down that
unspeakable path with those unspeakable loads; I myself found the
descent difficult enough, and as one's thigh muscles are the brakes on
such a gradient I know that mine will be very stiff tomorrow.

Soon after we left Siglis a cloud sat on the mountain and the chilly,
driving mist made me feel quite homesick for Ireland when I saw it
move across the green turf and grey rocks. By the time we got to the
Gurung tea-house another real deluge was in progress, so we each had
two glasses of the ginger brew while waiting for it to ease off. On the
way down the sole of one of my canvas boots had come partly adrift,
and now Tsiring – at sixteen the youngest of the party – noticed this
unimportant detail, registered horror, demanded the boot, produced
a large needle and strong thread from his pocket and expertly repaired
the damage while we were drinking our tea. As good nomads these
Tibetans set out on even the briefest trek equipped for all such
emergencies.

They also have a commendable passion for buying hens and chickens
and, as they had each acquired at least two birds in Siglis, every roll of
mats now contained its quota of poultry – which complained loudly at
halts, to the wonderment of the Gurung farm birds.

Next came that damnable river, which had risen so much since
yesterday that our crossing via the boulders could not be repeated.
After a long search we came on a place, much further upstream, where
by a combination of rock climbing and jumping we could quite safely
cross – without loads. Everyone then unloaded, some of us went to the
other side and each roll of mats was passed from hand to hand up the
rocks and over the water and down the rocks to level ground – an
operation which delayed us more than an hour.

Knowing that no other danger spots lay between us and Toprung I now went ahead of the rest, grateful for an opportunity to be alone for a few hours. Already the sky was clear again and the sun dazzled on a sparkling exuberance of growth; even Ireland could not surpass the brilliance of the green that clothed these mountains. But even since yesterday the rains had wreaked havoc on the path above the paddy-fields, and somewhere amidst those minor landslides I took a wrong turning which eventually brought me to the village – after many bewildered wanderings in various directions – from below instead of above.

On those lower slopes I had loitered to watch the rice planters at work. This one week in the year is the most critical period of the Nepalese farmers' lives, when transplanting takes place after the original shoots have suddenly sprung up and the first rains have irrigated the terraces. Each tiny field has a hole in the dyke through which the water pours out until a foot's depth is left, when the hole is adroitly blocked with mud and the ploughing begins. Next the dyke is re-opened to allow the surplus water to flow away and in the residue of soft mud the young shoots are transplanted, before another closing of the dykes brings the water level back to six inches. I had never before realised what swift and skilful labour is required for this operation. When you see every individual tiny wisp of rice stalk being planted by hand you begin to understand why the entire population of a village has to slave at the task from dawn to dusk. Men and boys do the ploughing on one level while half the women and girls bend over the dry terraces, gently but speedily uprooting the tender shoots and throwing them onto the terrace above, where the rest of the womenfolk replant them, about six inches apart, at the most incredible speed; so rapidly do these workers' hands move that you can hardly see them. It's consoling to think that no machine is ever likely to be invented for a job that demands such a combination of skill, speed and gentleness.

The general standard of health in all these villages is pretty low – though not as low as in the average Indian village. This morning I spent half-an-hour talking to the compounder at the tiny, ill-stocked Siglis dispensary. (No hospitals, doctors or nurses are to be found outside the Kathmandu and Pokhara valleys; and even within these valleys most of the worthwhile medical care is provided by missionaries.) This young man, a native of Kathmandu, was the only person in Siglis who spoke any English but, unlike the majority of Kathmandu-born officials who find themselves stationed in the hills, he did not complain about his present 'primitive' surroundings. Instead he gave the impression of being genuinely interested in his work, though he admitted that with his limited knowledge and experience and his minimal medical supplies he could really do very little to alleviate local suffering. He told me that venereal diseases – either inherited or contracted – were responsible for most of the villagers' complaints. His estimate was that eighty-five per cent of the population was riddled with VD – hence so many blind, deaf, deformed or imbecile children. Whether or not Siglis is an exceptional village in this respect I wouldn't know; one can only hope so.

To my sleeping-bag now – but I fear *not* to sleep, remembering what our previous night at Toprung was like.

22 JUNE – POKHARA

It was another hellishly buggy night, as I had expected, and at 5.30 a.m. when the rain had just ceased, I set off alone, leaving the Tibetans to their lengthy preparation of a *tsampa* breakfast. An early meal is contrary to local trekking custom but the Tibetans, unlike the Nepalese, are used to a meal soon after waking, and because of this party's poor condition and heavy loads I thought it advisable for them to fill up before starting for home.

The next two hours provided one of those strange interludes – curiously apart from the rest of existence – which occur only when by some blessed chance a heightened receptivity coincides with a rare degree of beauty in one's surroundings. I know that I shall never forget this morning's walk through the forest. There seemed to be some magic in those short hours, some wonder beyond what was apparent to the senses.

Half-a-mile beyond Toprung I was walking through a density of high greenness with which man has never tampered – an entirely solitary world where supple lengths of grey vapour, weaving between

great trees, seemed to possess an eerie substance and purpose of their
own. A dawn hush still lay over the mountains, and on this mantle of
silence were embroidered the urgent rushings of new-born streams,
and the myriad harsh or melodic bird cries that are the voice of the
forest. Far below me a motionless pillow of cloud hid the depths of the
valley and beyond this gulf the dark blue outlines of the opposite
mountains were half-revealed, then obscured, then again half-revealed
as their sheaths of mist shifted – until quite suddenly the sun was
dominant, and the long, smooth lines of these crests lay free against a
clear blue sky. Now the whole scene was changed by this vigorous
golden light that came pouring over the mountaintops. As the warmth
rapidly increased one could feel the earth's eager response and around
every corner were freshly-blossoming shrubs, their white, blue and
deep pink flowers unfolding as one watched, to bloom with a most
sweet radiance against the dark green of the undergrowth.

Only when I reached the 'marble village', and paused to de-leech
myself, did I come out of my trance. Between this village and the valley
floor the track had been so transformed by floods, and the landscape so
altered by new growth that I got lost twice, in a mild way, and was
eventually forced – by the remains of a real landslide about halfway
down the mountain – to find a new route to the river. I left signposts of
specially arranged sticks for the Tibetans, to save them from repeating
my optimistic mistakes in search of short-cuts, and this evening I was
gratified to learn that these markers had served their purpose.

This detour involved a descent through literally pathless forest, a
long scramble down terraces of muddy paddy-fields, the fording of a
waist-deep, violent river and then the ascent and descent of a new hill
(which by this stage felt extraordinarily like a mountain). And all these
manoeuvres were simply in order to reach another point along the
river where it was possible to cross back to the main Pokhara track
from which the landslide had deflected us.

It was 4.30 p.m. when I at last got home, painfully hungry and with
both boots blood-filled from leech bites. 'Going for a walk' in Nepal
really is quite something!

6

Animal Spirits

Yesterday my pup Tashi briefly joined this multiplying household. Though a happy and healthy infant her growth has been almost imperceptible during these past weeks, and when Ngawang Pema insisted on handing over possession I very much doubted her readiness to leave home. Tibetans suckle their own offspring until the mother's breast has been repeatedly lacerated by sharp teeth so I thought it unlikely that the minute Tashi had already been prepared for life without Mum – and the next twenty-four hours proved me right. She was cowed, miserable and resolutely on hunger strike; her piteous whimpering would have taken a tear from a stone, so this morning, after a sleepless night for all concerned, I returned her to Mum with my compliments.

One hopes that soon she will grow just a little. At present she is so furry-toy-like that on several occasions last night, when she moved suddenly, I imagined myself to be at last in the DTs. An appreciation of religious music would also help; as yet she is positively allergic to it and the lama's sacred melodies had an extremely deleterious effect on her. Every time he started a new bell-and-drum duet she compulsively accompanied him, producing noises that sounded incredibly like the cacklings of a hen which has just laid. Yet Tashi makes music too, with every movement, because like all Tibetan pups she had seven tiny tinkling bells tied around her neck on the day her eyes opened. These serve a dual purpose – the keeping of evil spirits at bay and the prevention of straying during nomad treks.

It's now 1 a.m. because this evening we attended an uncanny ceremony at the camp – the exorcising of evil spirits by Dawa, a monk magician.

When the ceremony began it was already dark outside, but the shelter was brightly lit by the flames of a huge log-fire and by the 108 butter lamps that flickered at the monk's right-hand side as he sat cross-legged on a little mound of yak skins, facing west, with about twenty relatives and friends of the 'possessed' around him.

Dawa spent the first fifteen minutes chanting more and more rapidly and wielding his drum and bell more and more quickly as he invoked the gods to enter into him and speak through him. Next he began to tremble all over – at first slightly, then in shuddering paroxysms as he turned north towards Tibet. At this point Thupten Tashi clutched my arm and whispered, 'The god is coming!' transmitting to me as he spoke a morsel of his own fearful belief. Now the acolyte, Dawa's young servant, stepped forward and placed on his master's head a bizarre cockade-cum-mask of bedraggled peacock feathers and streamers of dirty, coloured ribbon. This signified that the god had taken possession of his oracle, and at once the monk ceased to be a familiar neighbour and the Tibetans prostrated themselves before him as before a picture of His Holiness.

During the few moments preceding the donning of the head-dress Dawa had been unmistakably going into a self-induced hypnotic trance and now, suddenly, he leaped to his feet, tossed the mask of ribbons off his face, and with staring eyes began to speak very angrily, loudly and clearly. At this stage my blood began to curdle slightly, for instead of using his native Dholpo dialect Dawa was now speaking Lhasa Tibetan, which is even further from our camp speech than BBC English is from the broadest Scots. I asked Thupten where this uneducated monk could possibly have learned such polished Tibetan and the answer was that he never had learned it, but that all mediums use it when possessed.

Soon my blood curdled still more, as Dawa became thoroughly infuriated and went rampaging around the hut shouting hoarsely and waving his arms wildly until everyone had fled except Thupten and the blasé acolyte, whose function it was to placate the god by respectfully prostrating himself, and throwing little bowls of water or handfuls of flour into the air.

Dawa's frenzied perambulations eventually brought him to our corner, where he stood over us shaking his drum and bell cacophonously while he roared maledictions; now I could see the foam around his lips, the sweat trickling down his face and the truly terrifying gleam in his eye. Then, swerving away from us, he kicked violently at the altar of cardboard boxes on which the votive lamps were burning; this seemed to me a very rash thing for a god to do in a bamboo hut, but luckily the little flames went out as their containers fell to the ground. Possibly gods can ordain safety precautions in conjunction with their tantrums.

Then abruptly Dawa subsided, trembling, onto his yak-skins, and as everyone came creeping cautiously back I asked Thupten why the god had been so angry. He replied that it was very necessary to condemn certain people in the camp for habitually having evil thoughts, which gave evil spirits a foothold in the community and caused many deaths. Other camp defects had also been censured, including disobedience of His Holiness's commands that the refugees should strive to be self-supporting, and our washing of children in the local river, which is the home of an important god who objects to this pollution of his residence. I was greatly intrigued by the undiluted animism of this last complaint – and indeed by the whole confusing conglomeration of Bön-po rites, ancient primitive magic and practical politics. I hate to think of His Holiness's reaction to any such ceremony; but at least he was being remembered, if only in his rôle as earthly leader of the refugees.

Next came the exorcism of the sufferers, and now Dawa was back to normal; although in theory he was still inhabited by a deity all the symptoms of trance had vanished. His first patient was Droma, an adolescent girl who complained of great pain in the chest and back. (She is at present being treated by Kay for acute indigestion.) This youngster sat in front of the monk for about ten minutes with her eyes closed tightly and a look of terror on her face – which did not surprise me, as she was being emotionally pulverised by a fearful description of the particular demon she was harbouring. Then she lowered her *chuba* – keeping her breasts covered with unusual modesty because she is unmarried and Dawa a celibate – and the

The Royal Hotel, Kathmandu; formerly a Rana palace

An old Palace, Patan; these sculptured gods become personal friends
when one sees them every day

Children in the streets of Kathmandu: a young vendor in front
of the Hanuman Dhoka temple

Patan Police Station

Among young Tibetans in Kathmandu an intelligent child sometimes voluteers to teach his contemporaries

In most regions of Nepal the children are happy, healthy and friendly

Main Street, Pokhara; here the Nepalese atmosphere matters
more than the shops

At Pokhara airport planes are merely tolerated

The locals never tire of gathering on the airfield

The sort of bridge one prefers not to cross

Kaski River, Pokhara

Pokhara from the Kaski Ridge

The truly religious old lamas accept their exile with dignity
and cheerful courage

Leaving a high village at dawn is always one of the day's best moments

Surviving many rides along Pokhara's main street was a good test
for my Russian bicycle

In these mountain farmhouses a warm welcome usually makes up for lack of comfort

Tashi in Ireland, June 1967

acolyte handed his master a saucer-sized copper disc which had been standing upright in a sacrificial bowl of flour. With this Dawa tapped her back vigorously, while making loud, yelping noises to frighten off the demon. (Had I been a demon they would certainly have frightened me very far off.) Next he spat all over her torso, muttering incantations between each spit – and then the exorcism was over. As Droma prostrated herself three times, before giving Rs. 5/- to the acolyte, I felt a slight sense of anti-climax; somehow one expects demons to move house less unobtrusively.

The next two patients were babies whom Kay has been treating for severe dysentery, but who are not improving because their mothers will insist on breast-feeding them.

Dawa's second trance was even more violent than the first and, though there was no verbal outburst when the god arrived, he flailed around the hut waving drum and bell wildly and once hitting me on the side of my bemused head. Yet no one fled during this display of divine wrath, though everyone cowered and covered their eyes with their hands as the medium approached them; evidently it is the god's spoken message that really frightens the people – and that most scared me, if scared is not too strong a word for the chilled unease felt in such a situation. After some ten minutes of violence Dawa abruptly sat down, and when his uncanny rigours and involuntary moanings had subsided the exorcism of the babies began.

The first one received the same treatment as Droma but the other, who is very debilitated, was subjected to a long and complicated rite. So far Dawa's face had been entirely hidden by his mask, except when the patients were being spat on, but now, as this naked baby was being presented to him by its terrified mother, he tossed back the streamers to reveal a subhuman, snarling expression, not at all modified by the flickering firelight. Then he leant forward with a jerk, giving a perfect imitation of a savage dog growling, and bit the baby between the shoulders.

The rituals that followed were exceedingly complex. With his left hand Dawa pressed to the baby's back the ends of those filthy ribbons that are always attached to prayer-drums, while in his right hand he held the drum and sucked vigorously at the ribbons where they were attached to its centre. After each suck he spat into a little brass bowl handed him by the acolyte, and then appeared to drink a mouthful of water from another brass bowl – though in fact I think he retained the water in his mouth to provide the next spit. This process was repeated eleven times, after which he did the copper-disc demon-scaring act as with Droma, before bending low over the infant and laying his head on its stomach. Then he jerked upright, tossed his mask back, spat once more into the bowl – and with the air of a grimly self-satisfied conjurer announced that the cause of the disease was now lying in the bowl for all to see. A murmur of admiration and reverence greeted this announcement and everyone crowded forward to gaze into the bowl, while the baby's mother wept and laughed with relief. Yet I myself again felt thwarted; it is disillusioning to find that an evil spirit looks like a dead water-beetle.

Finally Dawa set about freeing himself of the god. A motionless, coma-like trance was followed by incantations and music that gradually worked up to the most frenzied crescendo of the evening – then suddenly the bell and drum were dropped and Dawa fell to the ground and lay twitching convulsively and grunting and groaning like a man who is attempting some Herculean feat. Then, after one last horrible gurgle, he relaxed and lay still, his eyes wandering around the hut with the slightly dazed expression of a normally tired man.

Immediately the spell was broken and the acolyte, reverting to being a servant, began to pour tea for us all. As an excited chattering broke out among the Tibetans Dawa slowly moved back to his seat, politely acknowledging the presence of Kay and myself in the normal Tibetan fashion – though previously he had given us no sign of recognition.

I can't say that this display impressed me as a religious rite, though I consider myself fortunate to have seen it. Recently, however, our genuine lamas have been praying a great deal over sick children or adults and these ceremonies are impressive. Usually the lamas improvise a temple in one of their tents, converting an American Surplus Food box into an altar on which they lay as many butter lamps as the patient's family can afford, and little bowls of cock's blood and rice and flour, and figures of gods – here made from dough instead of the traditional butter – and the inevitable conical *tormas*. Then two or three of them sit at right angles to this altar and, fortified by buttered tea, spend all day chanting reverently from the scriptures and producing beautiful, eerie melodies with their drums, bells and human thigh-bone trumpets. These sessions are sometimes concluded by the printing of prayers on the skin of the sufferer, over the affected part, using the wooden printing-blocks with which prayer flags are made.

However, though Dawa's activities were hardly edifying they should not be regarded as sheer fraud. His trances were undoubtedly genuine, and what he said during his 'sermon' revealed a sincere, if not very sensible concern about the camp's welfare. Admittedly his medical hokey-pokey had all the hallmarks, to Western eyes, of a blatant fake designed to dominate the people by fear and earn dishonest pennies, but in these contexts it is never wise to assume that what seems self-evident to Western eyes is therefore true. In his book *Adventures of the Mind*, Dr Arturo Castiglioni observes that 'the magician's voice is in reality nothing but the echo of the voice of the hopes and desires of the crowd ... their (the magician's) tricks are employed (tricks that are often necessary to the effect and are sometimes practised even in the most modern medical suggestion) to increase their power and success. But faith is indispensable; only the certainty of accomplishing the desired result ... can determine great success. Men with a critical and developed spirit are never true magicians ... only confidence in the success deriving from his own personal power, or from the supernatural factors to which he attributes his power, can exercise the spell that compels crowds.' Therefore those accusations of charlatanism so readily made by foreign observers are hardly fair. Magicians like Dawa do indeed use their special aptitudes to make money; but so do Harley Street specialists, and if the magician is not deliberately deceiving he cannot be censured for claiming a fee which, judging by tonight's performance, he has certainly earned the hard way.

3 JULY

Yesterday I returned from a hectic four-day visit to Kathmandu; it's difficult to decide which was the more exhausting part of it – the refugee business that took me there, or the excessively alcoholic social whirl that on four consecutive nights marked my return from the wilds.

After seven weeks in Pokhara the city seemed a good deal more like a capital than when I first arrived, and now that the rains have started the whole fertile valley is lush with new beauty. The weather reminded me of showery, warm midsummer days in Ireland, when light breezes send lots of grey-white cloud moving slowly across a very blue sky. Everything everywhere looked exuberantly green, the people seemed to have an access of vitality and the air was blessedly dust-free. Yet even the rains have their disadvantages, and now the whole city reeks still more odiously of stale urine; but that is an unimportant detail compared with the golden light that comes slanting between clouds on to freshly leafy trees, tumultuously blossoming shrubs, neat, vivid paddy-fields, glowing red-brown houses and the burnished roofs of pagodas by the score.

I had booked my return seat for 1 July, but that morning the monsoon was going full blast so my forenoon was spent writing and my afternoon strolling about the valley beyond Jawalkhel.

Here it struck me as paradoxical that the Newars, who created one of Asia's greatest cultures and who as farmers remain far in advance of most other Nepalese tribes, still do all their tillage with a short-handled, shovel-like iron hoe identical to that used five or six thousand years ago. Yet that oxen-drawn wooden plough used so skilfully by the hill-farmers would be perfectly suited to the broad, flat fields of the Kathmandu Valley. Hardly less extraordinary is the cultivation in the valley of virtually every kind of vegetable and fruit known in temperate and sub-tropical zones, while throughout the rest of Nepal, even in similarly favoured areas, almost none of these foods is produced.

I arrived back here early yesterday morning, and after lunch decided to re-establish communications with Tashi. Then reasoning that she merits refugee status, being the daughter of bona fide exiles from Tibet, I took the rest of the day off to help this particular refugee to adjust to her new environment. She spent most of the time on my lap while I wrote letters, and hours passed before her look of puzzled distress began to fade. Then, towards evening, the hoped-for happened and she wagged her tail. Admittedly it was a brief and doubtful wag, but a wag's a wag for all that, and this manifestation of dawning contentment enchanted me.

Another night of whimpering would have been excusable, yet when I lay on my straw mat Tashi came toddling along and climbed, with an effort, on to my stomach where she curled up matily and went fast asleep. Unmistakably I had been accepted, and it was not directly her fault that I failed to sleep equally soundly last night.

Before Tashi's advent the rats had not disturbed me more than once or twice a night, but in the small hours of this morning I came to the morbid conclusion that they would regard a plump pup as a nice change of diet and from then on it seemed my inescapable duty to remain at least semi-alert for rescue purposes. So it seems unlikely that I will enjoy another night's sleep until Tashi has at least attained rat-size.

As yet she is much too young and insecure to be left alone in new surroundings; this morning she wailed piteously when I went out to the field for three minutes so, taking the hint, I carried her everywhere today in that cloth shoulder-bag which is habitually worn by all inhabitants of Nepal. The effect delights both camp and village – a minute black-and-tan head and a pair of very bright eyes peering out of a pouch at navel level. When I called on Kay and said, 'I feel like a kangaroo today,' she promptly replied, 'You look like one too.'

6 JULY

Yesterday the whole camp was in a ferment of preparation for today's celebrations of His Holiness's thirtieth birthday: and ferment is very much the *mot juste* as half the work consisted of making *chang*, which normally is not available in this camp. It had been horribly humid and overcast since morning – the first such day of the season – and at four o'clock the rain came bucketing down. This was wretchedly bad luck, as already an enormous photograph of His Holiness had been brought from the Khamba headquarters in the bazaar to The Annapurna, and in the intervals of supervising *chang*-fermentation everyone dressed up and went to pray before it.

This morning the heavy rain continued until after ten o'clock. Our ceremonies had been due to start at 7 a.m. but when I went to the camp at 6.30, to see how the new huts were withstanding their first real test, the preparations – interrupted by rain yesterday – were not half completed.

Along the cart-track that bisects the camp two rows of carefully-laid white stones marked the route down which His Holiness's picture would be carried from The Annapurna, and small cairns of stones had been built to support the platters upon which incense would smoulder as the picture passed; but the two big tents, rented from the Indian Army camp to serve as temple and kitchen, were not yet erected. However, cooking had already begun in the biggest of our remaining camp tents and I passed a few giant cauldrons of boiling cotton-seed oil, into which hundreds of circular Tibetan pastries were being dropped, allowed to simmer for a few minutes, and then fished out on the end of forked sticks, which various dogs licked with relish in between fishing operations.

When the heavy rain eased off the entire camp went marching up the length of Pardi Bazaar. An hour later they came marching back behind the four camp chiefs, who were carrying the palanquin – made from tea chests – that contained the gaudily coloured photograph of His Holiness under a canopy of traditional orange cloth. (It is a fortunate coincidence that the recent Japanese expedition used canvas of the exact hue prescribed by the Mahayana School for such ceremonies.) No attempt had been made to reproduce the Tibetan flag – which has an extremely involved pattern – but a tattered standard of red, blue and yellow was being borne on a bamboo pole at the head of the procession; and it was an oddly moving sight to see the camp marching along behind, all out of step, and to hear them singing their stirring National Anthem, all out of tune.

As we entered the camp clouds of incense came towards us – the more pungent because of the muggy, windless air – and I made some remark to Kay on the pleasantness of this aroma; but she replied curtly that she hated it. And then it struck me how much easier it is for anyone who has been brought up a Catholic to 'take' Tibetan ritual, which for so many non-Catholic Christians is merely a revolting mess of incense-burning, bead-telling, genuflecting, incomprehensible chanting, and all sorts of crude superstitions like throwing blessed water around and lighting joss-sticks in front of religious pictures. Watching Buddhist ceremonies makes one realise how close Catholicism has remained to the East – which means that in this era of religious 'getting together' the Catholic Church has a shorter journey ahead of her, on one level, than some other Christian denominations. It seems odd that the majority of northern European Christians have felt compelled to turn Christianity into a bleak, sterilised affair, with a high resistance to the germs of mystery and of awe. And often people who have been brought up in this tradition of 'common-sense Christianity' become uneasy at ceremonies that allow for those unknown and 'un-guess-able' elements which lie at the heart of every religion. Yet their brisk scorn of 'all this nonsense' seems to betray an unadmitted fear that the whole thing may be more complex than they would like to think.

The six camp lamas – between them representing the Nyingmapas, Gelugpas and Sakyapas – received the palanquin into the temple tent with music and chanting. Then the photograph was placed on its altar and Kessang offered it a volume of scripture, a bowl of rice, a massive *torma* and a bell surmounted by a statue of Dorje. Next Kay and I were given little handfuls of raw rice to throw at the picture, and then the lamas, the other guests and finally every man, woman and child came to lay a white scarf before it, each bowing low after their presentation. Obviously none of our nomads had ever before taken part in such formal ceremonies and, though there was no lack of devotion, their etiquette simply wasn't equal to the occasion. I pitied Kessang who, as Master of Ceremonies, was responsible for maintaining some semblance of order and reverent behaviour. Most of the men attempted their obeisances while wearing bearskin or wide cowboy-type hats – a *faux pas* in itself, and one which was made almost intolerable for Kessang by the gales of laughter that greeted the frequent falling off of hats at the crucial moment. Then, when the women's turn came, many of them attempted to obtain special blessings for their infants by placing them on the pile of scarves that now lay in front of the photograph, from where they could touch the image of His Holiness. But Kessang was more lenient about this breach of etiquette and merely made disapproving noises, without taking action. Then came the best sight of all – scores of tiny Tiblets marching up with their scarves and, having presented them, folding their hands and bowing solemnly before turning away.

During this long drawn-out rite the six lamas and four monks (including our magician Dawa) were continuously chanting prayers while beating drums, blowing conches and ringing bells. Occasionally one of them would stop to swallow some tea or eat a mouthful of the boiled, sweetened rice that was among today's rather alarming delicacies; but only when the scarf presentations had been completed did they down instruments and really get to work on the banquet – of which even my ascetic lodger partook, though with more restraint than the rest. And all this time Tashi lay silent in her bag, so it seems reasonable to deduce that her appreciation of music is maturing faster than her body.

After lunch wooden jars of *chang* appeared, their brass ornamentation highly polished for the occasion, and this development prompted Kay to make her excuses and retire with dignity. A couple of hours later I also retired, without dignity, but feeling very happy indeed after four or five pints of what James Morris has so aptly called 'that species of alcoholic porridge'.

During the afternoon the drizzle turned to another downpour that has not yet eased off; but when I went on my evening tour of the camp I found everyone happily dicing for Tibetan currency, so they are enjoying themselves after all.

12 JULY

Kay's medical statistics are certainly proving the unsuitability of this climate for Tibetans; between 1 January and 27 May there were only three deaths, but since then there have been eighteen, the majority from dysentery.

Today one baby died while its parents were bringing it to the Shining Hospital. They at once returned here with the tiny corpse and stood weeping in the middle of the road beneath my window; when I went to them the mother was still holding the infant to her bare breast in the frantic hope that after all it wasn't really dead. I had to emphasise that it was and gently force her to cover the little face from the swarming flies – whereupon the father threw himself full length on the muddy road and began to sob his heart out. I then took them up to my room and gave them neat whiskey, which merely made them choke and seemed to do no good; yet perhaps it did help them over the shock. This baby was the youngest of a family of five, but they couldn't have been more grieved if it were their only one. However, it's likely that their grief will soon fade; most of these primitive Tibetans feel such things intensely for a brief period and then recover overnight.

The general decline in camp health during these past weeks has been most depressing. Even the toughest are now afflicted with rheumatism, dysentery, boils, abscesses, scurvy (vitamin C deficiency), swollen legs (vitamin B deficiency) and a variety of worms. Nor am I immune; what I had imagined to be two septic bed-bug bites on my right leg are in fact scurvy sores and I have an impressive cluster of five boils on my behind – all small, but not conducive to comfort.

This morning when I cycled – painfully – to the Military Hospital, I saw the most harrowing sight of a lifetime – a two-year-old Gurung girl at such an advanced stage of malnutrition that she simply didn't look human. Her mother has had mastitis for the past five months, and apparently no attempt was made to wean the child. The family lives four days' walk away, and this morning mother and daughter arrived at the hospital in a large *dokar*, having been carried down to the valley on father's back. The woman's breasts were in an appalling condition; it's impossible to understand why she didn't come for treatment months ago. And the little creature's skin was like that of a nonagenarian – yellow, dry, creased and just hanging on the sharp bones, while enormous glazed eyes stared without seeing from the tiny skull. One had the nightmare feeling that the child had already been dead a long time, though it was still capable of small, feeble movements. The idea of euthanasia repels me, yet today I found myself involuntarily longing to suffocate this little girl.

One notices quite a number of drunks around here, many lying senseless by the wayside, almost visibly enveloped in *rakshi* fumes. Often too they are to be seen swaying and stumbling along the streets, provoking angry frowns from the orthodox Brahmins and good-humoured jeers from the more tolerant masses.

At the hospital today the doctor told me that stomach ulcers caused by over-indulgence in *rakshi* are among the commonest local complaints. Personally I would have thought mere *indulgence* sufficient to ulcerate any stomach, since this Nepalese potion is even fouler than my 'refined' Pineapple Wine, against which the doctor also warned me, saying that it tends to produce sudden, total blindness.

Tonight the monsoon is being positively hysterical; coming home from supper at Kay's I was wading knee-deep through rushing water, in pitch darkness. On such nights umbrellas are just a nuisance and in any case mine, being an Indian model, leaks fluently, while my storm-lantern (also an Indian model) goes out within seconds of encountering a storm. I only hope my roof doesn't spring too many new leaks. At present rain is coming through in just three or four places, which constitutes a manageable situation.

16 JULY

Tashi is proving to be a true Tiblet. On the third day of our joint life I decided to test her powers of self-propulsion and she followed to heel perfectly, proceeding in a series of absurd rubbery bounces.

A week ago she had her first swim, in the lake. I hadn't meant her to join me but when the poor little mite saw me swimming away from the shore she gave a scream of horror and, after a moment's terrified dithering on the bank, plunged gallantly into this new element. Her silly up-curling tail remained high and dry, and began to wag ridiculously above the water as I turned back to express appropriate appreciation of her loyalty.

By now the writing is on the wall. I can no longer delude myself that when leaving Pokhara it will be simple to find a kind home for Tashi and say a fond farewell. Obviously my future career, for the life-span of one dog, is going to be hideously complicated by Quarantine Regulations, International Canine Vaccination Certificates, By-laws governing the Import and Export of Livestock and Rules affecting the Transport of Domestic Pets by Land, Sea and Air. In a word, I've bought it – and all for ten-and-sixpence!

Even now there are complications, for Tashi has strong views about squatting only on grass, and she consistently spurns the statutory box of clay. Therefore, small pups being very lavish of urine in tiny instalments, much of my time now goes climbing down and up the ladder answering her calls of Nature. Even at night, when she awakens me by nipping my nose, she insists on bouncing across to the grass on the opposite side of the road instead of squatting sensibly in the shelter of the verandah – a fetish which means that at this season I spend half the night towelling her.

Her capacity for destruction is tremendous and, as my room affords nothing which is both destructible and within reach, she much enjoys visiting Kay's room. There she wreaks havoc on precious Kleenex sent from London, on beloved pots of cacti which have been driven all the way from Mysore, on vitally important documents and on priceless plastic bags irreplaceable within a radius of a thousand miles. Kay's forbearance is endless and she merely remarks that 'pups will be pups', but as I take the old-fashioned view that a certain amount of repression benefits the young of all species Tashi is regularly beaten on these occasions. However, she imagines that my hidings are a sort of pre-bedtime game, and one's austere disciplinary mood receives a severe shaking when she rolls over on her back, ogles expertly, and holds her right forepaw in her mouth –

this being a trick calculated to disarm the most unfeeling of dog-trainers.

Yet on the whole Tashi is obedient, and today was the first time she disgraced me in public, forcing me to pretend cravenly that we were total strangers. One of her obsessions concerns shoe-laces, which she believes to have been tied in every case so that she may enjoy the satisfaction of untying them. But outlets for such a mania are few in this region of bare feet and therefore she rejoiced at today's appearance on the airstrip of a very correctly attired Chinese Communist Delegation. (What they were delegated to or from I never discovered.) When the plane landed and the twelve comrades emerged many of Pokhara's VIPs were there to greet them, most of Pokhara's armed police were there to protect them (from Tibetans?), and immediately several Kathmandu and Peking press-photographers came scuttling around to arrange groups to prove how dearly the Chinese and Nepalese love one another.

During these preliminaries Tashi had been calling on friends nearby – one of whom habitually wears shoes – but now she came bouncing along to make sure I wasn't going too far astray. The photographers had just attained perfection – Chinese arms around Nepalese shoulders, solidarity smiles on all faces – when Tashi suddenly realised that she had a whole row of stationary shoes at her disposal. Ecstatically she raced up and down the line before deciding to be formal and begin on the leader of the Delegation – so that as camera shutters clicked an irritated frown replaced a solidarity smile on the most important Chinese face.

A very curious feature of this Chinese 'courtesy call' was its length. After precisely seventeen minutes the Delegates re-entered their plane – never having left the airstrip – and headed back to Kathmandu. Perhaps the Nepalese authorities felt that it could be dangerous to allow them through the bazaar, where armed Khamba guerilla-fighters, on leave from the frontier area, are always to be found. And undoubtedly these Tibetan soldiers would enjoy nothing more than a busman's holiday.

As I was writing this last paragraph a head appeared through my trap-door and I recognised a pleasant young man who lives nearby and whose dysentery I treated successfully last week. A moment later he was in the room, followed by his mother, who complained of a violent pain in the right breast. Even by lamplight it was obvious at a glance that she had a very neglected abscess: but in case I didn't get the message she shot a stream of pus from the nipple right into my face – a proof of infection I could have well done without. Dispensing three aspirins, I strongly advised her to go to the Shining Hospital tomorrow and explained that I could do nothing to help. Unfortunately most Nepalese and Tibetans believe that just because you have a white skin (or had before you came to Pokhara) you can perform medical miracles.

This morning Krishna, my landlord, told me that soon I must move to the room next door, which has now been vacated by Thupten Tashi. These two rooms are to be let to Krishna's newly-married brother-in-law, who will set up his own minute shop downstairs – doubtless stocking cigarettes, matches, rice, soap and biscuits, like all the other minute Pardi shops.

24 JULY

Last night in the small hours I was awakened by the most blood-curdling wails, sobs and shouts. They seemed to be coming from the lean-to at one side of the house – a shack which shelters a tailor's family of five, though it consists only of a grass roof, two bamboo-matting walls and an earth floor. Evidently someone was either being murdered or going mad – both common fates around here – but as in neither event could my intervention help I promptly went asleep again. A couple of hours later the eerie sounds recurred, while I was breakfasting, and by then a group of expressionless villagers was standing on the street staring into the shack. Joining it, I saw that the tailor's old mother had indeed gone mad and was being held down with difficulty by her son and daughter-in-law, while their baby lay screaming unheeded on a pile of filthy rags in a corner. Then suddenly the seizure was over, the old woman lay panting but still and the neighbours drifted silently away.

Many events which would be regarded as crises at home are witnessed with indifference here. A few days ago I saw a man attacking his wife outside their house; as his rage increased he tried to pick up a heavy stone for quicker results, but his son, aged about twelve, struggled desperately to restrain him, and eventually mother and son were victorious. That afternoon I again went up the street and saw husband and wife sitting in their doorway amicably stripping corn-cobs together. Yet in our countries a likely result of this fracas would have been the husband's arrest, the wife's removal to hospital for shock treatment and the son's removal from his unsuitable home to an institution.

Initially I had been ashamed of my own placid lack of reaction to such scenes: it seemed my duty at least to feel alarmed or upset. But it appears that we unconsciously and very quickly take our cues from our environment, and in Asia there is felt neither the need to evade life's grimmer aspects nor the obligation to become involved in the misfortunes of others.

Last week I had my own little experience of how close physical violence lies to the surface of Nepalese life. I had gone to the bazaar, taking with me as porter a gentle fourteen-year-old boy named Pema, and as I was haggling about the price of dahl for the Tiblets' Lifeline-subsidised midday meal I heard jeering shouts and looked out to see Pema being attacked by about twenty small Nepalese boys. At first I paid no attention, thinking 'boys will be boys', but when Pema was thrown on his back in the gutter and the gang began to stone him I realised that this was in fact a minor race riot. (Tibetans are understandably very unpopular in the valley.) Leaping down from the shop I went round an intervening house to surprise the gang from the rear, grabbed their leader and was about to thrash him when a screaming fury of a woman frantically attacked me. With one hand she tried to loosen my grip on her terrified son while with the other she beat me over the head, using her empty *dokar* as a weapon. At once a dense crowd gathered round us – amused, curious and, as far as one could judge, quite neutral; the main thing seemed to be that a free entertainment was being staged. I soon wrested the *dokar* away and hurled it into the crowd but Mamma, though unarmed, was not deterred (more power to her) and she continued to shriek abuse at me and to pull and scrape at my arm, which now has a deep four-inch scratch as souvenir. Yet despite her 'tigress-in-defence' efforts I managed to give the little bully four hard ones with my cycle pump before releasing him.

Unfortunately there was no interpreter to explain that had twenty Tiblets attacked one Nepalese boy I would have been equally angry with the Tibetans; so the incident was bad for Irish–Nepalese relations. It was also bad for the reputation of the local missionaries. Bazaar gossip is such that before leaving Pokhara, an hour later, I was told that one of the Shining Hospital nurses had just beaten up (almost unto death!) a helpless little boy who annoyed her by begging for money. Somehow I wouldn't have thought that even a Nepalese crowd could possibly mistake me for a missionary.

Yesterday I moved house, which took me all of fifteen minutes. The move should have happened four days ago, but this being the rice-planting season Krishna hasn't once opened his shop during the past week, and he only appeared yesterday morning for long enough to hand me my new key.

The three differences in this room are: (1) a red mud floor (freshly plastered by Krishna's mother since Thupten left), (2) a tiny back window that does open, and (3) eight leaks in the tin roof instead of four. But (1) and (2) more than compensate for (3). Two open windows lower the temperature and smooth mud provides a much more comfortable bed than unsymmetrical boards – though it also raises the floor level by about a foot, so that my head almost touches the roof. Today I plugged the leaks with candle-grease and so far this device is working quite well.

Inevitably Tashi fancies that the mud floor was laid specially for her to dig up, which she did with great gusto when briefly left alone yesterday. This would be bearable if I were a Nepalese housewife – the local women lay a new floor weekly – but in my case excavations have to be severely discouraged or we'd soon be living amidst a heap of rubble.

Clothing is the one essential obtainable here at a reasonable price. Recently I bought seven yards of brown cotton for nine and fourpence and now my tailor neighbour has made me a pair of shorts and two shirts for five shillings, so I've acquired three new garments at a total

cost of fourteen and fourpence. Kay says that wearing shorts and shirt
of the same drab material makes me look like a convict – but who
cares?

31 JULY

Yesterday I developed acute dysentery and retired to bed early; but
as my new neighbours had just moved in this didn't do me much
good. I haven't yet got round to taking a census, but going on aural
evidence the family includes an aged bronchitic grandparent of
uncertain sex, a discontented infant with a rasping, penetrating wail
and several adults who disagree peevishly about most subjects that
come up for discussion. To add to it all Tashi insisted on yapping
shrilly at regular intervals. I tried to explain that we were no longer
paying rent for the next-door room, but she didn't even begin to get
the point and her hackles never subsided the whole night through.
However, the rain was so heavy and continuous today that no work
could be done and I slept for most of the time; at this relentless phase
of the monsoon ordinary life here comes to a standstill.

7

Conflicting Views

21 AUGUST – POKHARA

The past three weeks have been dominated by illness and wetness. I had planned to go to Kathmandu on the 7th of August but for ten days, from the 6th, Pokhara reverted to its pre-aeroplane isolation – perhaps fortunately, since I was then being victimised by a particularly debilitating belly-bug.

Had one *known* that no plane could come for ten days this isolation would have been quite pleasant; but when one is due to leave on the first available plane and has to keep a constant watch on the sky, lest an unexpected flight should arrive, the prolonged uncertainty becomes decidedly wearing. Yet I was in a favoured position – living beside the airstrip – compared with those would-be passengers who were enduring a damp, aimless existence at The Annapurna, where the seasonal shortage of supplies was defeating even Kessang's ingenuity.

By the 8th of August no less than nine foreigners were awaiting the Kathmandu plane. Alan MacWilliam sat there champing to get to Delhi for urgent consultations; Peter Johnson lounged disconsolately in a corner ticking off the wasted days of his fortnight's leave which, after eighteen months' Peace Corps work in a remote hill village, was to have been spent under Calcutta's bright lights; a diabetic Indian engineer lay on his charpoy predicting – correctly – that his insulin supply would never hold out; a visiting American female missionary paced up and down the verandah insisting that the deficient diet was sapping all her energy – though her perpetual motion contradicted this – and, to refine the tension, a German couple who had been doing soil research near by were accompanied by three bored and petulant children – and were themselves un-soothing because they persistently ascribed the absence of planes to Nepalese inefficiency. By the end of these ten days The Annapurna's atmosphere had become so charged with frustrated animosity that it was dangerous even to look at any of the would-be passengers, much less address them, and only a Tibetan proprietor could have retained his poise as did Kessang.

During this period the whole valley lay inert beneath water, providing an extraordinary contrast to the usual noisy 'to-ing and fro-ing' that starts daily at dawn. For most of the time our Pardi 'street' was knee-deep in brown floods and soon grass began to grow freely on the mud floor of my little hallway – luckily for Tashi, who was thus spared frequent swims to her customary squatting site.

My first action on arriving in Kathmandu on the sixteenth of August was to book a return seat for the twentieth; but no RNAC flights took off either yesterday or today and it was only through Swiss kindness that I got home this afternoon in a microscopic Pilatus Porter.

When the three Swiss and I reached Gaucher Airport at 9 a.m. we were told that the forecast seemed doubtful and we spent the next four hours waiting in the so-called restaurant, from whence the pilot made periodic excursions to survey the sky. At 1.30 p.m. a favourable radio report came through from Pokhara but, since Kathmandu remained completely cloud-obscured, my private opinion was that tomorrow should be regarded as another day. Yet the pilot declared cheerfully that it was worth having a bash at it, meaning that we could turn back if conditions worsened.

Flying in a Pilatus Porter is rather like being in a winged motor car; there is room for a passenger on the front seat, and one literally does get a bird's eye view of people working or walking on the hills below. Yet for me this trip was a most ghastly experience. As we climbed over the city I was unable to distinguish that narrow gap in the mountains which is the only exit for Pokhara flights and I badly needed the fifteen-minute respite of clear weather that followed our escape from this inferno of vapour. Then another menacing wall of cloud loomed up directly across our route and as we went into the middle of it I thought of my dear ones while the pilot yelled to

Kathmandu, 'We may be turning back, stop. Just seeing how far it
goes, stop. Hold on for two minutes, stop. Am warning Pokhara,
stop.' All of which sounded to me remarkably like Famous Last
Words – stop! Yet oddly enough, after those two (very long) minutes
the vapour did begin to thin, and Kathmandu was told that everything looked lovely in the garden. Next Pokhara was advised that
now they could safely send a plane back – which meant that when we
plunged into another cloud ten minutes later I suffered the extra
terror of imagining a collision with the returning Dakota. But
mercifully the Pokhara Valley itself was unclouded and we landed
here at 2.30 in bright sunshine.

I received an astonishingly warm welcome from my Pardi
neighbours. Obviously they have at last accepted me, on much the
same basis as they accept the serenely smiling blind beggar-boy who
wanders alone round the valley, or the ragged Indian lunatic who
speaks Oxford English and sits in tea-houses for hours on end, holding
heated discussions with himself about the relative merits of Hinduism
and Christianity.

31 AUGUST

Last month I discovered that Bhupi Sherchan – a young Pokhara
friend of mine who is Nepal's best-known poet – possesses a copy of
Ekai Kawakuchi's *Three Years in Tibet*. This is the rarest of all books
on Tibet and I have long been scouring the bookshops of Britain and
India for a copy of the English translation, published by the Theo-
sophical Society of Madras in 1906. At first it seemed as inexplicable
as it was thrilling that the valley's meagre stock of English volumes
should happen to include a Kawakuchi; but then Bhupi told me that
this copy was presented to his grandfather by the author who, on his
way to Tibet, had received much kind assistance from the powerful
Sherchan clan – one of the richest merchant families in Nepal.

During the earlier part of this month, while animation was
suspended, I spent much of my time reading Kawakuchi and came
really to love this brave, eccentric and very devout Japanese Buddhist
monk, who combined profound learning with the most engagingly

childish foibles. In 1900, having mastered the Tibetan language, he disguised himself as a lama and risked his life by illicitly entering Tibet to study the country's religion. Then, having serenely survived many arduous and varied adventures he went home to write this unsurpassed account of life in Tibet at the turn of the century. And his book so enchants me that I must quote a few relevant extracts before reluctantly returning it to Bhupi.

In March 1899 Kawakuchi passed through this valley and wrote: 'Pokhara looked like a town of villas at home, the site being chosen because of the beauty of its natural scenery. Bamboo-covered ravines, flower-roofed heights, rich in green foliage, picturesque because of a rushing and winding stream, itself set in the midst of high mountains – such were the characteristic features of Pokhara. The stream's waters are milky white, probably on account of their carrying in them particles of mountain clay. In all my travels in the Himalayas I saw no scenery as enchanting as that which enraptured me at Pokhara. Another thing notable about that place was that it was the cheapest spot in Nepal for all kinds of commodities.'

With all of which, apart from the last sentence, I heartily agree. And as the rise in prices and addition of an airstrip have been the only major changes in Pokhara since 1899 one is comfortably aware that were Kawakuchi to return here in his present incarnation he would at once recognise his 'enrapturing' valley.

Further on in the same chapter he reaches Tsarang, the home of many of our camp Tibetans, and then he writes:

'In point of uncleanliness, Tibetans stand very high among the inhabitants of the earth, but I think the inhabitants of Tsarang go still higher in this respect. In Tibet people wash themselves occasionally, but they almost never do in Tsarang. In the course of the year that I lived there, I only twice saw a person wash himself, the washing being confined even then to the face and neck. The skin all over the body has on it a peculiarly repulsive shine of polished dirt, so to say; but what can they do when it is a custom to laugh at persons who wash their faces nice and clean, and to deride them as being very dirty in their habits? Not only in their appearance, but in all they do, the natives seem to have absolutely no idea of cleanliness. To say that they think nothing of making a cup of tea for you with the same fingers with which they have just blown their noses, is to give only a very mild instance of their filthiness; and I have no courage to dwell here on their many other doings, which are altogether beyond imagination for those who have not seen them done and are too loathsome even unto sickening to recall to mind. The natives hereabouts are merely creatures of animal instincts; they think of nothing but eating, drinking and sleeping, their minds being otherwise filled with thoughts pertaining to sensual love. They occasionally spend their evening in listening to a lama preaching, but only occasionally. They change their clothing but once a year, and if any of them is brave enough to wear the same suit for two years, that person is made an object of high praise. And as they never wash their wearing apparel it is always shiny with grease and dirt. Indifferent as they are to their appearance, they are very painstaking in preparing food, as also in making their sleep comfortable. And their ruling passion is that of carnal love, and that applies to all ages from the very young to the very old. Like all uncivilised people they are intensely superstitious; to them a lama is omnipotent, for they believe he can cure diseases and divine all future events.'

With most of this, too, I agree – though one doesn't notice our Tsarangs being inordinately disposed to 'carnal love'.

Anyway our Japanese friend has a 'thing' about sex, and consequently about Tibetan Buddhism in general. Towards the end of this same chapter he writes very scathingly on Padma Sambhama and the Nyingmapas: 'His teaching is a sort of parody on Buddhism proper, and an attempt to sanctify the sexual relations of human-kind, explaining and interpreting all the important passages and tenets in the Sacred text from a sensual standpoint, and in the Tibetan rhetoric in which I took lessons I found this lewd and detestable teaching largely incorporated.' At which point one begins to wonder if the Japanese monk – alias Tibetan lama – was not in fact a disguised Presbyterian clergyman!

This morning the sky was cloudless when I cycled up to the bazaar at six o'clock – and what a sight the mountains were in that clear, early sunshine! One appreciated them all the more, not having seen them for so many weeks; even Roget – if he were among those present – would be unequal to those Himayan snowpeaks. They *are* majestic, and I can't help it if everyone else has said so already. This really is the only adjective that begins to convey the impression received as one cycles up from Pardi, going straight towards Machhapuchhare itself – a king of snow and ice soaring far above the rest, high and mighty, into the blueness.

3 SEPTEMBER

Today I had my first quarrel with local officialdom; however successful I may be in social contacts with Asians I seem doomed to repeated failures in professional contacts, where resounding ethical clashes so often occur. This is an enormous problem, to which one can rarely find a solution both honourable and practical. Common sense and tolerance dictate some degree of flexibility and on minor points I do accept the irritating necessity to jog along in a haze of compromise. But then comes some major point that compels me to act according to my own principles, and it must be bewildering for the Nepalese when I suddenly revolt and begin rigidly to oppose them. Perhaps it is a mistake ever to compromise, even on minor points; yet one's work here would come to a standstill if one didn't. I can't claim that any reasoned decision is taken at the moment when I stop jogging along; I merely rebel instinctively against an utterly repugnant course of action, and from that point on the certainty that one is right by one's own standards makes further compromise impossible.

This whole problem centres on the difficulty of determining the extent to which we are entitled to impose our standards on an Eastern people. My own feeling is that normally we are not entitled to do this to any extent, and I would be the first to protest if others were bullying the unfortunate Nepalese. Yet when Eastern nations misguidedly insist on importing Western institutions that are wholly unsuited to their society, and expect us to provide the essential funds and personnel, then surely we *are* entitled to demand a minimum of conformity to our standards. However, in most cases this is an unrealistic demand, and therefore many Western field-workers, with a far wider experience of the problem than mine, have by now concluded that the whole elaborate structure of Aid to the Developing Nations should be dismantled and either forgotten or reconstituted.

It was obvious this afternoon that our 'frankness' appears to the Nepalese as simply the most atrocious form of bad manners. They feel shocked, hurt and saddened when a spade is called a *spade*, and today they were clearly writing me off as an unspeakable barbarian from some caveman civilisation – which indeed I am, in many ways, compared with them. Yet my natural aggressiveness was being rigorously curbed in their honour and I referred to that spade very gently – though I couldn't quite bring myself to call it an agricultural implement. However, this offensive frankness at least gives Asians the opportunity to understand our reasoning, whereas we are forever groping in twilight towards some faint understanding of theirs.

Only once has a Hindu sincerely tried to explain to me his thinking on honesty, and that explanation was not very illuminating. I was staying with an English couple in Uttar Pradesh when this young Brahmin came to dinner. He was a most delightful person – warm-hearted, courteous, witty and well-informed – and during the past two years he had been virtually adopted by my elderly friends. Soon we all began to discuss the hoary topic of Indian dishonesty and in an effort to enlighten us the young man said: 'Look at it this way – I'm an educated Brahmin and a very good friend of this family, yet if I came into the house when it was empty and saw Rs. 100/- on top of that bureau, I'd almost certainly steal it, but if I only knew that the Rs. 100/- was locked inside the bureau I would *never* steal it, even if I could easily break the lock and was sure of not being caught.'

Naturally enough this concrete example was received with some rather half-hearted laughter, whereupon the young man frowned impatiently and went on: 'You don't like to believe me, but this is true. The theft would have been the fault of whoever left the money lying around. I'd feel I'd done wrong but I'd think I couldn't be expected to resist such a temptation. And then the carelessness of the owner would counterbalance my own guilt and I'd be happy.'

By this stage my host and hostess were plainly feeling upset so I hastily changed the subject, much as I longed to pursue it. The only perceptible vestige of decency in this exposition was the admission that some guilt would be felt, though it could be suppressed so expeditiously. Possibly the uneasiness revealed by so many Hindus in their relations with Europeans is partly based on envy of the values upheld by our more obstreperous consciences. Individual Hindus cannot be blamed for following their traditional code; yet when that code is so out of harmony not merely with Christian morality, but with a universally applicable natural law, they are bound to suffer from the repercussions of their too easily quieted consciences.

These clashes of standards are a normal hazard in the East and what most disheartened me today was the full realisation of how ill-equipped the Nepalese are to tackle organisational problems. Only when one has had a close up view, over a considerable period, of how their minds work can one appreciate the crucial difference between a race with a tradition of logical thinking and a race with no such tradition. And this is the chief obstacle to successful co-operation on any project. Ordinarily we completely take for granted our heritage of logic, since any moderately intelligent Westerner will think coherently, if not profoundly, about a given problem; but even the best educated and most intelligent of the Nepalese seem to lack this method of approach. Their various theories may be sound, and their various practical schemes constructive, but any co-ordination of either theories or schemes is non-existent and would require a major miracle rather than a Western adviser. Instead of looking at all of a problem first, and then dealing with its component parts in relation to its entirety, the average Nepalese deals with each aspect as a separate issue and makes various decisions which, if they were acted upon, would promptly cancel each other out – so perhaps it is fortunate that in Nepal decisions are rarely or never acted upon. But coping with this sort of thing day after day is enough to depress the most ebullient and I don't wonder that so many Western workers simply give up trying.

These disillusioned experts often dismiss the Nepalese as being colossally and irredeemably stupid; yet this is a most unjust over-simplification. Here we are not up against inferior brain-power, but brain-power that operates on a different fuel, travels on a different gauge line and is going in a different direction; and it may be that the illogical Nepalese will have the laugh on us at some not-too-distant date, when they are as happy as ever and our civilisation has tripped itself up and broken its neck in the progress race.

5 SEPTEMBER

It is interesting that many of Pokhara's leading citizens profess to be Communists; this morning one of them openly discussed with me his sympathy for China, and he is the fifth to do so. None of these men is poor and three of them are among the richest in the valley, and are continuing to do very well under the present regime, so their new allegiance cannot be attributed to discontent. But – significantly – all five have received that fatal half-education, clumsily modelled on a Western pattern, which cuts the mind adrift from its traditional moorings without beginning to equip it to steer safely through alien waters. And now their support of Chinese Communism is being rather self-consciously flaunted as proof of both an *avant-garde* outlook and of ability to withstand Western pressures. This last point seems to be of major importance, and one finds an obsessional defiance of the United States in their attitude. Invariably they argue – more or less coherently – 'America hates China and we resent American efforts to dominate us, so let's show these dollar-splashers that it's not as easy as they might think to buy us.' Clearly this childish yet forgivable reaction against America is the Nepalese Communist's most powerful incentive, and it is surprising that the inevitability of such a development was not foreseen years ago. On the one hand are the Americans, full of pity and dollars and naïve enthusiasm, supplemented by a pathological hatred of the Chinese and a total incomprehension of the Nepalese; to these 'do-gooders' the spending of money on a country is the obvious way to 'rescue' it, but as yet the Nepalese seem quite unprepared to follow where the dollar leads. Then, on the other hand, one has the Chinese talking across, instead of down, to their Nepalese 'brothers', sharing with them a state of undevelopment which they can justly claim to be improving through their own efforts, preaching opposition to a capitalism of which the Nepalese know nothing except that Americans are capitalists, and smoothly gearing their propaganda to Asian thought processes and emotional reactions. It would be strange if those Nepalese who sincerely believe that their country needs reform did *not* look north-east for support.

In Kathmandu there are several Nepalese-run Chinese Communist bookshops which sell propaganda literature in Nepali, Hindi and English. Many of these publications are incongruously luxurious, yet the prices remain artificially low. Books that would cost twenty or twenty-five rupees if imported from the West are to be had for five or six rupees, and I recently bought for one rupee (eightpence) a well-produced, hardback volume of Rewi Alley poems entitled *Who is the Enemy?* This was published last year by the New World Press, Peking, and the blurb begins – 'Rewi Alley is a citizen of New Zealand and of the world. He is now coming to the end of his first four decades in China.' And immediately one wonders if the implication is that Chinese Communism bestows an exclusive longevity which will enable Rewi Alley to enjoy a second four decades in China. The final sentence of the blurb says that these poems 'are quite frankly political', and this is so true that at no stage do they come within light-years of being poetry. Some of them are defaced by a jeering, almost obscene blasphemy that makes the Western reader wince; but the majority – especially those on the Vietnamese war – do have that beauty which sparkles from sincerity whatever its setting. Only a fanatically obtuse reader could dismiss them as mere crafty propaganda. On every page the writer conveys his absolute commitment to the peasants of Asia and his unwavering faith in the benefits that Communism can bring them; and one feels the strength and warmth of a real compassion consistently coming through these semi-hysterical phrases. Too often we think of Communism as a cold, systematic, conform-or-die ideology that inhumanly sacrifices the individual to the theory; yet the writings of Rewi Alley and of many of his 'comrades' show that it is as essentially human as any other political phenomenon in the history of mankind. Throughout this little book one hears the thumping of its indignant, puzzled, aggressive heart, and one knows that many of these people do care for the poor, however misguidedly, and whatever brutalities may result from their passion of loathing for all 'Imperialists'.

Last night we citizens of Pardi were treated to some Western-style propaganda when a British Embassy official staged an open-air film show to enlighten the locals on Life in Modern Britain. The films were so ludicrously inappropriate that one marvelled at the responsible authorities ever having fallen into such an abyss of idiocy; but at least the performance afforded me a splendid evening's entertainment, as I sat there viewing it through the eyes of a Nepalese peasant.

Life in London was represented by the Trooping of the Colour, so the audience must naturally have assumed that city to be a most civilised place, where the majority of the male population wear gorgeous uniforms and ride around on glossy horses – always in military formation for reasons best known to themselves. Next we saw rousing shots from a performance of *Macbeth* produced on Cornish cliffs in Elizabethan costume, with a bloody dagger much in evidence – which latter detail will no doubt have done a lot to strengthen the links of friendship between the Gurkhas and the Great British Public. This was followed by the Quatro-centenary birthday celebrations at Stratford-on-Avon, showing scores of robed Lord Mayors from all over Britain, and next came the Eisteddfod, showing dancers from many countries in their national costumes, with bevies (or should it be covies?) of druidically-garbed druids in the foreground. Then, as a Grand Finale, we were given the Highland Games, with kilts flying while bagpipes squealed. Such is the image of Britain Today as the Pokhara Valley is seeing it this week. Doubtless my neighbours now think that the clothes worn here by Westerners are designed for tropical use only, and they must certainly imagine that Britain has at least as many national holidays as Nepal.

8 SEPTEMBER

This evening it was my turn to prepare supper and when Kay arrived at half-past seven, carrying her rarely-used transistor radio, she was breathless with excitement. For an instant after her announcement that a war had started I experienced a sick 'This-is-it' feeling, but as she went on I realised that the war is just more bickering than usual between India and Pakistan. Undoubtedly it will cause many sadly unnecessary deaths on the battlefield and some inconvenience here, but it is hardly a war in contemporary terminology.

Already the bazaar price of kerosene has gone up to two pounds per gallon and there is a possibility that all internal RNAC flights may be stopped because Nepal is dependent on India for her petrol supplies. We have just spent two hours listening with great difficulty to snatches of English Language news giving very dissimilar interpretations of the situation from Pakistani, Indian, Nepalese, Chinese, American and British viewpoints. Peking is being even more lurid than usual and describing America as 'a vicious wolf' and 'the most rabid oppressor mankind has ever known', America is being no less puerile on a slightly more sophisticated level and everyone else is also reacting according to form. The whole thing leaves one sunk in depression. I myself believe in Pakistan's moral right to Kashmir and, as one of the 'Fighting Irish', I would say 'Good luck to them' if I thought the Pakistani Army had so much as an even chance of securing that right by force. But this futile skirmishing can only bring further misery to two already destitute countries.

Yet the country I pity most at the moment is poor little Nepal, who is now shaking in her shoes (or would be if she wore them!) between China plus Pakistan and India plus America. The English Language news from Kathmandu was struggling desperately to be neutral but betraying an unmistakable pro-Chinese bias – perhaps partly because there is a Nepalese Mission in Peking just now and the delegates' families want to see them again. However, we are in no danger here. Even if a full-scale conflict were to develop between China and India it is most unlikely that Nepal would be directly involved in any fighting.

Tonight Kay is understandably worried. She had been planning to drive her jeep down to South India at the end of the month, but by then no petrol may be available for civilian use; so she will probably leave within the next few days.

15 SEPTEMBER

Kay took off on the eleventh and must now be on her way down the Rajpath. Jill Buxton is the only other grandmother of my acquaintance who would blithely drive a twenty-one-year-old jeep single-handed from Kathmandu to Mysore, through a country at war. Whatever else may be said about Britain's export trade there's nothing wrong with its line in grandmothers.

Today the war is a week old but Peking's jamming is so efficient nowadays that no news trickles through from the Big Wide World. This seems healthy; presumably anything too drastic would have made some slight impression, even on the Nepalese.

The bazaar black market is now thriving; obviously Nepalese merchants are born profiteers – once they get a whiff of war beyond the horizon everything becomes a racket overnight. In theory the Government has imposed price control, but in practice Kathmandu's laws never do impinge on Pokhara's daily life.

This morning I myself was out to corner Russian tinned milk for the eighteen Tiblets who are suffering from malnutrition and who, since Kay's departure, have been coming to my room early every morning for their egg-flips. I did manage to get forty one-pound tins; but these won't last very long so I also got thirty tins of the Indian product, though this is far inferior to the Russian and costs even more.

At the moment I am a bit shaken, having just seen the killing of a rabid dog on the village street. When leaving the camp after my evening tour I heard the most frightful shrieking sounds ahead – and then a herd of buffalo came galloping wildly towards me across the common-land. People were fleeing in all directions and a moment later I saw a very nice dog, belonging to a local trader, racing round and round in circles making this hideous noise. At once I looked frantically for Tashi, who was well behind, frolicking with other Tibetan dogs, and having rushed back to pick her up I stood near the tents wondering what would happen next. There wasn't long to wait: three young men climbed on to the roof of a house, with armfuls of sharp-edged bricks, and the grim execution was soon over. But the fact that this poor little creature was one of Tashi's best friends is creating a certain amount of suspense.

By now Tashi has become quite an elegant young lady, her earlier furry cuddlesomeness having been replaced by a silky strokability. Her general architecture is reminiscent of a Dachshund whose parents' genes have been a little wide of the mark; she has a ridiculous brown feathery tail which curls up and over her back and her regular white and tan markings are very handsome indeed.

On the delicate question of Tashi's breed there are several schools of thought. When she was two months old a local 'expert' pronounced her to be a smooth-haired Tibetan terrier; but I have always questioned this diagnosis. Then, a few weeks later, a visiting Indian, who obviously knew something of Eastern breeds, defined her as a Miniature Himalayan Sheepdog – which theory is reinforced by her breeder's occupation of shepherd. Privately, however, I am of the opinion that she is a perfectly good Tibetan mongrel. Yet if one is besotted enough to go to the immense inconvenience and expense of transporting a dog from Nepal to Ireland one has to pretend, as a face-saving device, that the dog in question belongs to some exclusive Central Asian breed of enormous snob-value. So, on the form which I have filled in this evening to begin the tortuous process of obtaining Irish citizenship for Tashi, her breed is boldly given as Miniature Himalayan Sheepdog.

A week ago the more tiresome aspects of being possessed by a Nepal-born dog began to obtrude on the idyll. I am due home in December and a letter of enquiry to the Irish Embassy in Delhi brought a fearsome array of lengthy documents by return of post. These made it plain that our Department of Agriculture is allergic to alien quadrupeds, and the pages of grim regulations are clearly intended to eradicate all the imprudent affections indulged in by Irish citizens abroad. But

an Irish Government Department should know better than to attempt
to thwart the desires of an Irish citizen. My determination to 'import a
domestic pet of the canine species [dog to you] into the State from a
place abroad' hardened rapidly as I read these formidable strictures;
even had I actively disliked Tashi they would have inspired me to
import her 'separately confined in a suitable hamper, crate, box or
other receptacle which must be nose and paw proof and must not
contain any hay, straw or peat-moss litter'. It was in an aggressive
mood that I completed the preliminary from and wrote the
preliminary letters to 'the approved quarantine premises' and the
'approved carrying agents', while Tashi lay peacefully asleep by my
feet, unaware that during the next few months a lot of people were
going to make a very big fuss about a very little dog.

8

A Thief and a Goddess

23 SEPTEMBER – KATHMANDU

Two days ago I came to a Kathmandu where, outside the Embassy compounds and The Royal Hotel, no one would suspect our southern neighbours of being at war. The Royal has been completely deserted by the seasonal swarm of rich tourists who briefly visit Nepal on their Round-the-World-Air-Trips, and poor Boris is looking very dejected. Because of his own legendary soft-heartedness it costs a great deal just to keep that vast hotel ticking over; all other hoteliers have dismissed most of their staff, but Boris argues – 'It's not the servants' fault that there's a war on. They work hard and loyally when I need them so how can I turn them out now?' No wonder they are loyal to him!

I spent three hours at the airport this morning excavating a consignment of Multi-Purpose Food from among the mountains of supplies that are now accumulating there. Ironically the present crisis has speeded up the arrival of goods from Calcutta; most passenger-flights have been cancelled so RNAC has taken to transporting the freight back-log instead of losing money on idle planes, and now the airport is crammed with bales, crates, chests and cartons of every description. The 150 tins of Multi-Purpose Food had been awaiting transportation at Calcutta Airport for the past seven weeks and might have been there for the next seven months had the more profitable passenger traffic not been stopped.

24 SEPTEMBER

Today I spent over nine hours at the airport waiting for 'a departure' that never departed. Weather conditions were suitable for the Pokhara flight so there was a possibility, from 8 a.m. onwards, that we might take off at any moment – if this, that or t'other did not intervene. But they did intervene – apparently all three of them – and at 5.20 p.m. the Pokhara flight was cancelled.

Then came the struggle back to Jawalkhel with my usual elaborate refugee-luggage. The present consignment is made up of three boxes of dried milk weighing 60 lb. each, six tins of Multi-Purpose Food weighing 40 lb. each and two boxes of medical supplies weighing 20 lb. each – plus a *dokar* of fresh vegetables for the Shining Hospital, weighing 30 lb. and a cloth shoulder bag of personal luggage weighing 2½ lb. Amidst the chaos of Kathmandu Airport it is not easy to guard so many separate pieces for nine hours; in fact this can only be done by building a pyramid and then sitting on it, like Patience on a monument, smiling at delay. It is even less easy to get it all back to base, while horribly aware that somehow it must be dragged to the airport again at dawn; the damnable thing is that no official Left Luggage Office exists either at the airport itself or at the RNAC Terminal in New Road.

At 5.30 I tried to scrounge a friend's car, but the telephones in the relevant district were dead. Then, at 6.15, the airport bus wheezed along, my luggage was loaded up and by 7.50 I had got it all unloaded and brought into the Terminal office, where I attempted to telephone Sigrid. Having failed I called for a taxi, loaded up again and finally arrived back here at 8.15, feeling crabbed.

25 SEPTEMBER

Life is getting easier; today I only spent six hours waiting at the airport.

Being Saturday this is Sigrid's day off, yet she most nobly rose at dawn and drove me and my beastly luggage to New Road, where we were told that the departure of the airport bus had been postponed from 8 to 10 a.m. I then said another provisional goodbye to this most long-suffering of hostesses, whose stoical endurance of my comings and not-goings is beyond compare; when I arrived back at

Jawalkhel yesterday evening she at once soothed me by seeming so pleased that I *hadn't* got to Pokhara!

The bus eventually decanted me and my baggage at the airport at 11.30 a.m. and, having reconstructed my pyramid, I perched hopefully on it until 5.30 p.m. when my patience was rewarded by an announcement that the Pokhara flight had again been cancelled for undisclosed reasons. I then repeated the luggage-shifting performance, which is now becoming merely another daily chore, and at the Terminal office I was advised to report there tomorrow morning at 6.30 and told that a seat was guaranteed for me – but there was no guarantee of a flight to Pokhara.

26 SEPTEMBER

Perhaps a flight did go to Pokhara today, but this passenger was not among those present. By a painful coincidence I've done it again and fractured two ribs in a bus – though mercifully they are not the two that were cracked a couple of years ago in an Afghan bus. Yet I mustn't let this become a habit . . .

The misadventure occurred yesterday on the way back from the airport but, as sometimes happens with rib injuries, the extent of the damage was not immediately apparent. This bus had distinct affinities with Afghan models, and all our luggage was piled high in the centre of the chassis, between the two narrow wooden benches. The driver was little short of a lunatic, and when a sacred bull suddenly ambled into view from behind a line of grass-carrying porters we were going far too fast to cope safely with this everday contingency. The sudden braking threw me violently against a tin of that dratted Multi-Purpose Food but, though the pain was momentarily severe, I thought no more of the incident until I woke in agony at midnight, about an hour after going to sleep.

Sigrid was still out a bridge-party – as usual not knowing whether her guest was here or there – but she came in soon afterwards, made calming noises, bound me tightly in sheeting and, by administering three codeine tablets and a glass of neat brandy, convinced me that this was the most minor of injuries. Then, after a slight battle about the advisability of my annexing the bed upstairs, I again lay on my Tibetan rug, beside a most sympathetic Puchare, and was asleep within moments.

This morning Dr Gyr sent me to the Nepal TB Centre for an X-ray to confirm his diagnosis of two fractured ribs; but on arriving there, after a torturingly joltful car journey, I found no X-rays can be taken until tomorrow as this is a National Holiday. However, I hope to be fit to fly to Pokhara on Tuesday.

28 SEPTEMBER

For about a week after The Event, simple rib-fractures have a way of feeling less simple each day; even had Dr Gyr not banned any travelling in the immediate future I would have cancelled my booking for today's hypothetical Pokhara flight.

Yesterday morning I dutifully kept my appointment for 9.30 at the TB Centre, only to be told that the generator had just developed a weakness and couldn't reasonably be expected to function before 1 p.m. Eventually, at 2.45, I was dealt with by a very pleasant but fascinatingly witless young radiologist who, when the picture had been developed, spent five minutes intently studying it – though even I could see at a glance that it didn't happen to include the particular ribs specified by Dr Gyr.

Last night the pain was acute but by now it has diminished considerably, after a day spent reading and sunbathing in the garden.

During Sigrid's office-hours her house becomes a sort of club where Donbahadur and his friends meet to sing and play on the long Nepalese drum, to teach each other curious versions of the English and German languages, to flirt blissfully with other people's wives, to drink tea and gossip affectionately about their respective employers – or to spend hours in the garden preparing kites for competitions, as they were doing today.

The kite-flying season opens after the monsoon and now, all over the valley, one sees 'defeated' kites hanging sadly from tree-tops or electric cables. Yesterday I watched three duels being fought simultaneously in the blue sky far, far above. Usually the strings are invisible and it's utterly absorbing to follow the extremely skilful manoeuvrings of these soaring, swooping, fluttering protagonists – whose owners are never seen, so that one imagines each kite to have an alert little built-in brain.

Donbahadur is a local champion and today he was preparing his kite for an important contest due to take place tomorrow, if the present deliciously fresh breeze persists. His string is over one hundred yards long and every inch of it, above the first five or six yards, has now been coated with the powdered glass which will perhaps cut his opponents' string tomorrow. This seemed to me a most tedious process, but clearly Donbahadur was loving every moment of it. His friend Tulbahadur, the milkman, helped him to extend the string to its full length, winding it tautly around trees and bushes, and then Donbahadur fetched from the kitchen Sigrid's best saucepan, in which he had boiled a mixture of flour, water and not too finely ground glass. This paste was most meticulously applied to the string and, when the sun had quickly dried it, every inch was expertly tested to ensure that the caked flour was holding each tiny splinter in place. Then, while the precious string was being gingerly wound back onto its reel, I unobtrusively took the saucepan to the bathroom to remove all traces of its lethal contents.

30 SEPTEMBER

This date will be remembered as my most horrible day in Nepal.

I had just sat down to breakfast when an odd exclamation came from upstairs and then a dead-pale Sigrid appeared through the little mock-cupboard door. 'I've been robbed,' she said. 'Everything has gone – jewellery, cameras, films – everything.' Immediately I felt a cold sickness at the centre of me, caused not only by natural distress on her behalf but by the immediate, devastating realisation that the burglar's success was entirely *my* fault.

Yesterday evening I was writing at the living-room table when a not very helpful section of my brain registered footsteps directly overhead. I thought vaguely, 'Sigrid must have come home while I was in the loo' – and went on writing. Moments later I heard bangings against the outside wall of the house directly behind my chair; but I was registering these sounds only superficially, and was automatically rejecting them, as one does all disturbances to concentration. My animal sense of hearing had assured me that they were either directly overhead or directly behind me; yet when Sigrid came in my malfunctioning human reason contradicted the evidence of my senses simply because it did not seem possible that anyone could have been upstairs. There is no valid excuse for this moronic behaviour but Sigrid, being Sigrid, now says 'not to worry', and claims that it is her own fault for always leaving cupboards unlocked and windows wide open. I might feel better this evening had she shown less magnanimity and given me my deserts.

When Donbahadur heard the news he was almost as upset as we were. Tulbahadur was in the kitchen (he seems to breakfast here more often than not) and immediately we all went to Patan in Sigrid's car.

The police station is among the oldest and loveliest of Patan's Newari buildings. In a wall-niche on one side of the main entrance stands a statue of Hanuman, the Monkey God, and this ancient sculpture is regularly smeared by the devout with red and yellow powder and paint. The eaves of the building are supported and the lintels decorated by very detailed carvings of naked gods and goddesses being no better than they should be – a form of art often alleged to be obscene, though to me it seems more witty than smutty. One can understand that it might not be considered the most apt sort of embellishment for a European police station; but if the Nepalese have retained enough balance to see the humour in sex this is surely a matter for congratulation rather than criticism.

Inside the building a rickety stairway led to the top-floor office of the Chief of Police; his unstable desk occupied one corner beside the small windows, the exquisitely carved shutters of which were lifted inwards and hooked to the low rafters during the day. The officer himself was fat, elderly and badly pock-marked, with a shaven head and steel-rimmed spectacles. On our arrival he gazed silently at us, his expression conveying some deep-rooted dislike for robbed mem-sahibs, and after a moment told us through Donbahadur that we would have to await the appearance of the police interpreter – who might or might not report for duty before lunch-time.

The four of us then sat on a bench near the window, and an hour later we were surprised by the arrival of Lal Rana, the young interpreter, whose relative punctuality made me suspect that the Chief's pessimism on this point had been a ruse to drive us impatient foreigners away. Lal Rana was amiable but inept; when Sigrid attempted to make her statement he – and all his colleagues – showed far less interest in the crime than they did in her and my ages, occupations, passport numbers, home addresses and next-of-kin. Then the interpreter proudly announced that the police had 'a panel of local thieves' whom they would now proceed to question – whereupon Sigrid suggested, a trifle acidly, that were they to pay just a little attention to her description of the stolen articles their investigations might prove more fruitful. At once it was generally agreed that a list of the missing goods would indeed be helpful; then Lal Rana suddenly got very excited, said that of course they could take fingerprints too and dashed off to collect the relevant apparatus. This was bought last month from the Lucknow police, who had decided to replace it by some rather more up-to-date equipment; and when I saw it I realised that the Lucknow police had not made their decision prematurely.

Four other police officers followed us back here on foot – two clad in shabby uniforms and two in vivaciously striped pyjamas. It was not clear to me which pair were the senior officers; one could interpret the wearing of pyjamas while on duty either as a privilege reserved for higher ranks or as a mark of lowliness in the force – and none of these five men seemed to have any authority over the other four. However, they all revelled in the crime and went prowling around Sigrid's bedroom with preposterously exaggerated caution, taking great care to wrap towels around their hands before touching the woollen curtains; but in the end it was Sigrid who observed the many burnt matches on the cupboard shelves and the floor, though neither she nor I – much less the police – was able to make any astute deduction from this clue.

We next went outside, to gaze on the place of entry, and innumerable photographs were laboriously taken with a gigantic camera that almost creaked. Then the police departed – 'to be pursued by investigations', as the interpreter put it; but the investigations were so obviously incapable of 'being pursued' constructively that Sigrid at once telephoned an influential Nepalese friend – and we soon received a message summoning us back to the police station.

There we found that a lavishly-uniformed and very tough-looking young Senior Officer had been sent from Police Headquarters at Singha Durbar to take charge of the case – and already his presence had transformed the atmosphere. Whenever this formidable youth moved a finger everyone gave a series of palsied jerks which were probably the local version of coming to attention, saluting and clicking heels; yet I can't say that from a practical point of view the efficiency of the establishment was noticeably higher. However, we did have our fingerprints taken, which was perhaps an advance in some direction; and then we were all questioned about our movements yesterday, while Lavish Uniform sat looking threateningly at his subordinates and listening to us without comment.

It soon became evident that the local police, unnerved by His Nibs' presence, were intent on proving Donbahadur the culprit. Sigrid and I simmered furiously as they persistently tried to trip him up; we would as soon suspect each other as Donbahadur, who has been on the verge of tears all day because his 'Memsahib's nice things gone'. Yet our angry intervention would not really have helped, so we confined ourselves to directing indignant or sympathetic looks at the officers or their victim.

It was almost five o'clock when we left the police station, having been dismissed by His Nibs as though we were a pair of rather unpromising recruits. Immediately Donbahadur suggested that we should consult a Hindu soothsayer who lives nearby and we agreed that this might be more – and couldn't be less – helpful than consulting the Patan police. After a complicated drive through narrow alleyways we stopped at the entrance to an untidy, shrine-crowded courtyard and found the Brahmin priest sitting cross-legged in a corner of his first-floor room. Before him stood a low table, covered with geometrical signs, and when Donbahadur had briefly explained our problem the soothsayer picked up a handful of dry earth, scattered it over the table, consulted a dog-eared book that had been lying on the ground beside him and began to draw or write in the earth with a four-inch glass cylinder. Meanwhile an old woman who was threshing rice in another corner went on tossing her trayfuls of grain, ignoring us, and the setting sun turned the chaff to a golden cloud.

Looking at Donbahadur, standing near the soothsayer, I was reminded of a European going to the doctor with some minor ailment, describing his symptoms, and then trustfully awaiting the scribbled prescription. This was magic in action, yet the atmosphere was utterly prosaic.

The Brahmin did not spend more than four or five minutes on his calculations. Then he laid down the cylinder and announced matter-of-factly that the stolen articles would not be sold immediately, but would be kept hidden in the thief's Patan house. He added that a young man who habitually wears black Western trousers and occasionally visits Sigrid's office had been implicated in the crime; and he concluded by foretelling that this young man would openly visit Sigrid's house at midday tomorrow. Donbahadur then paid the Rs. 1/- fee and followed us downstairs, translating the Brahmin's remarks when we reached the courtyard; and even he had to admit that this consultation had not got us very far.

2 OCTOBER

Yesterday, at 12 p.m., a young man in black pants walked into the living-room with a message for Sigrid; and he does go to her office occasionally on business, though he has never before been to her house. His appearance in the doorway made me feel a little odd for a moment, as black Western trousers are not commonly worn here, and Donbahadur, when called from the kitchen to take the message, concealed his agitation very inadequately; but the snag is that one can't have a man arrested on this sort of 'evidence'.

There were no other robbery developments until this afternoon. Today, being Saturday, Sigrid spent her time in the bazaar, doing private detective work, and as I was reading in the garden Lal Rana came rushing excitedly towards me. When he heard that Sigrid wouldn't be back until dinner-time he hurriedly explained that there was a suspect now loitering in the road just outside the gate and that he very much wanted to know if this man had been seen around the house or garden in the recent past. I immediately stood up – too quickly for comfort – and was already half-expecting an extension of the coincidence when I came face-to-face with Black Trousers outside the gate. By now I felt too addled even to try to sort any of it out. Though the young man greeted me most effusively I fancied some awkwardness in his manner; yet I firmly told myself that this was probably imaginary and, on returning to the garden, I merely reported his innocuous visit yesterday. Whereupon the interpreter departed, saying that he would return later to interview Sigrid again.

One result of Black Trousers' appearance at midday yesterday has been the complete restoration of Donbahadur's faith in the soothsayer; last evening he went to him twice for more high-powered consultations, and in consequence the case is now being given the full magical treatment. Yesterday an image of dough was baked and today the Brahmin is busy chanting sinister incantations over it – these being calculated to make the thief shake violently and incessantly until he has been arrested. (Donbahadur has of course warned the police to look out for a man who can't stop shaking.) Yet if Black Trousers is the culprit something must have gone wrong – either with the baking or the chanting – since he was quite unshaky this afternoon.

The other part of the campaign is being conducted here; inside Sigrid's bedroom cupboard a big bowl of incense has been smouldering aromatically all day, and over both the cupboard door and the room door strangely-inscribed pieces of paper have been nailed to the wall. No doubt this is the ultimate in childish superstition: yet it is evident that both Sigrid and I are suffering from an excessive responsiveness to atmosphere and are taking the *puja* much more seriously than either of us would admit, even to the other.

By now the whole police investigation has acquired that patina of unreality which characterises most aspects of life in Nepal; if the circumstances were different one could thoroughly enjoy this weird kaleidoscope of improbable police-stations, detectives clad either in pyjamas or much-beribboned uniforms, uncannily accurate sooth-sayers, archaic equipment, boyish enthusiasm, blatant corruption and utter inability even to attempt to find a thief.

At present Kathmandu's weather is the only pleasant feature of life. The nights are refreshingly chilly and every morning the valley is filled with a thick grey mist that recalls autumn at home. All day the light has a glorious, exhilarating clarity, and towards evening it is especially lovely. At half-past six today, when the valley was already dark, two billowing masses of cloud to the east were still glowing a deep pink – and beyond them in the far distance the world's highest snow-peaks were also lingeringly pink against a starry, royal-blue sky.

4 OCTOBER

For the past eight days the whole country has been celebrating Dasain (also known as the Durga Puja) and by now we foreigners are really feeling the draught. The GPO has shut down completely; three days ago the electricity supply expired and we were informed that it could not be revived until 6 October; Singha Durbar has put up its shutters, leaving various Top-Level negotiations in a state of internationally inconvenient suspension; and almost all servants, peons and chokidars are *chuti*, making communication extremely difficult – only now do we realise how much we depend on peons delivering chits when the telephones are unwell. The whole thing is irresistibly enchanting and I am particularly taken by the idea of a capital city where the GPO closes down uncompromisingly for days on end to give everyone a chance to say their prayers; one wonders if there is any other capital in the world so immune to the practical pressures of modern life.

My rib-injuries have been stationary, at a rather painful stage, during the past few days. At first I had attempted to cultivate a stiff-upper-lip disdain for painkillers, but I have long since come down from that particular high horse and am now devouring them greedily every three hours. Today I took a double dose at 5.30 a.m. before setting off with Sigrid and Donhabadur to watch the annual sacrifice to Durga at the Kot; yet I soon realised that this precaution had been unnecessary, since the ceremony to placate the Black Goddess of Destruction is a more effective painkiller than any number of tablets.

There is a certain flavour peculiar to Nepalese functions that I can never define in a word; it is made up of casualness, gaiety, indiscipline and a wonderfully unsophisticated spontaneity – which mixture might be expected to provoke among Western spectators a patronising amusement. Yet somehow it doesn't, because in spite of everything these functions are *adequate*. The Nepalese are not trying to do something and failing – they are just not trying. And the chief impression received is of an elated unconcern and freedom – probably nothing will go according to plan, but anyway the plan didn't matter much in the first place, so who cares?

The setting of the Durga Sacrifice is unexpectedly drab; on three sides the Kot – a military square – is surrounded by new concrete army buildings, lamentably roofed with that corrugated iron which so often disfigures the Kathmandu scene. We sat on one of these roofs, looking towards the ancient slum house that forms the fourth side of the quadrangle; half its tiled roof collapsed long ago, and an eager crowd was watching the scene from the top floor. Under the long verandah on our left a shoddy strip of striped matting had been placed beneath a sofa and two armchairs; these were covered in a spectacularly repulsive chintz, as though they had come direct from a refined seaside-resort guest-house, and beside them were placed three slick 'contemporary' occasional tables, each supporting a peacock-blue tin ashtray. On either side of this suite stood rows of plain wooden chairs – completing the arrangements made for the reception of HM The King and assorted members of the Royal Family, who were expected to arrive at any moment.

An uneven line of twelve soldiers faced the Royal Enclosure, each holding a bugle. At irregular intervals these youths bugled what sounded vaguely like signals – but nothing specific ever seemed to happen as a result of their odd noises. Despite the fact that this is an exclusively military occasion everyone was in mufti apart from these buglers, and a group of soldiers on the flat roof to our right who formed a brass band.

By seven o'clock the scene was set on the parade-ground. Innumerable very young bullock-calves and frisky kids had been led or carried into the arena, and many of these sacrifices were now being stroked soothingly and fed with greenery to make their last hour a happy one. Three rows of furled flags were standing upright, some twenty yards apart, and enigmatic chalked signs had been drawn on the ground around them. There were no statues or other religious emblems in evidence, and one had the impression, when the sacrifices started, that they were being made directly to the flags. Strong wooden killing-posts stood at about a yard's distance from each row of flags and beside these were heaps of dry clay for scattering on the ground when it became too slippery with blood. There were a number of other foreigners sharing our roof-top, and already the women among them had begun to wail sentimentally about the poor little darling kids who were soon to be so cruelly slain. How unrealistic can you get! I'm perfectly certain there wasn't a single person there who had ever declined a plate of roast lamb.

On the ground, at the base of the flagstaffs, men were laying circular trays piled with fruit, vegetables, eggs, bread, grain, flowers, leaves, little mounds of red and yellow powders – and sometimes a sod of earth from which young rice was sprouting. These men were of every sort, from ragged beggars and peasants who brought tiny tin trays, meagrely laden, to prosperous merchants and senior Government officers whose enormous brass trays were almost too heavy to be carried single-handed.

Donbahadur had told us that the King himself would kill a white calf at seven o'clock, thus opening the ceremony; but at half-past seven we decided that His Majesty must have remembered another engagement. By then three young privates, clad in off-white singlets and blue denim shorts, were busily beheading calves at each post, using a larger and less curved edition of the ordinary kukri. The animals' heads were tied to the posts and held steady by one man, while another gripped the hindquarters; personally I would have been very nervous indeed were I holding the head, and seeing that fearsome weapon flashing down so swiftly within inches of my own neck. Yet in the course of over fifty killings we didn't see even one slight miscalculation, each head being severed with a single clean stroke. As the heads fell they were thrown towards the bases of the flagstaffs, where for moments they lay with ears violently twitching and mouths opening and shutting – a sight which slightly unnerved me at first, as I am not accustomed to watch sacrifices. All the bodies were dragged around the flags in a circle, with blood spurting, and when they had been brought back to the slaying-post they were flung together beside the heap of clay. Many of these carcasses continued to move for an astonishingly long time after death – and they were not merely twitching, but kicking so vigorously that it was difficult to drag them on the ritual round. I longed to be able to experiment by leaving one on its feet after decapitation; probably it could have walked quite a few steps before collapsing. Stories about perambulating, headless bodies have never previously convinced me, but now I find them quite credible.

Shortly before the slaying started the buglers and the brass band had begun to play different tunes simultaneously; one could just discern that each was murdering a popular European march, yet the musicians themselves were obviously being reduced to paroxysms of joyful pride by their own performances.

At about 7.45, when the three privates had got well into their stride and lots of blood was flowing smoothly, a Very Important Person wearing horn-rimmed spectacles and a benign expression came wandering alone into the arena. At once the killings stopped and everyone began to salute wildly, like so many toy soldiers gone mad. Then twenty men who had been mingling with the crowd, clad in ordinary Nepalese costume, plus swords, agitatedly began to unsheath their weapons – and as these no-longer-bright swords were held aloft in a crooked row one could see that at some stage the dew had rusted them. The brass band now stopped playing and while the buglers blew a fanfare the VIP, looking faintly embarrassed, solemnly turned to salute the empty sofa and chairs. Then, as the fanfare blasted its uncertain way to its ragged end, the swords were lowered and the VIP lit himself a cigarette and sauntered over to talk to a group of men just below us.

Now the tempo of the ceremony quickened, as more and more

animals were led in for sacrifice and the kukris flashed faster and faster and gory men ran around the flags with their carcasses, instead of walking, and piled trays almost obscured the flag-staffs. Then, to augment the excitement, two members of the brass band exchanged their instruments for ancient muskets which they frequently fired deafeningly in the air – while their colleagues and the buglers continued to vie with each other by massacring Sousa.

Smells are always a prominent feature of Nepalese events, and this morning these were cumulative. When we first arrived at the Kot it was permeated merely by the everyday stench of stale urine: but then people began to burn incense on tall, bronze stands beside each row of flagstaffs, and soon we couldn't decide which was the worse – urine or urine intermingled with incense. Next came the pleasant pungency of clouds of gunpowder smoke and, as the ceremony proceeded, steaming rivulets of fresh blood thoroughly confused the issue. Yet – oddly enough – by that time the total effect was quite appetising.

An old Rana army officer was sitting beside me, looking gloomy, and when I made some enthusiastic remarks about the general scene he said curtly that this ceremony is not what it was. During the Rana regime it had been compulsory for every citizen of Kathmandu to sacrifice *something* – if only a pigeon or sparrow – in honour of the Goddess Durga, but now tiresome democratic ideas have infected the atmosphere and the King has announced that only those who really wish to placate the goddess need do so. Possibly she is feeling a little peeved as a result, because it is estimated that the number of sacrifices has dropped to about 25 per cent of the pre-1951 figures; yet she may realise that this is a consequence of prices rising, rather than of devout fear diminishing. In 1950 a chicken cost half a rupee, but now an egg costs three-quarters of a rupee and a chicken twelve or fifteen rupees.

When we left the Kot at nine o'clock the slaughtering was still in progress – the original three privates having been replaced by three others – and Donbahadur said that it would continue for many hours; but the air of festive excitement had already faded and one felt that the rest of the ceremony would be a mere routine killing of animals such as might occur in a butcher's yard.

Donbahadur now announced that he was going to buy a chicken to do *puja* for Memsahib's car. He explained that all the valley's motor-vehicles are included in todays' ceremonies, to ensure that Durga will not use them during the coming year as instruments in her destruction campaign; and considering how recently motor vehicles were introduced to Kathmandu this reveals surprising adaptability on the part of Nepalese Hinduism. The chicken was duly bought on our way back to Jawalkhel and Donbahadur spent the next hour threading a long garland of yellow flowers to lay on the car bonnet, mixing the inevitable coloured powders with water from the sacred Bagmati River and sharpening the carving-knife. Then the three of us processed out to Sigrid's little beige Volkswagen – closely followed by Puchare, who is always interested in chicken killings from irreligious motives.

Donbahadur opened the ceremony by sprinkling coloured holy water all over the car and laying flowers and fruit along the front bumper. Next he laid the garland on the bonnet, before drawing with his fingers weird hieroglyphics on the dusty doors and wheels, while praying *sotto voce*. Then came the big moment, when he took the chicken from Sigrid and cut its neck over the flowers and fruit. Finally he again went slowly around the car, letting the blood trickle onto the roof, sides and wheels – obviously where Durga is concerned it's always a case of 'the bloodier the better'.

Our part in the ceremony brought it to a companionable conclusion. A little pile of rice lay on the sacrificial brass tray and when this had been mixed with blood Sigrid knelt before Donbahadur, who stuck a lump of the concoction on the middle of her forehead and put a red flower in her hair. My turn came next, before Donbahadur applied the same treatment to himself. The blood congeals very quickly and even now (10.30 p.m.) my piece is still in place – which indicates that Durga will not destroy me during the year ahead. Unfortunately, however, Sigrid's mark fell off quite soon, so now poor Donbahadur is slightly apprehensive about the fate of his beloved Memsahib.

To complete our celebrations we had the chicken for lunch; it was very tastily curried, but conspicuously anaemic.

5 OCTOBER

Quite suddenly my ribs have begun to mend; today I needed no painkillers and my seat to Pokhara has been booked for the day after tomorrow.

This afternoon I took a test-walk to Patan, and on the way, while passing along a narrow street of three-storey, mud-brick farmhouses, I saw a madwoman dancing and singing – with distinctly lewd overtones – in front of one of these houses. She was surrounded by a little group of smiling, but not leering, onlookers, and many other interested spectators were leaning far out over their carved balconies up and down the street. Almost everyone was dressed in festival style – complete with vivid *tika* marks in the centre of the forehead, garlands of fresh flowers around the neck and bright blossoms in the hair – and one immediately sensed that the madwoman's display was being accepted – not cruelly, but casually – as a sort of bonus minor entertainment quite suitable to a day of relaxation and rejoicing. Lunatics are a common enough sight in a country where there are no mental homes, and many of them reveal their insanity by these frenzied and often slightly *risqué* outbursts of song and dance. In Europe the sight of a madwoman roaming the streets would now arouse the most extreme pity, embarrassment and horror, so it does seem a little strange at first to observe onlookers enjoying this pathetic exhibition. Yet though they laugh, and sometimes engage in what appears to be deliberately provocative repartee, one is aware of no derision or real unkindness; indeed the onlookers are obviously sharing in the lunatics' crazy pleasure in singing and dancing – and one wonders if some of these mad men and women are not better off than our hidden lunatics, who must live for ever in discreet isolation from their fellows.

At Patan the Durbar Square was thronged with holiday crowds, full of the joys of life, and on walking up a statue-lined side-street I met an extraordinary little procession slowly making its way towards the main temple in the Square. It consisted of fourteen men dressed up as women, each wearing a huge, painted mask from which hung fantastic cloaks of waist-length horse hair, dyed red, green, pink, yellow and brown. These goddesses were preceded by two men, one of whom held aloft an enormous blazing torch, from which flames were leaping dangerously over the heads of the crowd, while the other carried in his arms a sheaf of bay-leaves surrounding what was evidently a very ancient, precious and sacred bronze plaque depicting Durga in various contortions of rage. The goddesses were walking in single file, with curious rhythmic jerky movements, and each one was accompanied by a normally dressed man who held 'her' right hand with his own left hand, while a large sword was carried jointly by the couple. The procession was followed by a man playing on a drum decorated with two pairs of mountain-sheep horns and at frequent intervals, when cymbals joined the drum, the goddesses stood still and their escorts moved away a few paces. Then, waving their swords, the goddesses danced briefly with slow, solemn motions of the arms and legs. At the conclusion of each dance devout people came forward from among the crowd and ritually fed the performers by pushing tiny wafers of wheaten bread under the masks into their mouths, and presenting them with water in what looked like earthenware coffee-cup saucers, which the goddesses smashed on the ground after drinking.

Even without these halts progress would have been slow, as the narrow street was packed with excited, reverent, laughing spectators who were continually pressing forward to touch the goddesses – and who were especially anxious to bring their babies and small children into contact with these divinities. I followed the procession for almost an hour, being accepted by the crowd with that gay friendliness so characteristic of Kathmandu.

As we approached the Square the throng became even denser, so for the sake of my ribs it seemed prudent to escape and I found a seat, on an elephant-god's pedestal, from which to see the ceremonial entry into the temple courtyard. Here I was surrounded by laughing, teasing, curious children – some of them quite old friends – who were flying balloons and eating sticky sweetmeats and whose ambitions to climb all over me had to be checked by an explanation that I was not in my normal state of resilience. Soon the big bronze bell in the centre of the

Square began to toll – with a sweet, mellow solemnity incongruously reminiscent of a European church bell – but though this was meant to herald the appearance of the procession there was neither sight nor sound of the goddesses half-an-hour later. It was now getting dusk and, as I feared for my ribs when walking home through rough, unlighted laneways, I reluctantly said goodbye to the children and left. Then, a few moments later, I passed the fourteen goddesses reclining on the verandah of a very scruffy teahouse, with their masks and wigs on their laps and cigarettes in their hands, while tea was being brewed to sustain them for the last lap to the temple.

9

Purifying Spirits

On arriving back here four days ago I experienced a very strong 'coming home' feeling: and since then it has been doubly difficult to accept the fact that soon I will be leaving for ever. I had expected to suffer the usual pangs when parting from the Tibetans, but only now do I fully realise the strength of my affection for Pokhara Valley in general and Pardi village in particular.

Tashi gave me a deliriously warm welcome and importantly led the way home from the camp – though after my long absence I had been prepared to find her allegiance at least partially transferred back to Ngawang Pema and his family, whose guest she had been. From her point of view my return was most inopportune because yesterday, incredible as it may seem, the precocious little hussy came on heat. Granted everyone and everything matures quickly in this climate, but for a few inches of puppyhood to come on heat at the age of five months and ten days really is taking precocity to extremes. Naturally I wasn't prepared (nor, presumably, was Tashi) so I'm very much afraid that the worst has happened. Yesterday afternoon she came in, after one of her gambols with the local hounds, looking slightly distraught – but at the time I attributed this to some tiff with a buddy and thought nothing of it. Yet now that the penny has dropped I suspect that she had just then lost her virginity and was registering a seemly degree of emotional upheaval. This afternoon, when she was taken for a frustrating walk on a chain, I had to use a stick in defence of her probably extinct virtue. One hates to thwart young love, yet altogether apart from the silly little thing's immaturity the legal implications of this situation are quite petrifying. It is difficult enough to import 'a

domestic pet of the canine species' into Ireland in an unmarried state –
but the imagination boggles as it has never boggled before at the
prospect of importing said domestic pet plus innumerable progeny;
and they would be innumerable if Tashi's fertility were to match her
precocity, just as they would be too adorable to leave behind if they
took after their mamma.

Now the nights are really cold here – and the days indescribably
beautiful, with clear skies over the Annapurna range – so Tashi insists
on coming into my sleeping-bag. At first I protested, thinking that she
would suffocate, but she refused to take 'no' for an answer; and
obviously she had had it all worked out beforehand, because on
admission she immediately burrowed down to the end and curled up
at my feet. Whereupon I decided that this was really quite a good idea,
since she forms a hot-bottle that never gets cold.

19 OCTOBER

All last night it rained heavily and the downpour continued until
3 p.m. today, like a revival of the monsoon. The locals say that this is
freakish in October, though from mid-November onwards the valley
does have occasional severe hailstorms.

Now that the so-called war is over tourists are again coming to Nepal,
and almost every day during this past week a special plane has flown
from Kathmandu to spew out on our airstrip a rigidly regimented group
of 'Round-the-Worlders'. These groups of course comprise the bravest
tourist spirits – the ones who have taken a deep breath and, against their
friends' advice, decided to risk two or three hours in Pokhara, bringing
hygienically packed lunches with them and drinking very little at breakfast-time because – 'My dear, we were *warned!* There simply *aren't* any
toilets in the place!' It is most unkind to laugh at such groups – but
impossible not to do so, when they emerge from their planes wearing
that same expression of bemused weariness, thinly veiled by a spurious
joy at the excitement of 'exploring', which I have so often seen on the
faces of similar groups being spewed out of luxury coaches in my own
'beauty-spot' home-town; and inevitably a regiment of Round-the-
Worlders looks even funnier in Pokhara than it does in Ireland. I feel

delightfully integrated with my neighbours when we stand in a row near the airstrip, being hypnotised by the latest Paris or New York fashions which, seen from a Central Nepal angle, appear even more grotesque than they actually are.

Usually the regiment is commanded by a buxom blonde 'guidette' (a monstrous word with which I have lately become reluctantly familiar) who wears 'sensible' shoes and strides ahead clanging an arty bronze bell – 'typical of Old Nepal' – to keep her troops in line. Unhappily few of the females follow her good example in footwear and crises become monotonous as the high-heelers get their deserts on our rocky tracks.

A few days ago one high-heeler caused me hours of tormenting curiosity. Her regiment was passing my house, at the non-U end of the bazaar, when she noticed me sitting on my doorstep doing nothing – a satisfying occupation now known to too few Europeans. At once she stopped to stare, as though I were a singularly repellent phenomenon on par with regional odours; then she called after a friend – 'Betty, *look!* Do you suppose she *lives* there?' And ever since I have been consumed by a desire to know the content of Betty's inaudible reply.

Yesterday a regiment of Round-the-Worlders was cut off from its base and trapped in Pokhara overnight by the abrupt change in the weather. I didn't have the sadistic pleasure of visiting our bug-infested doss-houses while the abandoned troops were quartering there, and my imagination is unequal to visualising their reactions to the 'service'. But this afternoon I did observe them – unwashed, unfed, and unslept – getting into formation on the airstrip in readiness for the rescue operation: and I must say they looked ripe for rescuing. One could see them cowering before the advancing spectre of dysentery – if they hadn't already brain-washed themselves into developing it – and their chic ensembles had taken it hard. That regiment will remember Pokhara long after the Taj has been forgotten.

3 NOVEMBER

A few days ago I gave my landlord a week's notice, and ever since there has been a 'purifying' campaign in progress in my room. This is being conducted with characteristic Asian disregard for privacy; at any hour of the day a bearded sadhu, laden with joss-sticks, sacred water, flowers, fruit and Sanskrit texts, may come scrambling up my ladder to seat himself in the middle of the floor – completely ignoring my presence – and perform interminable rituals to cleanse this room of the pollution caused by its untouchable resident. Despite his pretence that I do not exist – which may be part of the rite – I have by now become quite attached to 'my' sadhu, whose expression is less grim and predatory than that of the average Brahmin priest. The main part of the ceremony consists of long chantings, interrupted at set intervals by the strewing of flowers in the four corners of the room and the placing of a piece of fruit and a small coin on the table right under my astonished nose. At first I wondered if these were presents to me – but apparently not, for they are removed at the end of each session, though the flowers remain to wither in the corners. (This lavish use of fruit, flowers and vegetables is to me one of the most pleasing features of Hindu rituals in Nepal; it gives them a simple beauty and grace quite absent from any of the Buddhist rituals that one sees practised in the camp.)

I have to admit that the general lack of privacy here does become slightly trying after a time. Of course one could simply keep one's door bolted: yet to do this would be much more than a physical locking-out of the neighbours, and seclusion could never compensate for the damage inflicted on one's relationship with the village. Unfortunately compromise is impossible on such issues: one must either totally accept or reject local customs.

The weather has been appalling for the past fortnight, and as this is rice-harvesting time these rains are likely to bring considerable hardship to Pokhara. They are also hindering the recently begun seasonal house-building activities, which are now giving a great atmosphere of bustle to the whole valley. Men are constantly passing to and fro, leading creaking bullock-carts piled with rocks and stones; and women and children are to be seen everywhere carrying colossal loads of grass for the roofs, or of clay for the walls, or forming teams of three or four to transport bamboo poles for the supports. It's all so simple – one day there is a vacant plot of land and a week later a family is moving into a solid, attractive new home. Of course in the interval even the four-year-olds have been working virtually day and night; it's enchanting to see them trotting sturdily along behind their parents, carrying miniature dokars of grass – the NSPCC might not approve, but these children look happily proud to be so involved in this important family undertaking. Usually the houses are not completed until their owners have moved in. Then the women plaster the walls and floors with red mud while the men are carving and attaching the wooden doors and shutters, and building an outside stairway of stone or timber, if the ground floor is to be used as a stable.

This afternoon the camp held a farewell party for me, and this was indeed a melancholy occasion. It rained greyly all the time, which seemed appropriate, but the Tiblets insisted on dancing in my honour under the dismal sky, and everyone ate prodigious quantities of delicious *moo-moo*, which had been boiled in oil and syrup, and drank endless bowls of salted tea mixed with real yak-butter.

5 NOVEMBER – KATHMANDU

I have now proved conclusively that one pain does indeed cancel out another; today I awoke with such an unprecedented hangover that this afternoon's dreaded departure from Pokhara meant nothing as compared with the activities of that personal Goddess of Destruction who seemed to be residing in my head.

In the course of a not abstemious life I have only once before had a hangover – at the age of twenty, after drinking a half-bottle of the cheapest Spanish brandy – but obviously it was the mingling of *chang* and *rakshi* that did the damage. Kessang and the Khamba community of Pokhara had invited me to a 6 p.m. Tibetan farewell party at The Annapurna, and a Pardi Gurkha friend had invited me to a 9 p.m. Nepalese farewell party at a Thakkholi eating-house in the village – and having gone to both parties and drunk multiracially I can't reasonably complain about the consequences.

The weather surpassed itself yesterday; at 4.30 p.m., after a day of heavy rain, Pokhara was subjected to a cloudburst that made the worst of the monsoon downpours look merely damp. This lasted for a whole terrifying hour, before stopping abruptly, as though a dam had been closed. Then we set out for The Annapurna, and Tashi had to be carried all the way; at no point on the track was the furiously tearing water below my waist and at one stage it rose to neck-level and I had to swim to higher ground, gripping Tashi's scruff with one hand. Perhaps after all it was fortunate that I spent the evening pickled in alcohol: otherwise I might have awakened with pneumonia instead of a hangover.

When Tibetans give a party it is nothing less than a banquet. At first, because of the party to come, I tried to back-pedal when offered solid refreshment, but everything was so delicious that self-control became impossible – and would in any case have been impolite when such an effort had been made for the occasion. By the time I stood up from the meal at 8.30 I could scarcely walk; and some of my fellow guests were quite frankly dozing off with their heads on the table.

The Thakkholi eating-house was scrupulously clean, as Thakkholi homes almost always are, and the ochre walls and floor glowed warmly by the light of twisting flames that came leaping out of a hole in the ground in one corner – rather as though we were on the edge of a baby volcano. There were ten of us officially present for the meal – but innumerable others drifted in and out of the background shadows – and we all sat cross-legged in a circle, on little squares of Tibetan carpeting. Luckily the main meal was not served until eleven o'clock, though we were nibbling incessantly at various tit-bits as we swilled the rawest of raw *rakshi*, ordered specially by my host from his village. He claimed that it was the most potent alcohol obtainable in Nepal (where no alcohol is exactly impotent) and today I am prepared to endorse this.

All the food was served on brilliantly burnished brass dishes of varying sizes – from minute ones for the hors-d'oeuvres to circular trays for the rice – and our 'nibblings' in fact amounted to quite a meal. We began with tiny strips of perfectly braised wild-goat meat – among the tastiest savouries I have ever eaten – followed by fried sardine-like fish from the lake, followed by two hard-boiled eggs apiece, followed by one fried egg, followed by an omelette containing intolerably hot chopped peppers that compelled me to spit it out with more haste than good manners. And all the time we sipped steadily at *rakshi*, more *rakshi* and still more *rakshi* until I felt as though a bonfire were burning in my guts – but by then I had passed the point of no return.

The main course consisted of a gigantic mound of rice, with curried vegetables and dahl. As it was being served the local prostitute wandered in, hoping for a customer at the end of our revels; but she could see at a glance that after this party no one would be in a fit state to patronise her, so she immediately dropped her professional manner and settled down merely to be sociable. I have always thought her the best-looking woman in the village; she has fine-cut Aryan features, fair skin, and glossy, jet hair. By fire-light she seemed quite beautiful – until one noticed that brittle unhappiness and unwomanliness which disfigures even the loveliest of her sisters in every country of the world. From her nose hung an enormous circular gold ornament, which compelled her to smoke her countless cigarettes through the corner of her mouth, and her clothes were ragged and filthy – though of such good material that one suspected them of having been acquired as payment for favours received. One could see that this addition to the party displeased the Thakkholi proprietress – though it was only when her own attractive sixteen-year-old daughter began to talk to the gate-crasher that an indirect protest was made by sharply ordering the girl to bed.

I cannot pretend to know at what time the party ended; but when two swaying neighbours escorted me home and pushed me up the ladder I was quite unable to distinguish one end of my sleeping-bag from the other – so I merely collapsed on top of it.

The next few hours were not restful; in the midst of sundry night-mares I awoke once and for some moments remained firmly convinced that I was no longer a human being but one of Jupiter's satellites – a singularly disquieting delusion, possibly exclusive to rakshi. And today my condition resembled a serious illness rather than a hangover – indeed I have never had any illness from natural causes that felt even half so serious.

Pokhara airstrip chose the occasion to break all its own records for 'erraticism'. Though I had been requested to report at 9.30 for a 10 a.m. flight our plane did not depart until 4.30 p.m. However, I was indifferent to this; it could not have mattered less to me where I was, or for how long, or why. I sat in The Annapurna, wrapped in a cocoon of malaise and misery, with my fellow-revellers – none of them looking too robust – and we drank cup after cup of heavily salted black coffee, which is reputed to counteract the worst effect of *rakshi* poisoning, and our long silences were broken only by staccato comments on how very dreadful we felt.

Today was a Public Holiday in Pokhara; I think someone told me that the valley was celebrating the wedding of the two banks of the Seti River. This sounds improbable enough to be a figment of my *rakshi*-ridden imagination – but even more improbable things *do* occur in Nepal. In any case, whatever the cause of the celebrations they were very elaborate, and on two occasions freight-planes returning from Bhairawa had to circle the valley for ten or twelve minutes while slow processions of hundreds of women crossed the airstrip. Everyone was dressed in their most brilliant clothes, and there was much singing and dancing and blowing of conches, and carrying of effigies of the Seti on flower-laden platforms. For hours these noisy, colourful processions wound around the valley and it seemed to me that the populace was in a most tiresome and unnecessarily frivolous mood. All that gay laughter, song and music penetrated to my brain as a series of demoniacal shrieks, and the blur of colourful clothes sent sharp arrows of pain darting across my forehead.

When I at last dragged myself on to the plane I seemed to be laden with white scarves from the Tibetans and flower-garlands from the Nepalese – but perhaps my condition was creating this compensatory illusion of popularity.

I began to feel a little less unhuman during the plane journey and on arrival a couple of stiff Courvoisiers speeded the cure; in the circumstances this could hardly be described as 'a hair of the dog', but the principle was perhaps the same.

And now I'm going early to bed.

On Foot to Langtang

9 NOVEMBER – KATHMANDU

I have spent the past few days trying to forget the Pokhara Tibetans and organising a fortnight's exploratory trek to the Langtang area due north of Kathmandu – though perhaps 'organising' is too strong a word for my sort of pre-trek arrangements.

Trekking parties here vary enormously according to the status, pernicketiness and physical fitness (or unfitness) of their members. The most elaborate are the comical Royal Progress of Ambassadors, who travel accompanied by scores of porters, a team manager to control them, a cook, a kitchen-boy, a guide, an interpreter, personal servants, quantities of imported food, cases of alcohol and every conceivable piece of equipment from a mobile lavatory to a folding wardrobe. The next and largest group are the lesser Embassy officials and Foreign Aid men, who travel in moderately luxurious parties numbering their porters by the dozen and forgoing lavatories and wardrobes – but bringing tents, tables, chairs, beds, larders and cellars; and then there are the hoi-polloi, who are too poor – or too sensible – to do anything but rough it.

I had planned to go alone on my own short trek, but Rudi Weissmuller, a Swiss friend who is familiar with the area, told me that this would be unfair on the locals because during winter they have no surplus food to sell to travellers; he also pointed out that I would be permanently lost without a guide, and advised me to go to the notorious Globe Restaurant to look for a Sherpa who would be willing to act as both porter and guide.

Had I not by now been semi-integrated in the Nepal province of Tibland it would have been difficult to find such a combination; the

Sherpas are being a little spoiled by the Big Time Expeditions and are no longer very enthusiastic about ambling in the foothills with ordinary mortals. However, through Tibetan friends I contacted Mingmar, a twenty-four-year-old native of Namche Bazaar who agreed to come with me for eight shillings a day – by Sherpa standards a sensationally low wage.

A month ago I applied to the Singha Durbar for a trekking permit, but inevitably I have spent most of my time during the past few days prising it out of the relevant Government Department. In addition to losing my application form these caricatures of bureaucrats had also lost my passport, so I just hung around the office waiting ... and waiting ... and waiting ... until at last I became a Public Nuisance. Then someone bestirred himself to excavate a mound of documents (doubtless losing several other passports in the process), and a battered green booklet inscribed EIRE eventually appeared. This was at once seized on by me – to the great distress of the clerk, who insisted that it belonged to a Czech stocking-manufacturer – and in due course the permit was grudgingly issued by a more senior clerk, who reprimanded me for not having made my application until the last moment.

This morning I again met Mingmar and gave him money to buy rice, salt, tea and a saucepan. He seemed considerably agitated by the scantiness of these provisions – not on his own behalf, but on mine – nor was he much consoled to hear that I myself was bringing twelve tins of sardines, twelve packets of dried soup, a tin of coffee, two mugs, two spoons and a knife. This was still not the sort of provisioning and equipment he expected of even the humblest Western trekker, and despite my assurance that I perversely enjoy hardship he remained convinced that I would fold up *en route* for lack of comfort.

Yesterday I spent an unforgettable afternoon wandering around Patan – beyond a doubt my favourite part of the valley. To me there is by now something very special about this disintegrating yet still lovely city; familiarity with the most obscure of its filthy little alleys and a positive sense of friendship towards its time-worn, grotesquely carved animal-gods has changed my original excited admiration to a warm affection.

The rice-harvesting is at its height this week and as I strolled around the narrow streets, feeling the local magic rising like a tide to engulf me, the air was hazily golden with threshing dust. Now Patan is to be seen in the rôle of a big farming-village and even in the Durbar Square, where a prim group of guided tourists was pretending not to notice the temple-god's penis, I had to pick my way carefully between mounds of glowing grain and stacks of straw. Most people quit all other work at harvest-time and return home to help – a delightfully sane arrangement of priorities which does nothing to speed the modernisation of Nepal. While the men cut the crop in the fields the women attend to the threshing, and outside every house along every street the family's rice supply for the next year was being heaped. Normally the surplus is sold to bazaar merchants, but unhappily there will be little surplus this year, for Kathmandu has also had vile weather during the last fortnight.

Perhaps there won't be time for me to visit Patan again, but I could have no lovelier a final memory than yesterday's, when the streets were one vast sun-burnished granary, with crimson skirts swirling above golden grain, and sheaves of shining straw being balanced on raven heads, and the untidy music of swinging jewellery sounding faintly as lithe bodies displayed a timeless art.

10 NOVEMBER – TRISULI

A typical Nepalese day, with lots more waiting. Mingmar and I had arranged to meet at 6 a.m., on a certain bridge; but we each went to a wrong one – unfortunately not the same wrong one – and by the time we had got ourselves sorted out it was 9 a.m.

Trisuli is a valley north-west of Kathmandu where the Indian Aid Mission is now working on a colossal hydro-electric project. A rough forty-mile track has been hacked out across the mountains and every day an incredible number of heavy, battered trucks carry machinery, piping and cement to the work-site. To my annoyance Mingmar decided that we would do the first stage of our trek – in what he most misleadingly described as 'comfort' – by taking a truck to Trisuli. I argued that my conception of a Himalayan trek did not include rides in motor vehicles; but it is against modern Sherpa principles to walk one yard further than is absolutely necessary, so I soon gave in and we set out for Balaju, the suburb of Kathmandu from which the Trisuli track begins.

This is the industrial area of the valley, where foreign aid has already done its worst and produced incongruous little factories, schools and blocks of 'workers' flats – not to mention a deep-freeze plant with a notice advising foreigners to book space for storing their PERCIABLE goods; even in the context it took me a few moments to decipher that one.

We waited here by the roadside for over an hour, during which I became more and more restive. It is easy to wait patiently when a situation is beyond one's control, but to sit around pointlessly when one could be happily walking into the hills is very galling indeed. Yet Sherpas are as obstinate as Tibetans, and it would have been impossible to convince Mingmar that some people do enjoy walking.

When a cement truck finally appeared we joined the twenty other passengers after a prolonged haggle about fares; obviously, though his own purse was not affected, it was a point of honour with Mingmar to secure the lowest possible rate from the Sikh driver. We then drove a few hundred yards up the village street, which is being newly paved, but soon our way was blocked by an ancient steamroller that looked as though it had been abducted from some Museum of Early Machinery. This fascinating object, having expired on the narrowest section of the embryonic road, was now resisting all attempts to push, tow or otherwise move it out of the way. Occasionally a scowling young Indian with set jaw appeared from somewhere, shinned up to the driver's seat and struggled violently with whatever it is that makes ancient steam-rollers roll; but nothing ever happened.

Meanwhile our driver was having trouble with the police, who could not make up their minds whether we should proceed to Trisuli (steam-rollers permitting) immediately or at 5 o'clock this afternoon. (It was not clear to me why the police were in control of our apparently innocent movements: but I have long since ceased to be surprised by the quirks of Nepalese officialdom.) No less than three times all twenty-two passengers and their luggage were moved out of the truck, and back into the truck, as the police vacillated. One feels that Lewis Carroll must have secretly visited Nepal; a strong 'Alice' atmosphere now enveloped the whole scene, and to Mingmar's alarm I succumbed to an uncontrollable giggling fit when, for the third time, we were ordered back into the truck.

At this point an Indian Senior Engineer arrived at the scene of the breakdown and did something so drastic that the steamroller gave a scream of terror, emitted unbelievable clouds of steam and moved at terrifying speed down the steep hill, grazing the side of our truck as it passed. Fortunately this development coincided with a police mood favouring our immediate departure, so off we went at full speed – 10 m.p.h. – up the hill over the half-made road.

One suspects Sikh drivers of fiddling their loads so that they can make a good profit on carrying passengers and our covered truck was only one quarter full of cement sacks; but, as these constitute a most unpleasant cargo with which to travel, I soon climbed out on to the roof of the cab and hung on there, obtaining splendid though terrifying views for most of the forty-six mile, six-hour journey.

This track makes the Rajpath look like the M1 and, as we crawled along, I reflected yet again on the unlikelihood of Nepal ever having a conventional network of roads, or of China ever wanting to annex a country that could be of no possible use, either agriculturally or industrially, to anyone. There is only one Himalayan range in the world, much of which happens to be right here in Nepal, and even the ingenuity of mid-twentieth-century technologists can do very little about it. The Chinese have just spent four million pounds on building their sixty-five-mile dirt track 'strategic highway' from Kathmandu to Kodari – on the Tibetan frontier – and no doubt they regard this final link in the Lhasa–India road as being worth every penny of these four millions; but the building, and even more the maintaining of commercial roads throughout landsliding Nepal is never likely to be considered economic by any government.

As we left Balaju I was brooding morbidly on yesterday's American jet crash, in relation to our flight home; but before we had travelled far on this track I could only think how very slim my chances were of ever again boarding an aeroplane. The snag is that when sitting in a corner of the box on a cab-roof one's seat is projecting beyond the wheels – which are only a matter of inches from the often crumbling verge – so at hairpin bends one imagines repeatedly that the lumbering vehicle is about to go over the edge. Recently I have been congratulating myself on having an improved head for heights but, though it is true that I no longer even notice 1,000-foot drops, and am only mildly impressed by 2,000-foot drops, I do still take fright on finding myself poised over 4,000-foot abysses while being driven by a slightly inebriated Sikh. Yet when I had adjusted to the singularity of this road – which is not to be compared with anything I have ever seen elsewhere – it became paradoxically soothing to go swinging around mountain after mountain, hour after hour; but the jolting was hellish, and tonight my whole body feels as though it had been put through a mangle. Such journeys are not the best sort of preparation for strenuous treks.

The soil in this area appears to be much poorer than around Pokhara. The main crops are millet and maize, but three-quarters of the land is an uncultivable – though gloriously beautiful – mixture of rock and forest.

During the day several trucks and two jeepfuls of Indian engineers came towards us *en route* for Kathmandu, and during the complicated manoeuvrings that have to be executed before vehicles can pass each other here our lorry went axle-deep into soft mud at the cliff-side of the track. Obviously there was going to be a long delay, while the more able-bodied passengers freed the vehicle with spades borrowed from local peasants, so I suggested to Mingmar that we should walk the remaining ten miles to Trisuli Bazaar: but the idea was spurned. I then briefly considered going on alone; however, Nepal being Nepal, the truck could suddenly take a fancy to return to Kathmandu with Mingmar and most of my kit on board – or some other inconceivable catastrophe might occur to prevent us from ever meeting again in this life.

I noticed that the four Tibetans among the passengers were the most willing and energetic helpers; they showed no resentment of the Sikh's peremptory instructions, which so antagonised the local farmers that they were understandably reluctant to lend their spades and finally charged for the loan.

Within the past decade there has been some deterioration in Indo-Nepalese relations, and by now, having studied at close quarters quite a number of individual Nepalese–Indian relationships, I feel that India must accept rather more than half the blame for this. Admittedly the Nepalese have the usual excessive – though attractive – pride of mountain peoples and are very quick to resent, or even imagine, minor slights; but it is unnecessary for them to over-exercise their imagination in this context for the Indians usually treat them with breathtaking tactlessness. As citizens of a country to which the British introduced railways, hospitals, electricity and postal services the Indians now affect extreme contempt for a city like Kathmandu – forgetting that Delhi might be similarly undeveloped had foreigners never meddled with Indian affairs. In a place like Pokhara the condescension of the resident Indians is beyond *my* endurance, let alone that of the Nepalese. Were it not so infuriating it would be funny to see how expertly these men reproduce the attitudes of the worst type of British sahib in India; and frequently too there is venom in their voices, for they seem to be compulsively avenging themselves on the Nepalese for the unforgotten hoard of trivial insults directed at their own countrymen in the past.

However, it is probable that in any case the Nepalese would have been hostile to India at this present point in history, because of our common human inability to accept assistance graciously. During the past six months a number of Nepalese have sulkily told me that had India not been given so many dollars by America she could not possibly have given so many rupees to Nepal – which makes one wonder just how much furtive animosity is provoked in materially poor countries by the lavishness of Western financial aid.

Our truck mishap had occurred when we were almost down to river level, and now long streams of late sunshine were making the savage clefts in the hills – relics of monsoon landslides – glow redly amidst the dark green of the forests and the pale golden-green of ripening millet. At this season there is no great urgency here about work in the fields, and as time passed a small crowd gathered around the truck to enjoy our little crisis. One woman was accompanied by her self-possessed five-year-old son who, feeling a bit peckish, had a long drink from his mother's breast – and then stood up, wiped his mouth, took a cigarette from the pocket of his tattered shift and strolled over to me to request a match. One hears that mothers should not smoke while breast-feeding their children: but apparently it is quite in order for Nepalese children to smoke while being breast-fed.

After seventy minutes of hard work the truck was at last liberated and we drove down to the valley floor where, at 1,700 feet, the air seemed thickly warm. Then, having crossed the river by a startlingly posh new bridge, we arrived at Trisuli Bazaar just as darkness fell and are spending the night in a ramshackle eating-house that calls itself an hotel – having evidently 'got notions', as we say in Ireland, since so many Indians came to work here. This small town is built on a steep slope directly above the river, and all the streets are smelly flights of steps. As usual in Nepal the men seem to spend most of their evening hours gambling intently, and it was difficult to get the hotel-keeper away from his cards for long enough to lead us to the top of a dark, narrow stairway. We have a most luxuriously furnished room to ourselves – with no less than three straw mattresses on the floor; but these are probably the headquarters of an army of bed-bugs so I have urged Mingmar to sleep on all three and am hoping that the army will concentrate on his impervious body. My own sleeping-bag has been laid in the centre of the mud floor, as far away as possible from the presumably infested walls.

11 NOVEMBER – IN A SHACK ON A RIDGE

After an undisturbed nine-hour sleep we woke at six o'clock and fifteen minutes later were on the track, Mingmar carrying sixty pounds (a light load for a Sherpa) and I myself carrying thirty pounds (a heavy load for an effete Westerner). Mingmar's load could be much lighter were his standards not modelled absurdly on those of the expeditions he has worked for; in addition to his flea-bag he is carrying an inflatable rubber mattress and a thick blanket, which together must weigh at least twenty-five pounds.

The Trisuli Valley would be very lovely had the Indian Aid project not already desecrated it with the roar of machinery, and with hillocks of cement and stacks of piping. Now monstrous bulldozers and angular cranes are bullying the river into submission, and one is frightened by the speed with which men can despoil beauty. I was glad when after two hours' brisk walking we had passed those scenes and recrossed the river to where our track began its climb. Here a hamlet of wooden houses stood just above the river and, though it was a little early for trekkers' brunch, Mingmar decided that we should eat now as we would come to no other settlement before dusk.

By the time we had finished our meal and set off up the first mountain (alias ridge) the sun was quite fierce and Mingmar was muttering impolite things about the heat. On being questioned he admitted that he was wearing woollen ankle-length underpants and nylon skiing pants under his denim jeans, plus a woolly vest, a flannel shirt and a sweater under his down-padded wind-cheater. As I was too hot in a thin cotton shirt and shorts the mere thought of this apparel weakened me and eventually I talked him out of two-thirds of his garments – leaving him still grossly over-dressed and considerably increasing his load. This Sherpa predilection for excessive clothing amounts to a mania; having acquired these status symbols from various expeditions they cannot bear not to wear them everywhere and all the time.

Today we were climbing most of the way, going north above the Kyirung River. Our track was never forced right down to river-level, though it often descended a few thousand feet to avoid the more intractable precipices and then climbed steeply again to its average level of about 5,000 feet; but at no stage was it as gruelling as the Pokhara–Siglis route.

Yet simply to say that we were going up and down hills all day gives a misleading impression of monotony; around every corner of the winding track one saw a new loveliness, or an already familiar and striking vista from a completely different angle. Sheer mountains rose beyond the narrow Kyirung gorge and we passed from thick forests to barren stretches of rock-littered moor, and from sunny, grassy glades, half-encircled by high grey cliffs, to cool, dim tunnels overhung by giant shrubs and filled with the tumult of waterfalls – while everywhere were patches of pungent herbs, and a glory of wild flowers splashing the mountainside with oranges, blues, reds, yellows, whites and pinks.

This region is virtually a no-man's-land between the Hindu-dominated area to the south and the almost exclusively Buddhist area to the north, and I felt ridiculously moved on coming to my first ancient wayside *chorten* – a sight which indicated that now I'm as close to Tibet, spiritually and geographically, as any ordinary traveller can be in this sad decade. These stone *chortens*, usually built in the middle of paths, are symbols of Nirvana; when walking around them Buddhists always keep them on their right and it is one of the signs of a Bön-po that he keeps them on his left. This was a very old *chorten*, with grass and weeds flourishing in the crevices between the stones; one could almost have passed by without noticing it, yet its very inconspicuousness seemed to symbolise most fittingly the often imperfectly understood but ever present Buddhist influence that guides all Tibetan peoples.

I arrived at this solitary hovel on the crest of a ridge forty minutes ahead of Mingmar, who is in rather poor shape today because of a nasty boil on his right cheek. Western travellers do not often trek around here, yet the seven members of the household accepted my arrival without showing a trace of curiosity, disapproval or welcome: their apathy took me back to that appalling train-journey through Bihar.

This hut is built of rock-slabs, with a plank roof anchored by stones, and the squalor makes it seem more like a nineteenth-century convict's cell than a home. I am not easily shaken by Asian standards of living, which frequently are not nearly as low, within their own climatic and cultural context, as affluent Western travellers imagine them to be; yet this degree of poverty is devastating by any standards. These people grow a little millet on the unsympathetic mountainside, but it is pitifully inadequate for their annual needs and tonight they had a supper of stewed nettles (known to them as stinging-grass), flavoured with chillies and washed down with *rakshi*. Seeing this fare Mingmar and I simultaneously suggested to each other that we should cook a double ration of rice, and on being offered the extra food they seized fistfuls of it from our saucepan and ate it ravenously.

There are two rooms here – an outer one leading on to the verandah and containing two plank beds, and an inner one with a fire in the middle of the floor, around which everyone crowds when darkness has fallen. Mercifully fuel is no problem and cheerfully-leaping flames do something to alleviate the general misery. When any object is being sought beyond the radius of the firelight a blazing brand is used as a candle, and crimson embers replace tobacco in the family hookah, which is passed silently from person to person; but the acrid wood-smoke (one of the causes of glaucoma) is very hard on the eyes and I can hardly see to write this.

In the darkness of the outer room a youngish woman is lying alone beneath a filthy blanket, moaning and coughing. Obviously she is in the last stages of TB, yet the rest of the family seem dully indifferent to her distress. A little while ago I gave her some aspirin, just to show an interest; she was pathetically grateful and now says she feels a little better, but the moaning and the rasping cough continue.

I've tried to find out which tribe these people belong to, but they don't seem to know themselves; Mingmar says that their dialect is almost incomprehensible to him, though definitely derived from the Tibeto-Burmese rather than the Sanskrit language-group. Their features are more Mongolian than Aryan and, as none of the universal signs of Hinduism are apparent in the hovel, I assume them to be nominally Buddhist – though at this stage of dehumanisation it is unlikely that religion plays much part in their life.

As I write the complicated shutters that serve instead of a door are being lifted into place and securely barred with long wooden poles; so now I must spread my flea-bag on the second plank-bed before the firelight has entirely faded.

12 NOVEMBER – THANGJET

We were on our way by 6 a.m., having slept from 8.30 p.m. – if you can call it sleeping, between the biting of bugs and what sounded like the death-throes of that unfortunate woman.

From outside the hovel, before we continued down the ridge, we caught our last glimpse of the broad Trisuli Valley, far away beyond all the hills we crossed yesterday; and now the valley was so covered in cloud that it seemed like a sea of milk, whose motionless waves were clinging to the bases of many mountains.

Five hours later we stopped for brunch at a tiny hamlet of filthy stone farmhouses. Here was the same absence of food – too acute to be called a mere shortage – and at least every second person, including the children, had goitre. The skin diseases were not as bad as one would expect them to be but significant coughs were prevalent, and eye infections very common. The shattering poverty of this region almost counteracts the splendour of the surroundings; yet Langtang has always been among the most backward areas of Nepal, so it would be unfair to generalise from what one observes here. The people are mainly Tamangs, who speak a dialect of Tibetan, and Dr David Snellgrove estimates that they moved across the main Himalayan range before the sixth century AD.

Like all Nepal's hill-people they have suffered from consistent governmental neglect, and even now, when some feeble effort towards responsible government is being made in other areas, as despised 'Bhotias' they are not receiving their fair share of attention. Also few Gurkha soldiers are recruited from this district, so army pay-packets don't help the economy.

My Swiss relief-map of Nepal puts Thangjet west of the Kyirung River but, with all due respect to Messrs Kummerly and Frey, it happens to be east of it – or else I'm too addled to know where the sun is setting. (However, even such distinguished geographical publishers can readily be forgiven for losing their grip when producing a map of Nepal.) At first I thought it probable that a more prepossessing Thangjet existed beyond the Kyirung and that this was merely Little-Thangjet-Across-The-River: but the locals deny that any other similarly named place exists nearer than Tange in Thakkholi.

This is my first Tibetan-style village and on seeing the neglected *mani*-wall and the decrepit arched gateway I again experienced the bitter-sweet thrill of nearness to the unattainable. Today we passed several more *chortens* and a few very tall prayer-flag poles – suddenly recalling the existence of gods and men in the midst of the mountains' isolation. And now, when I look up from my writing, I can see a large, tumbledown *chorten* in the middle of the village 'street', with white prayer flags fluttering beside it in the cold evening wind. It gives me a special pleasure to see these flags flying against their natural background, instead of merely indicating refugee settlements; yet here one has the sad feeling that a long separation from the mainstream of Tibetan Buddhism has reduced local religion to a rather perfunctory following of superstitious customs.

We arrived at Thangjet just before 3 p.m. after a much tougher walk than yesterday's, and when Mingmar decided to call a halt, though the next village was only three hours away, I mutinously suggested that we should go on. In reply he pointed to a mountain north of another river and said, 'Look at our track.' Obediently I looked – and stopped feeling mutinous. Thangjet is at 8,000 feet and to get to the next village we must descend 5,000 feet to river-level, before climbing to 9,000 feet, at which point the track rounds the flank of the opposite mountain – and for all I know continues to climb.

Thangjet consists of about a hundred and fifty slate-roofed houses, and, being one of the main halts on the Langtang–Kathmandu route, it sports an astonishingly clean doss-house, run by a cheerful Thakkholi woman. The place is a lean-to rather than a building, with an inner wall of stones, loosely piled together as in Connemara, an outer wall and roof of bamboo-matting and no gable-walls. The result, at this height in mid-November, adds up to a Cold Night; but luckily Rudi Weissmuller insisted on lending me a windcheater, which I will wear with my slacks as pyjamas.

There was a treat for supper – boiled buffalo-milk poured over my rice instead of the usual soup. This establishment is also a tea-house – the hallmark of Thangjet's sophistication! – and when darkness had fallen some half-dozen men, wrapped in ragged blankets, came to sit around the fire and drink glasses of tea. As they spoke in Tibetan I could follow some of the conversation, which was all about yetis. Our hostess and Mingmar denied that any such things exist, but the locals and our fellow lodger (a Tibetan trader) believed in them very firmly and only disagreed about the yeti's nature: some maintained that it was an animal, while others insisted that it was an evil Spirit incarnate. Two of the villagers claimed to have seen small yetis, about the size of a five-year-old child, and at this stage I offered, through Mingmar, my own opinion that the yeti is indeed an animal, unknown to zoologists, which lives at exceptionally high altitudes and very sensibly declines to be captured.

At present I am sitting in unparalleled comfort on the Tibetan trader's wool-sack, which measures five feet by three – though the significance of this statistic cannot be appreciated by anyone without first-hand knowledge of these Nepalese tracks. John Morris has written '... but I must emphasise that the paths in the hills of Nepal cannot in any way be compared with even the roughest tracks in the more remote parts of Europe: they are merely the result of people having walked over the same route for many generations.' Indeed they are – and 'path' would be too flowery a description for much of the route we covered today. I now see that quite apart from carrying food Mingmar is essential as a guide. No doubt one could find the way eventually, but this afternoon we were climbing over fantastic wastes of colossal, wobbling, jagged rocks, through which my eyes could detect no vestige of a track; and the most disconcerting thing about this terrain is that when one is heading for a northern destination the *right* path often goes south and the *wrong* path north.

I am being fascinated this evening by the passers-by, who walk up and down the rocky, steep street carrying long branches of blazing wood at arm's length – street lighting, Thangjet style!

13 NOVEMBER – SHABLUNG

The gods were against us today, and an individual who calls himself 'The Police' has forbidden us to go north-east from here into the Langtang Valley. It's another of these Nepalese muddles – or is it? According to this unsavoury bit of humanity – whose uniform consists of cotton underpants and a torn Western shirt and who is the only Brahmin in the village – my permit says that we can go to Gosainkund Lekh, but not any further north. The document, being written in Nepali, is of course unintelligible to Mingmar and me – so we can't argue. Admittedly it is very possible that within the Singha Durbar a request for a Langtang permit would elicit a Gosainkund

Lekh permit, either through stupidity or for political reasons, and 'The Police' may now be luxuriating quite justifiably in this rare opportunity to exercise his authority against a Westerner; but it is equally possible that he sees here a glorious chance to land a fat bribe. However, unfortunately for him I am quite happy to turn south-east in the morning instead of north-east: the real frustration is not being able to go due north, where Tibet lies less than five hours' walk away.

Among the more dramatic contrasts of this trek are the frequent swift transitions from season to season. When we left Thangjet at dawn it was winter: sharp air stung our faces, the early light was metallic and the fields were colourless and quiescent. Yet by three o'clock it was high summer in Shablung and we sat arguing with 'The Police' under a deep blue sky, among blossom-laden almond-trees which seemed like pink clouds that had drifted to the cliff edge. Here long grass grew lush beneath flowering shrubs, above a flashing green river, and the air was soft with warm content. We had enjoyed an autumn zone too, during our long descent, seeing shining red, black and brown berries and nuts, and walking through the crispness of crimson, orange and russet leaves.

After our very tough climb on leaving Thangjet we had been glad to stop for an early brunch at a four-shack Tamang hamlet half-way down a mountainside. Here the poverty was grim enough, yet the people seemed alert – indeed, almost gay – and they showed both a normal curiosity and a shy friendliness.

The population of these stone-walled, grass- or plank-roofed shacks was thirty-six and there was a prodigious number of charming children who seemed surprisingly fit, apart from the inevitable eye-infections. I asked if coughs were common here but apparently they are not. The health of these settlements is largely controlled by chance; if one tubercular trader spends a night in a house he can infect the whole community.

While Mingmar was cooking I watched part of the millet harvest being threshed. On a level, hard-earth terrace in front of one of the shacks an elderly man was rhythmically pounding the grain with a thick six-foot pole; beside him fluttered tall prayer-flags, beyond him was an abrupt drop of 3,000 feet and in the background shone the snow-peaks of Tibet. When the grain had been sufficiently pounded the womenfolk collected it in large, oval wicker baskets and, having taken it to another terrace, spread it out on round wicker trays and tossed it so adroitly that all the chaff quickly flew off. This looked easy, yet when I tried to do it half the grain fell to the ground and half the chaff remained on the tray – to the delight of the onlookers.

While we were eating Mingmar added to my cartographical confusion by declaring that the east–west river which we had just crossed is the Kyirung. Logically the Kyirung should be the north–south river which this torrent joins below Thangjet, which we have been following up from Trisuli and which rises some thirty miles north of the Tibetan frontier town of Kyirung. I note that Messrs Kummerly and Frey have cautiously refrained from naming this river above its confluence (where we stopped for brunch the first day) with what I had perhaps mistakenly assumed to be the young Trisuli, which rises a few miles north-west of Helmu. The whole thing is rather intriguing – and personally I like vague maps that leave one free to speculate.

No less intriguing in its way is the amount of rice consumed daily by Mingmar. Though lean, and hardly five foot tall, he gets through three-quarters of a pound of the stodge at each meal. Two ounces go to make the average rice pudding so you can imagine what twelve ounces looks like when cooked and heaped on a big brass platter. I myself would be immobilised for a week after one such repast – but Mingmar cannot understand how I walk so far and so fast on a mere ladleful of rice and a small tin of sardines. Neither can he understand my impulse to leap into glacial torrents whenever possible. Admittedly these waters *are* cold, but it is a supremely satisfying sensation to immerse one's sweaty, weary body beneath a white rush of iciness – and then to emerge, tingling, into warm sunshine.

Shablung is only about 3,000 feet high, yet it has an even stronger Tibetan flavour than Thangjet. It is not marked on my map, nor is the considerable torrent that flows from the north-east and here joins the Kyirung – or the Trisuli, as the case may be. The village stands on a little plateau just north of this tributary, which is spanned by a wood and rope suspension bridge, and it is in the shadow of the next high ridge. The Kyirung is crossed by a rope pulley-bridge, on which men hang by the arms high above the water, and beyond it there is a long strip of cultivable land along the lower slopes of the opposite ridge; so the people are relatively prosperous, though the inherent Tibetan filthiness keeps the appearance of squalor well up to local standards. Millet and maize are the main crops, and herds of cattle, goats and sheep graze on the higher pastures. Shablung also has a school house, of which the villagers are inordinately proud; but naturally it is not now staffed, nor likely to be in the foreseeable future.

To outsiders there is an exhilarating atmosphere of siege about all these isolated settlements. They are at the furthest possible remove from the industrial areas of Europe where scraps of countryside, disfigured by pylons and wire-fencing, are only grudgingly tolerated by those to whom financial profit comes first. Here in the Himalayas it is Man who is just tolerated, in meagre communities at infrequent intervals, where the mountains relent enough for him to survive by the exercise of heroic labours – and also by the exercise of much more intelligence than is recognised by those theorising agricultural advisers who come East in droves, laden with university degrees, and who would be dead within a month if left to fend for themselves on a potentially fertile Himalayan mountainside.

Tonight we are staying with a delightful family whose home, like all the others in Shablung, is roughly constructed of stone, with a plank roof. Animals are housed on the ground floor and from the street one ascends a shaky step-ladder to a five-foot high doorway which leads to a single room, some twenty-five feet by twenty, with a large stone fireplace sunk into the uneven wooden floor at one end. Over this projects from the wall a smoke-blackened canopy of bamboo-matting laid over wooden slats – something I have never seen elsewhere; it is about five feet above the fire and appears to be used as a hot-press-cum-larder. These houses all have decorated wooden façades which vary considerably in artistry, though even the best of them are more crudely executed than the famous Newari carvings.

At the moment I am sitting in the little window-embrasure making the most of the fast-fading daylight and being attacked by a vanguard of bed-bugs who are too greedy to wait for darkness. From the rafters above hang three bows and a quiverful of arrows, and my unashamedly romantic soul rejoices at the idea of staying with people who still regularly use bows and arrows to shoot wild goat. This household consists of parents – Dawa and Tashi – who are in their early forties, and nine children; the eldest is aged eighteen and the youngest six months, which seems to indicate careful if not restrictive family-planning. All have survived, which must be rather unusual in these parts, but at present the three eldest are away tending flocks on the high pastures, from which they will soon be descending for the winter.

Now Mingmar has lit one of our candles and I have moved to sit on the floor. Beyond the fire Tashi is lying on a pile of piebald dzo-skins, naked from the waist up, feeding the baby. Her muscular torso is copper coloured in the flame-light and shoulder-length, lousy black hair draggles round her face as she beams at the infant while it happily sucks. Meanwhile the other children are tumbling in the shadowy background, like a litter of exuberant puppies, and Dawa is chopping with his kukri at a hunk of fresh mutton – making my mouth water at the prospect of *meat* for supper.

The manifold uses of the kukri fascinate me. One can do anything with it, from beheading an ox or felling a tree to sharpening a pencil or peeling a potato – not to mention killing men on all the battlefields of the world. The nonchalance with which these heavy, razor-sharp weapons are handled by small children is quite terrifying; if they made the slightest miscalculation they could very easily slice off one of their own limbs.

This evening I myself found use for the kukri as a surgical instrument. Mingmar has been unwell all day, the boil on his face having grown to carbuncle proportions, so I lanced it with the sterilised tip of Dawa's kukri and squeezed out an awe-inspiring amount of pus. It must have been causing him agony and making him feel as weak as a kitten – but like a good Sherpa he never complained. When the operation was over we were each given a mug of thick brown *chang*, made from millet instead of the more usual rice or barley. It tasted sour and was full of vaguely alarming foreign bodies; but the alcohol content was gratifyingly high and I did not say 'no' to either the second or third rounds.

Earlier this evening the Nyingmapa village lama came to greet me. He is a tall and very handsome man of about thirty-five, whose swinging maroon robes well become him; but he seemed a good deal more interested in trade than in theology and I doubt if he contributes much to the spiritual life of the community.

14 NOVEMBER – A GOMPA ON A MOUNTAIN

This is the first evening that we have arrived at our destination exhausted rather than pleasantly tired; we left Shablung at 6 a.m. and by 5 p.m. had climbed more than 10,000 feet.

On recrossing the suspension bridge outside Shablung we went back towards Thangjet, and in my innocence this slightly puzzled me, as I couldn't remember seeing any track branching off to the east. Here flat, narrow, maize fields lay on our left and I was enchanted to see a troop of giant silver langurs having their breakfast among the crop. These monkeys do a lot of damage and are always stoned on sight by non-Hindu farmers, so they fled when we appeared, moving most gracefully with long, loping strides.

Leaving the maize fields behind, the track curved around an almost sheer mountain until Shablung could no longer be seen, and as I was walking ahead a whistle from Mingmar recalled me. I found him pointing towards one particular section of the mountain for no apparent reason, and he said 'Here we go up'; which we did, for the next ten hours.

Before long I realised that the rough track from Trisuli in fact represents a Nepalese main road. This hardly discernible path, which Mingmar had never used before, was so steep that for the first hour we were not really walking, but pulling ourselves up through long thick grass (there were no trees and few shrubs), using our hands as much as our feet. Soon Mingmar had been left far behind and I was alone, feeling like a lizard on a pyramid and rather proud of my newly-acquired ability to follow the illogic of an almost non-existent track. Often I stopped to rest and look round, and unhopefully I took a few photographs, knowing full well that my unique incompatibility with cameras made the effort a waste of money. Moreover, this incompatibility was now being aggravated by an aversion to the falsification of mountain photography. In such surroundings even the most expertly-wielded camera cannot help but lie, and once the reality has been seen the preservation of fragments seems futile. Also it distresses me to break up visually the wholeness of a Himalayan landscape in an effort to see it as a series of 'good pictures'. So I soon freed myself from my camera and surrendered to the purity of the light, the foaming strength of the already distant river, the heaving complex of mountains on every side and the tantalising cleft that leads to Tibet, drawing one's eye to that ultimate glory of snow-peaks blazing coldly along the near horizon.

Soon I began to wonder why *any* path existed here, since it seemed unlikely that even Nepalese humans would settle on such a slope; but then suddenly I found myself scrambling on to a wide, level ledge, where a crop of unripe barley was overlooked by two solid stone farmhouses.

As I walked across this ledge – luxuriating in a movement that was not upward – I fancied something fairy-tale-like about these austere, improbable, grey dwellings. It seemed as if they must be inhabited by witches, whose broomsticks could provide a helicopter service to Shablung; but in reality the settlement consisted of twelve delightful Tamangs, including a young monk from the Gosainkund Lekh Monastery who was visiting the home which he had left at the age of nine. Only this youth had ever seen a Westerner; yet even before Mingmar arrived, to give a lucid explanation of my presence, everyone had welcomed me warmly, though wonderingly.

The origins and patterns of such settlements fascinate me – where the people came from, why they chose to live in so remote a region, where their sons find wives and their daughters husbands, and how far afield they go on trading trips. I asked all these questions, through Mingmar, but got no satisfactory answers to the first two. Questions about *why* people had settled on this plateau they clearly regarded as absurd; there was land to be cultivated, and water and fuel near by, so it was an obvious place for humans to live – and apparently it was not as isolated as passers-by might imagine. During the summer people from Langtang go to and fro to the yak pastures higher up, and both Thangjet and Shablung are, after all, quite near. In reply to my other questions I was told that marriages are not arranged, the young people choosing their own mates from these neighbouring villages or from the summer settlements of herds-people. Barley is their only saleable commodity and most of this goes to the Langtang folk, who are glad to have an easily accessible supply to supplement the potatoes and radishes that they grow for themselves beside the yak pastures. In exchange they give yak-butter, tea and salt, and for the rest this little community is self-supporting, producing its own *tsampa, chang*, potatoes, radishes, chillies and goat cheese, and weaving its own blankets and garments from goats' wool.

These people clearly felt no allegiance to any government, north or south. The surrounding mountains were their nation and their world, and no outside event could be said to affect them much; yet the Dalai Lama's flight to India and the subsequent Communist persecution of religion in Tibet had undoubtedly made some faint impression on their minds. I tried to find out – without implanting any disturbing ideas – if they feared a Chinese take-over of Nepal, but obviously the possibility did not worry them; either they had never considered it or they felt – probably rightly – that such a development would not make the slightest difference to them on their remote little ledge.

While Mingmar was cooking I sat smoking in the sun, and when I threw away the butt four waiting children dived for this precious prize which was won by a little girl who somehow coaxed two more puffs out of it. The adults then gathered to look wistfully at my packet of 'Panama' – a luxury Indian brand costing 8d for twenty. No one actually asked for a cigarette, but when I handed the packet round every face glowed with delight.

After our meal Mingmar and the monk held a long discussion about the track, and as we set off Mingmar informed me that from here onwards there was only a yak-path. I said that this sounded satis-factory, since yak presumably create a more distinct trail than humans; but according to Mingmar such infrequently used paths soon fade away, especially among dead leaves.

An easy twenty-minute climb brought us to the edge of a forest, where all signs of our path vanished, and after a moment's hesitation Mingmar admitted that he had no idea whether we should now continue upwards or go around the mountain. He only knew that our destination was on the other side of the ridge – and as the ridge in question stretched away vastly to north and south this degree of knowledge was not very helpful. Eventually he decided that we should try rounding the south flank and for the next half-hour we wandered along on the level, sometimes imagining that we had found the yak path, but soon realising that all these faint trails had been made by wood-gatherers from the settlement. Then suddenly we came to a sheer 5,000-foot drop into a side valley and at the sight of this abyss Mingmar shrewdly remarked that we were going in the wrong direction – so we promptly turned back.

Personally I was not at all averse to these haphazard wanderings. Here the trees were wide spaced – many had been felled – and in the brilliant midday sunshine the shrubs and ferns of the undergrowth filled this high silent world with rich autumn glows. We passed several open glades where amidst tawny, tangled grasses I saw the gleam of wild raspberries, strawberries, cranberries and blackberries – and stopped to eat them in fistfuls, with a view to stocking up on Vitamin C.

There was a strange familiarity about this scene 10,000 feet up in the Himalayan foothills. If one did not look beyond the immediate cosiness of the warm, mellow woodland one could imagine oneself in an Irish wood on a sunny October day – though however sunny that October day might be one would still need to wear more than the shirt and shorts that were adequate here in mid-November.

When we got back to where our path had vanished Mingmar took off his rucksack, announcing that he was going to look quickly in various directions for some trace of a yak-trail – and soon he came trotting triumphantly back, having found unmistakable signs of the creatures' progress. This path climbed very steeply, around the northern flank of the ridge, and in general it was visible only to Mingmar's eyes; had I been alone I would have denied its existence.

Here the forest was a twilit cavern of immensely tall and very ancient trees which repelled the sun and created an atmosphere of chill gloom. Many of these monsters had been blasted by lightning or uprooted by gales and we were slowed by having to scramble under or climb over the rotting, giant trunks that so often lay across our route. Soon my faith in this track was wavering and I suspiciously asked Mingmar how yaks were supposed to negotiate such obstacles. He replied that they jumped over them and, never having seen a yak in action, I felt in no position to argue; but it seemed to me that for this purpose a Grand National winner would be more appropriate than a yak.

The ground here was thickly covered with soft, slippery, black leaf-mould, and before long there was crackling ice underfoot, for we were climbing steadily. Now it was growing colder every moment and I staged the reverse of a strip-tease show, stopping repeatedly to put on socks, slacks, a vest, a sweater, a windcheater, a balaclava and gloves.

At about 12,000 feet the forest began to thin and then the path levelled out and became plain for all to see, curving past a herdsman's wooden hut and leading to a windswept, sunlit yak pasture. Now freshly covered snow-peaks were visible directly ahead – no more than a mile away as eagles fly – and I rejoiced at our emergence into this brilliant world of blue, gold and white.

Already I was feeling the lack of oxygen (no doubt because I smoke too much) and was finding it difficult, when climbing, to keep pace with Mingmar. After a ten-minute walk across the plateau we came to a fork in the track, where one branch continued around the mountain and another climbed steeply towards the summit. Some instinct (or perhaps it was only my hammering heart) told me that the *gompa* path went around, not up; but Mingmar, pointing to three *chortens* on the summit path, said 'up!'. So up we went, to the 13,400-foot summit, where there was no sign of any *gompa* and the icy wind almost stripped the skin off our faces. Moving a little way down I sat in the shelter of a yak-house and said rather breathlessly, 'I suppose we may call *this* a mountain-top?' – but Mingmar replied firmly that it was no more than a high hill-top; apparently in these parts only permanently snow-covered peaks qualify as mountains.

By now the sun was about to disappear behind the ridge beyond the

Kyirung and we still didn't know where the *gompa* was: but I was too
exhilarated by the magnificence of the scene to worry. Apart from the
snow-peaks our hill-top was the highest point in the area and, despite
its relative insignificance, I felt a surge of triumph while surveying the
countless lower ridges that surrounded us on every side like the
immobile breakers of some fantastic ocean.

Then, wandering over to the eastern edge of the plateau, I saw the
shining roof of the little *gompa* some 1,000 feet below us – approached
by that track which went around instead of up. Now I was glad that we
had taken the wrong fork, but poor Mingmar almost wept on realising
that our final climb had been unnecessary. No track led directly down,
and were we to follow our original path darkness would fall long
before we reached shelter – so we decided to attempt a descent in as
straight a line as possible.

The *gompa* had looked quite close from the summit but it took us
over an hour to reach it, and that descent was almost as exhausting as
the upward climb. At first the slope was densely covered with an odd
sort of bushy undergrowth, about five feet high, which had
extraordinarily springy and progress-resistant branches; yet without
these the way would have been even more difficult – they provided
something secure to clutch at when we were in danger of hurtling to
eternity on the steepest stretches.

When the gradient eased we entered a weird forest of dead trees,
some very tall, some mere broken stumps. All the branches had been
lopped off, and at first I assumed that a half-hearted forest-fire had
recently swept the hillside; but a closer scrutiny revealed no trace of
burning so I can only suppose that some obscure disease attacked this
forest long ago. Whatever the cause, the effect was extraordinarily
sinister in the twilight, and it would not have greatly surprised me had
we come upon Dante and Virgil standing on the brink of an abyss
watching souls being tortured.

The young monk had told us that the five Nyingmapa lamas who
spent each summer in the *gompa* had recently left, so we expected to
find the place deserted – but to my astonished horror we discovered
three small children in a stone hut beside the temple. They are aged

about eight, six and three and they haven't seen their mother for over a fortnight; nor do they expect her back until next week. Yet this strange, solitary existence, in a region to which very few travellers come between October and April, doesn't seem to disturb them in the least. They know nothing of the world beyond their mountainside and would probably be more frightened by a street-scene in Kathmandu than they are by these long, cold, dark nights spent huddled together in a heap of dried bracken. Named Tsiring Droma, Dorje and Tashi Droma they are typical little Tiblets, black with dirt and full of the joys of life – though understandably a little in awe as yet of their Western visitor.

However, despite the apparent contentment of these diminutive waifs I can't help feeling that their mother must be unnatural by any standards. When alone they have nothing to eat but raw white turnips, which grow on a small patch of fertile soil near the *gompa*, and in this region hungry snow-leopards have been known to kill children during the winter. (As I write the Babes-on-the-Mountain are ravenously devouring some of our rice and Knorr's tomato soup.)

This hut measures about 20´ x 8´ and the low ceiling-beams don't allow me to stand upright. Both they and the thick stone walls have been so tarred by many years of wood-smoke that they now look as though newly painted with shiny black varnish. Since I sat down here in a corner by the huge mud stove – on which the lamas' cooking is done – a faint, steady, dripping noise has been puzzling me and I have just now realised that it is coming from a huge earthenware jar in which *arak* (the Tibetan poteen) is being distilled for the edification of Their Reverences next summer.

Normally, while their mother is away, these children sleep in a little empty yak-house at the edge of this level shelf of ground, where the rats are less troublesome than in the hut. When alone they are unable to light a fire, having neither matches nor flint (which deprivation seems the only vestige of commonsense shown by the missing mother), and now they are delightedly spreading malodorous dzo-skins on the floor in front of the stove. Already it's freezing hard, and the sky is trembling beautifully with the brilliance of the stars.

15 NOVEMBER – THE GOMPA

Yesterday evening I suspected that diarrhoea was on the way and by this morning my prognosis had been proved correct. I would have attributed this to mountain-sickness were Mingmar not similarly afflicted, which indicates a dysentery bacillus acquired *en route* – probably in the course of our potations at Shablung. I was out four times during the night, which in this weather is enough to give one chilblains on the behind, and by dawn I had got to the stage of scarcely being able to lift my head. Poor Mingmar was no better and we both had massive doses of sulphaguanidine tablets for breakfast, and at three-hourly intervals during the day; as a result we are now rapidly recovering, though neither of us could look at food this evening. (Not that there's much to look at.) We spent all day lying in hot sun – sheltered from the wind by three *chortens* that stand beside the yak-house – overlooking a tremendously deep valley that lies between our mountain and the dazzling snow-peaks opposite. Occasionally we stirred to help each other to our feet for the next instalment, and every few hours Mingmar staggered to the hut to brew the tea which our dehydrated bodies craved.

Last night it froze so hard that our water was solid ice this morning; the *gompa*'s water supply comes from a stream some miles away and is cleverly brought here through a line of hollow tree-trunks, finally trickling from the last of these 'pipes' into a large brass jar.

The Babes-on-the-Mountain really are adorable – I'd love to kidnap them. Tsiring Droma, the elder girl, today spent hours sitting near us slicing white turnips, which she then spread out on a bamboo mat so that the sun would dry and preserve them for use later in the winter. The rest of her time was spent with Dorje, the boy, practising the writing of Tibetan – a startlingly erudite pastime explained by the fact that these are the offspring of the lamas, who share one wife or concubine between them and who evidently take quite seriously the educational – if not the material – welfare of their family. Both children show great reverence for their tattered school books, which are pages from the ancient tomes of Buddhist scripture stored in the *gompa*. A deep respect for every object connected with their religion is ingrained in all Tibetans, however illiterate or uncouth they may be, and this respect is also extended to the religious objects of other faiths – an example of true civilisation which adherents of other faiths could profitably emulate.

On the last lap of our trek to the summit yesterday we saw – to my surprise – innumerable pheasants, but around here the only birds visible are a pair of ravens, who spent much of the day perched on top of the prayer-flag poles, croaking companionably.

There was a most dramatic sunset this evening – ribbons of scarlet above distant, deep blue mountains, and higher a width of clear pale green, and higher still tenuous sheets of orange vapour swiftly spreading across half the sky. But Mingmar did not share my enthusiasm for this display, saying it presaged a blizzard tomorrow.

16 NOVEMBER – THE GOMPA

How right Mingmar was in his weather forecast! We reckon we're lucky to have got back here safely this evening.

Both of us were in good form on awakening and we breakfasted then, having eaten nothing yesterday. When we left here at half-past seven the sky was cloudless and the snow-keen air intoxicating; but already Mingmar was studying the wind and being gloomy in consequence.

About a mile from the *gompa* I saw my first leopard-trap – a crude contrivance of wooden stakes built around a deep pit and looking as though it would delude none but the most seriously retarded leopard. Yet Mingmar assured me that this model is very successful.

We were now on the main Thangjet–Gosainkund Lekh track, beside which the *gompa* is built, and for about an hour we walked around the mountain just below the tree line, passing many herdsmen's huts and yak-houses. Then we came to a wide expanse of moorland, sloping up to a minor glacier, and here began an easy hour's climb towards the 15,800-foot pass. Today I found myself well adjusted to the altitude, and I irritated Mingmar by frequently taking off my knapsack and scampering up the low ridge on our left to revel in an unimpeded view of the Langtang range, now thrillingly close. Because of these detours it was almost eleven o'clock as we approached the steep, final lap of the upward path, which here was barely distinguishable beneath new snow. And now we had our initial warning – a grey veil suddenly wisping around the snow-peaks to the south-east. At once Mingmar hesitated, looking rather uneasy; but then – to my surprise – he decided that we should at least cross the pass and survey the weather-scene on the far side, where it might possibly be clearer. However, his optimism was not justified. As we reached the top so did the blizzard and we were almost lifted off the ground by an icy blast. Five minutes earlier the sun had been shining, yet now we were deep in that odd, muffled gloom which seems to belong neither to night nor day, and the thick flurry of flakes was reducing visibility to a few yards. When we quickly turned back our fresh footprints had already been obliterated, and within fifteen minutes we were very thoroughly lost. There seemed no real cause for alarm, with five hours of daylight remaining and the tree line quite close; yet to be blundering around so unsurely in this sort of terrain does put one slightly on edge, and I was relieved when we suddenly emerged into sunshine on an unfamiliar plateau.

Hereabouts a hill is not simply a hill, but a succession of similar-looking ridges, and it's only too easy to go half-way down the wrong ridge before realising one's mistake. This we did twice, while searching for the main track, and by the time we had found it both of us were feeling the weakening effect of yesterday's intestinal contretemps; so I then produced my emergency ration of rasins, which we chewed while ambling leisurely downwards, our chilled bodies luxuriating in the warm sunshine.

The children were delighted to see us again and their pleasure quite made up for the disappointment of not being able to continue towards Gosainkund Lekh. Less than half-an-hour after our return the sky again clouded over and as I write it is snowing heavily outside – a cosy sight, as the five of us crouch around a blazing pyramid of logs, eagerly awaiting our rice and soup and boiled turnips; but it would have been pretty grim for the Babes-on-the-Mountain had they been alone this evening.

Mingmar has decided that our best plan for tomorrow is a return along the main track to Thangjet, where we will rejoin our original route. Having followed it about half-way back to Trisuli we can then branch off to the east and explore that high pocket of Sherpa settlements which lies towards Helmu, returning to Kathmandu down the valley of the Indramati River.

17 NOVEMBER – BACK AT THE SHACK ON THE RIDGE

The woman who was so ill here last week died a few days ago, leaving four little children motherless; but as they all look and sound tubercular they may not be long following her.

Today's nine-hour walk provided superb contrasts. When we left the *gompa* at 7.30 a.m., having given the children a final hot meal, snow lay a foot deep on the track – yet three hours later we were walking through groves of bamboo and banana-trees. I long to give some not entirely inadequate description of the glory and variety of that 8,000-foot descent, during which we saw many deer and pheasants but not one other human being; yet perhaps it's best to know when you're beaten.

Such a continuous descent on a very rough path is much more exhausting than any but the steepest climbs. This morning the nimble Mingmar was always far ahead of me, and he remarked that the majority of Westerners do find these descents very difficult, since we lack that inherent sure-footedness which enables the locals to skim so efficiently down stairways of insecure boulders.

From river-level a 4,000-foot climb took us to Thangjet, where we stopped for brunch. Since our last visit the tea-house has been enriched by a sack of sugar, but as it cost sixpence per teaspoonful we did not indulge.

This afternoon we saw a group of about twenty men and boys transporting newly-cut bamboo poles from the forest to their village – a distance of some five miles. Each load consisted of thirty eight-foot poles, divided into two bundles which were harnessed to the shoulders with long strands of tough jungle-grass. I could hardly believe my eyes when the first four men came racing at top speed down the precipice above our track dragging these unwieldy loads – which made an oddly musical clatter as the ends swept swiftly over the rough ground. At the junction with the main track the men had to do a sharp turn but even then they never slackened speed; and on approaching one of the many shaky, narrow, plank bridges that here span racing torrents they accelerated even more, so that their loads would have no time to slip over the edge and pull them into the water. Rarely have I seen a more impressive display of nerve, skill and strength; these men aroused the sort of admiration that one feels when watching a good toreador in action against a brave bull. Among the last to cross the bridge was a boy who looked about twelve but was probably at least sixteen. Perhaps this was his first bamboo expedition and he did not quite make it, one side of his load slipping off the planks. For a horrible moment it seemed that he must topple into the water; but he had kept his balance by some miracle and now he stood still, straining against the weight of the bamboo, while the man behind him struggled out of his own harness and rushed to pick up the hanging load. He then helped the boy to get safely over by walking behind him, holding both sides of the load clear of the bridge.

We followed the bamboo team for an hour, and their endurance, as they hauled these loads uphill, was even more impressive – if less spectacular – than their downhill sprints. Repeatedly one wonders just how these seemingly undernourished bodies manage to achieve physical feats that would be far beyond the powers of most well-fed Westerners.

18 NOVEMBER – SERANG THOLI

What a day! If we are not getting anywhere in particular we are certainly getting off the beaten track – and very nearly off every other track too! By now Mingmar has given up pretending to know exactly where we are, or where we will be by tomorrow night. He says that this whole expedition is 'a bad trek'; yet our erratic wanderings suit me very well indeed – I feel blissfully happy all day and every day.

We set off this morning at six o'clock and for the first two hours were following the main track back towards Trisuli. Then we turned east and, having twice lost the faint path, eventually came to a small Tamang village where we stopped for a badly-needed brunch; the morning's climb had been tough, and by now I am beginning to suffer slightly from protein-deficiency.

This village, of some fifty houses, was almost deserted because the millet harvest has just begun. After brunch Mingmar tried to get some idea of where we should go next, but the only available informant was a deaf nonagenarian who insisted on directing us back to Trisuli; so we were left to the sluggish inspiration of our own senses of direction.

By 3 p.m. we had descended to river-level, where we were confronted by one of those nightmare tree-trunk 'bridges' which demand the skill of a trapeze-walker. Admittedly this specimen was only twenty feet long – but it did look terrifyingly insecure, being casually held in place at either side by little piles of loose rocks, while its width could barely accommodate a single human foot. After one glance I funked it completely. Forty feet below the water was churning violently through a boulder-filled channel and even my trick of crossing such bridges *à cheval* seemed inadvisable. Merely to see Mingmar tripping lightly over almost made me ill and when he returned to take my knapsack I also handed him my shirt, shorts and shoes, informing him that I was going upstream to find some point at which I could either wade or swim across. Then it was his turn to feel ill; he went quite pale and said 'You'll drown!' 'Very likely,' I agreed. 'Yet somehow I prefer drowning to falling off that unspeakable contraption you call a bridge.'

It was easier than I had expected to find a fording point. Some quarter-of-a-mile upstream – where the river was about 100 yards wide and ten feet deep – a little dam had been built, and though the current was still strong here it seemed that by swimming diagonally above the dam I could just about make it to the other side. Fortunately my self-confidence when *in* water equals my lack of self-confidence when *over* water; I always enjoy a challenge from this element and poor Mingmar, who had anxiously followed me upstream on the opposite bank, was suffering most from tension as I dived into the icy, clear green pool. By the half-way stage I had the measure of the current and knew that there was not the slightest danger; yet I didn't dare ease off for long enough to yell reassuringly to Mingmar and until I stepped onto the rock beside him he remained convinced that I *must* drown.

After this refreshment by immersion I was in excellent form for the next lap – a long, long climb up the steepest cultivated slope we have yet seen, where there was no path and we simply pulled ourselves somehow from one narrow terrace of ripening millet to another.

Tonight we are staying in a Tamang hamlet at 7,500 feet, where the slate-roofed houses are built of ochre mud and stone as in the Hindu villages around Pokhara. At the moment the populace are almost pushing each other over a precipice in their efforts to see me; and Mingmar is hardly less of a curiosity, for we are now far from the main tracks and few of these people have ever before seen either a Western female or a Sherpa porter in all his sartorial glory.

The filth of this house is extreme and the stable seemed so much less filthy that I chose it as my bedroom and am now leaning against the warm flank of a reclining buffalo. One hopes that bed-bugs will be fewer here than indoors: and the cow-bugs that must inevitably frequent Nepalese cattle are not so likely to be interested in me.

19 NOVEMBER – SENTHONG

Leaving Serang Tholi at dawn we climbed steadily to the summit of a 9,000-foot hill. Ordinarily the sun comes over the mountains to us, but today we went over a mountain to the sun and it was wonderful to step from cold early shadows into warm golden air, and to see the new, gentle light lying on a wild tumble of deserted mountains.

By ten o'clock we had negotiated two of these mountains, following a faint path that frequently vanished. Then we came to a tiny settlement, on the verge of another cultivated hillside, where we ran into caste trouble for the first time on this trek. When Mingmar inquired where he might cook our brunch we discovered that this was a very orthodox Chetri village in which we, as untouchable non-Hindus, would not be admitted to any house; but eventually we found a woman who consented to cook for us, provided we remained outside her compound.

The conscientious Mingmar was frantically worried at the idea of anyone but himself cooking for me, and he swore that after this meal I would get every disease in the book. However, I consolingly pointed out that my immunities are abnormally well-developed, by Western standards – and also that Chetris are cleaner, as well as more intolerant, than Tamangs. Yet I must admit that this village was loathsomely smelly, and our rice did look and taste as though cooked in a pretty sordid pot. None of the people we have stayed with (apart from the Thakkholi woman at Thangjet) ever practises the art of washing up – unless one counts the licking of platters at the end of a meal, which happens to be the labour-saving device that I too employ when living alone in my own home.

From half-past eleven we walked almost continuously for six hours – first down to river-level, next up and over an 8,800-footer, then two-thirds of the way down this 'hill' until we came to Senthong, where there are a few Tamang households among many Chetris. It is an odd sensation, when looking for lodgings, to go from door to door asking what the family religion is and receiving cold stares from the Hindus. The Tamangs here are very much poorer than the Chetris and are unmistakably the outcasts of the village; but equally unmistakably they are a far nicer group of people than their Hindu neighbours. I don't resent being shunned by orthodox Hindus, who can't reasonably be expected to fraternise with the likes of me, yet it is sad that Hinduism, despite the breadth of its basic philosophy, has in practice the effect of blighting many potentially valuable human contacts – whereas Tibetan Buddhism, however imperfectly understood by the masses, has the precisely opposite effect.

Tonight I have again chosen the cattle-shed as there simply isn't space for me inside this tiny house, which shelters a complex family of eighteen children and six adults. I discovered last night that cattle are noisy creatures with which to sleep because of their extraordinarily tumultuous digestive processes, which seem to go on all night like a thunderstorm.

20 NOVEMBER – LIKARKA

This morning I was awakened at half-past four by the ancient, soothing rhythm of millet being ground between the stones of a hand-mill. It was still dark and quite cold, and for the next hour I lay drowsily warm in my flea-bag, looking up at the golden throb of the stars and listening to the little stirrings of the village. The rice harvest had everyone on the move early, and as Mingmar and I made our way down to river-level soon after dawn we passed families already threshing grain on the wider terraces of the paddy fields. Here bullocks are used for the threshing, but at Serang Tholi – where the people also have cattle – we had seen the operation done by hand, each separate sheaf being beaten vigorously on the ground until every grain was shaken loose.

Were I only allowed a single adjective to describe Nepal I would have to use 'varied'. No two villages are quite alike in language, dress, customs, attitudes, architecture or surroundings, and one could not possibly refer to 'a typical village' of this region. Doubtless the isolation imposed by the terrain on each settlement is responsible for this most pleasing diversity, which makes one realise anew how horribly our Western uniformity impoverishes life. And an equally rich variety is found in the landscape; at every turn one is confronted by new, tremendous vistas of unimaginable beauty as though Nature, when creating these mountains, had been exercising the subtle imaginative power of a great musician elaborating on a simple basic theme.

Today has been the most strenuous of the entire trek. This morning's river was a wide seething torrent, spanned some 80 feet above the water by a swaying, decrepit suspension bridge; but luckily the hand-rails were sufficiently intact for me to feel no fear of the crossing, and at 7.15 a.m. we began the upward climb. From river-level – 3,400 feet – until we had crossed an 11,800-foot pass there was no respite on level ground, and even Mingmar had to admit that he felt 'very tired' at the top – a sensational confession.

We had stopped soon after nine o'clock for an hour's brunch-break at a three-house Tamang settlement, and these were the last dwellings seen until we crossed the pass at midday and descended some 1,500 feet to this region of scattered Sherpa houses.

After the savagely steep climb up it was a relief to find ourselves looking down from the top of the pass over an easy green slope. Here huge grey boulders were strewn on the grass, patches of unmelted snow gleamed in shady spots, and flocks of long-haired, sturdy goats grazed in the care of a little boy who lay alone on a slab of rock, thoughtfully playing a flute. From this point the circular valley – some fifteen miles in circumference – appeared to be quite shallow, though later we saw the ravine in the centre through which a river flows away to the south. Immediately above us, to the north, a jagged mountain was only thinly wooded with giant pines, but about a mile beyond the sunny expanse of pasture dense forests darkened the sides of the valley. And here I felt more than usually aware of that special tranquillity always experienced at these heights – a depth of peace impossible to describe or explain, but reaching to every fibre of one's being.

Our destination was a little settlement already visible on the far side of the valley and it looked so deceptively close that now we dawdled along, relishing our walk down the easy incline. Half-an-hour's ambling brought us to a sheltered hollow where we saw two Sherpa dwellings, with freshly-printed prayer-flags flying between them. There was a well here, beside the path, and pausing to drink from it I noticed something that almost paralysed me with astonishment – wrapping-paper off a bar of Lifebuoy soap. I beckoned to Mingmar, and we stood staring at this baffling manifestation of 'civilisation' as though we were the first men on the moon and had found an empty match-box there before us. Then, continuing towards the houses, we came upon two gorgeous silk saris spread on the grass to dry – and next we saw a most beautiful young creature, wearing a pink sari and golden slippers, with attractive bazaar jewellery in her glossy hair and on her slender neck and arms. This vision was leaning against a low stone wall, talking to an older woman with a weather-roughened face whose muscular body was clad in the filthiest of rags and who obviously had never washed in her life.

Mingmar and I did not even attempt to conceal our curiosity; having greeted the women we too sat on the wall, and in reply to questions were told that three years ago the girl had gone to Bombay to be trained as a nurse and was now home on a month's leave. 'Careers for Girls' are of course unheard of in these parts and it was inexplicable to me that this youngster should have had sufficient education to undergo a nurse's training. Evidently there was a story here, but neither mother nor daughter was very communicative and we could find out nothing more.

I wondered how the girl's relatives were reacting to the appearance in their midst of such unprecedented elegance and sophistication. Would they feel proud of her, or uneasy, or a little scornful of her fussiness and daintiness? Certainly the girl herself, by so scrupulously maintaining 'Bombay standards' against the heaviest of odds, was affirming her belief in the superiority of her new mode of life. She was most affectionate towards her mother, yet she did look rather strained, and it seemed likely that the immediate impact of the return had been disquieting and that she was secretly and guiltily looking forward to her departure.

Meeting this girl helped me to understand why Asian villagers who have had a medical training are so reluctant to return to those areas where help is most needed. For them the sheer novelty of both the material and mental opportunities of urban life is overwhelming, and in such a totally new world they become new people, continually discovering unsuspected potentialities within themselves. Some people accuse them of allowing improved conditions to 'go to their heads'; yet this seems an unfair description of the natural excitement caused by widening horizons. The comparative values of what is lost and what gained by migration to a city is not relevant to this argument. These young people are usually conscious only of gaining, and at this stage of individual development are as self-centred as babies, reaching out with both hands for all the advantages of education and unaware that their own good fortune imposes on them a responsibility to help their fellows. It seems unrealistic to demand, from this generation of newly-educated Asians, the self-discipline that would enable them willingly to relinquish their brave new world. Such a sacrifice would require a much riper fruit of education than any that they can be expected to bear; and this is one of the main obstacles that for years to come will hinder Health Programmes in Asia – however generously the West may finance them.

Before leaving this curiously pathetic mother and daughter we had asked about the path through the forest; yet within an hour of entering the twilight beneath the trees we were more lost than one could believe possible. I had expected quite a clear track between the two settlements, but if any such exists we never found it. For over two hours we went scrambling up and down precipitous slopes, through thick, thorny undergrowth, and repeatedly we were thwarted by impassable ravines. At half-past four we knew that less than ninety minutes of daylight remained and now Mingmar was getting really frightened; he had begun to pray non-stop, using that odd Buddhist hum which sounds rather comical until one has become familiar with it. Neither of us had any idea of the way back, so we decided to continue the struggle forward – and then suddenly we came on something that had once been a track, though now it is in a dangerous state of disrepair. Having nervously followed it through two deep dark ravines – even Mingmar was nervous, to my immense gratification – we emerged at last on to another wide stretch of level turf; and twenty minutes later, after crossing several fields of buck-wheat, barely and potatoes, we were relaxing with this charming Sherpa family.

Their house is similar to the one we stayed in at Shablung, though the living-room is twice as big and very much cleaner. Dry maize-cobs hang from the rafters and handsomely carved cupboards line the wall that faces the low door and two tiny windows. If one can judge by the array of silver votive bowls, and silver-bound wooden tea-cups, the family must be quite rich by local standards. Against the wall in one corner leans a four-foot-high copper-banded bamboo churn for making buttered tea, and in a little room leading off this is the family chapel, where eleven tiny butter-lamps flicker cosily beneath a grimy but very lovely *thanka* representing the Compassionate Aspect of the Lord Buddha.

This family consists of a grandmother, her son, his wife and five adorable children who stopped being shy of me in record time. As I write, sitting on the floor near the fire, the two younger ones are standing beside me, leaning on my shoulders and intently watching that strange procedure which covers clean paper with a nasty mess of squiggles.

As soon as we arrived here I sat in the window-embrasure to enjoy one of the most beautiful sunsets I have ever seen. This house – at 10,400 feet – faces due west, and I was overlooking range after range of dusk-blue mountains, beyond which the ghostly snows of the distant Dhauligiri Massif were just visible against a crimson horizon. Above this sunset flare was a blue-green ocean of space, in which the golden boat of Venus sailed alone; and higher still the zenith was tinged pinkish brown. Truly this was a most noble scene, so still with peace and so vital with beauty in the ebbing of the day.

On a more mundane level the evening was scarcely less memorable, because we had potatoes and milk for supper. Perhaps only a compatriot could appreciate the gastronomic ecstasy into which an Irishwoman can fall when served with potatoes after living on rice for a fortnight. Yet Mingmar seemed equally thrilled; though he can eat rice in such abundance, potatoes are the staple food of the Sherpas in their home district. He successfully consumed thirty-three large specimens and was quite concerned when, after twelve monsters, I reluctantly declined a third helping for sheer lack of space. Indeed this four-house-settlement is a veritable food-paradise; we have been able to buy five eggs, which we will hard-boil and take with us tomorrow as both our rice and sardine supplies are getting low.

21 NOVEMBER – A FARM ON A HILLTOP

I am willing to concede that this *is* only a hill-top, since we are now down to 6,000 feet. The hill in question is a spur of one of the giant mountains that overshadow this valley on both sides, and after the silence of the heights it's quite disconcerting this evening to hear the roar of the nearby river.

Oddly enough it was Mingmar who felt poorly today, after yesterday's marathon. This morning's easy ten-mile walk was mainly downhill and we stopped frequently; yet he made heavy weather of the few inevitable climbs, and when we arrived here at half-past two he suggested that an early halt might be good for *me!* Perhaps he over-indulged in *chang* last night, forgetting our dire experience after the Shablung binge.

Soon after leaving Likarka at 6.30 a.m. we crossed the steep wooded ridge that rises sharply behind the settlement and that loveliest of valleys was out of sight. About an hour later I saw my first herd of dzo – and was vaguely disappointed to find they look exactly like cows with very bushy tails. They were being guarded by a pair of enormous, ferocious-looking Tibetan mastiffs who almost foamed at the mouth as I wandered through the herd taking photographs. Mingmar says that these dogs are trained to kill intruding humans; during the day they are usually tied to wooden stakes with short, heavy chains and they wear large, clangorous iron bells around their necks. But at night they roam free and are far more dangerous than wild animals; I know several Tibetans whose faces have been horribly disfigured by their attacks. Today I felt decidedly apprehensive when we had to pass a herd in charge of an untied dog; but the enraged creature was restrained by two tiny children who flung their arms around his neck and told him to be quiet. I didn't really expect him to obey – yet immediately he subsided and began to wag his tail at the children, ignoring us as we sidled past.

Soon afterwards we met a youth returning to Likarka from his first trading expedition to Kathmandu. He had received a Rs. 100 note in payment for wool, but being illiterate and having never before handled big money he was not at all sure what this signified. When he stopped us to ask for a definition Mingmar said that such a large note would be useless in this area, so I changed it for twenty Rs. 5/- notes, to the boy's delight; he evidently imagined that his father would be much better pleased by twenty notes than by one! He then showed us what had once been a very good Swiss watch; it had been sold him in Kathmandu for – he thought! – Rs. 50/- and was still ticking, but the minute-hand had come off the day before – doubtless because he had been playing too vigorously with the winder. (He had of course no notion how to read the time.) I advised him to leave it alone until he next visited Kathmandu; but then there ensued a lengthy discussion between him and Mingmar on the advisability of exchanging watches. Mingmar's would have been the better of the two even had the boy's been perfect; yet the Sherpa trading urge is so strong that apparently a losing deal is preferable to no deal at all and finally Mingmar accepted the broken watch, plus Rs. 25/-, in exchange for his own Omega.

Half-an-hour later we stopped again at one of those 'dairies' fairly common in this area, where small herds of dzo are looked after by cheerful shepherdesses who make Tibetan-type cheese and butter. I intend bringing home a piece of the cheese, which has to be seen to be believed. It is harder than any rock except granite and is said to be still edible three centuries after it has been made – if one knows the technique required for eating granite-hard substances.

This 'dairy' was a little bamboo-matting hut on a grassy slope encircled by the forest and here we each enjoyed a long drink of butter-milk, and a platter of whey fried in butter and pleasantly tainted by the smoke of the wood-fire. Several very young dzo calves stood near by and completely captivated me. At this age they have their father's thick coat and are bundles of furry huggableness, with huge melting eyes and affectionate licks for all and sundry.

Several other brief delays were caused by Mingmar stopping at every farmhouse *en route* to enquire if there was any butter for sale; his mother died a year ago and now he wants to make *tormas* and burn lamps in honour of the anniversary. His trader father had two wives, one living in Namche Bazaar and the other in Lhasa. When he died Mingmar was only four and was brought up by both his mother and his step-mother, who themselves traded extensively between Tibet and India. Lhamo, his twenty-two-year-old sister, now looks after the family trading concerns and Pemba, his elder half-brother, runs one of the Tibetan hotels in Kathmandu – assisted by his own mother. This morning Mingmar bought two pounds of Tibetan cheese for her, as he always brings back a present of her favourite delicacy when he has been away on trek. So between butter for his dead mother and cheese for his live step-mother our progress was considerably slowed.

Obviously his sister Lhamo is Mingmar's favourite; he repeatedly refers to her with affection and pride, saying what a clever businesswoman she is and how much he is looking forward to seeing her, after a year's separation, when she comes from Lhasa to Kathmandu next month, en route for Calcutta. These Sherpas certainly get around – and they seem to need no passport for all their travels between Tibet, Nepal and India. Of course, Lhamo now flies from Kathmandu to Calcutta, and for all I know travels by truck in Tibet. She has two husbands so far – one who looks after the family farm near Namche Bazaar and one in Kathmandu, who also has another wife permanently resident there to comfort him while the tycoon Lhamo attends to her International Business. No wonder Sherpa relationships are not easy to sort out!

Our last and longest delay came soon after midday, when we paused to watch a religious ceremony being conducted outside a stone hut on a ledge. For some time before reaching this ledge we could hear the wonderful melody of drum, bell, cymbals and conch-shell – music that made me feel very homesick for the Pokhara camp, and that sounded even more stirring against its natural background. I tried to find out what the ceremony was all about, but even if Mingmar knew he clearly did not want to discuss it with an outsider; so I stopped probing and contented myself with imprudently drinking four wooden bowlfuls of the best *chang* I have ever tasted.

The elderly lama conducting the ceremony was dressed in black instead of the usual maroon robes, and his young monk assistant wore layman's clothes. Both sat cross-legged on the ground, with their backs to the hut wall, and the Scriptures were laid before the lama on a low wooden table. His Reverence held a bell in his right hand and a *dorje* in his left – the *dorje* being frequently abandoned when he needed another swig of *chang*, which he favoured instead of the buttered-tea consumed endlessly during ceremonies by the more orthodox lamas. At right angles to the wall stood a painting of the Lord Buddha with the usual *tormas* and butter-lamps laid before it, and in front of this was a hanging drum, some three feet in circumference, which a tall, slim youth, clad in the local kilt, beat regularly in time to the chanting. About thirty people sat nearby in a semi-circle, laughing, chatting, drinking *chang* and eating cold sliced potatoes. The atmosphere was gay and friendly, and we were made to feel so welcome that we remained with the little group for over half-an-hour, each of us giving an offering to the lama before we left.

The young mother of the Sherpa family with whom we are staying tonight recently spent three years as a coolie on the roads in Assam, and Mingmar told me that it is common for the people of this area to emigrate temporarily to India and work in road gangs with the Tibetan refugees. Then, having saved up more money than they could ever earn in Nepal – and increased it on the way home by astute trading in Kalimpong – they return to settle down here. I attempted to discover whether they are officially accepted into the road gangs as Nepalese citizens, or whether they masquerade as Tibetan refugees; but my questions on this subject were plainly regarded as indelicate so I did not pursue the enquiry.

Tonight Mingmar at last knows where we are and says we will be back at base by midday on 24 November. The track from here to Kathmandu is familiar to him, which seems sad; it has been sheer bliss wandering lost-like from mountain to mountain.

22 NOVEMBER – A HOVEL ON A MOUNTAIN-TOP

This is the *most* squalid lodging we have encountered on the whole trek; it is even filthier than the children's hut beside the *gompa*. The small room is windowless and now that darkness has fallen a bullock, four goats, seven hens and a cock are sharing the apartment with a family of six, plus Mingmar and me. Here we are again above 9,000 feet and the night-air is so cold that the door has been shut fast, allowing no outlet for the billowing wood smoke, which is making me cough incessantly and having the usual excruciating effect on my eyes; but as compensation these gentle, cheerful Tamangs are exceptionally likeable, and their anxiety to make me comfortable is all the more touching because of the irredeemable discomfort of their home.

Today's walk was another marathon, and by brunch-time I knew why Mingmar had not been keen on going further yesterday afternoon. We started the day's adventures at 7 a.m. with quite a hazardous fording of a fiercely-fast, waist-deep, icy river. Here Mingmar was the terrified one – for a change – and as we waded across together he clung to me so frantically that he very nearly unbalanced us both. We needed every ounce of our strength to keep upright against the force of the water and it was so extremely difficult to retain a foothold on the large, constantly shifting stones that I didn't really think we could make it without a ducking.

At times the water had been up to our armpits and now we were painfully cold; but that was soon cured by a ninety-minute climb up a precipitous, slippery and very narrow path through dense scrub. Here it was my turn to be terrified; the snag was that I couldn't see the crumbling path through the thick grass and undergrowth – but I could see very plainly the drop on the right, though I didn't dare look down for long enough to estimate its depth.

By about half-past nine we had left this unwholesome path behind and gone downhill again towards the river. We stopped for brunch at a stinking, fly-infested hovel near the junction with the main Kathmandu-Gosainkund Lekh track; and an hour later we were on this highway, sharing it with groups of heavily-laden Tibetans, Tamangs and Chetris and feeling already halfway back to the bustle of metropolitan life.

For the next four hours we continued gradually but steadily downhill, following the river. At times the path led over stretches of colossal boulders, or through bright widths of fine silver sand, and once we crossed a dilapidated suspension bridge that swayed uncertainly 150 feet above the water. One feels slightly impatient about the neglect of these plank bridges; with so much forest on every side there can be no shortage of raw material for their repair.

At three o'clock we reached a village which boasted the first shop seen since our departure from Trisuli. Here we asked for tea, since our own supply expired a few days ago, but the shop stocked only ancient, flyblown, Indian sweets and unsmokable cigarettes and mildewed biscuits – of which we bought two packets for consumption on the spot.

Next we again climbed steeply for three hours – up and up and up, with the shining snow-peaks to the north becoming lovelier every moment. Here the lower, richer slopes are cultivated by Chetris or Newaris and the upper, more barren slopes by Tamangs. The whole region seems very densely populated – and smelly in proportion – when compared with the lonely mountains now behind us. One of the incidental joys of lonely mountains is the absence of that overpowering stench of human excrement which is always present in the more populous parts of Nepal.

These insect-plagued lodgings are beginning to prey slightly on my nerves – and it's not difficult to foresee that tonight is going to be a bug-classic. Since leaving Trisuli I've not had one unbroken night's rest and, though the locals do not suffer to the same extent, I hear them scratching and muttering in their sleep every night. So the bugs must do real damage to health by making sound sleep impossible.

23 NOVEMBER – KATHMANDU

We achieved yet another marathon today, which got us here ahead of schedule – and what a welcome I received from Tashi! Like most Tibetans she is very soft-spoken so she didn't bark or yelp, the only audible sign of rejoicing being that peculiar, rapid sniffling noise with which she always greets my returns; but for the first few moments it seemed that she would wriggle out of her skin with joy, or that her over-wagged tail would come adrift – it's nice to be so important to somebody.

This morning I saw my first total eclipse of the sun, which lasted from about 8.15 until 9.30 – and in honour of which today is yet another public holiday throughout Nepal.

We left our hovel before dawn, since last night even Mingmar was unable to sleep for bugs, and by eight o'clock we had reached the top of a 9,000-foot hill, after an easy climb through crisp, early air. From here we were overlooking a long, deep, narrow valley, and our path now continued almost level for some two miles, before plunging abruptly down to a small village by the river.

As we were scrambling down from the ridge-top to join this path I noticed something very odd about the quality of the light, and simultaneously I registered an unnatural drop in the temperature. Overtaking Mingmar I said, 'What on earth is happening? The light's gone funny, and it's so *cold!*' To this obtuse question a native English-speaker might have been forgiven for replying that nothing was happening *on earth*; but Mingmar merely said, 'The moon is having a meal.' I stared at him for a moment, wondering if he were going dotty – and then I realised that the dottiness was on my side, for when he pointed to the sun I saw that about a quarter of its surface had already been obscured by the 'hungry' moon.

What an appropriate place this was for experiencing the eerieness of a solar eclipse! As we walked along that path, so high above the valley, we could hear conches being blown wildly and cymbals and drums being beaten frenziedly, while all the lamas and priests of the little villages far below shouted and wailed and screamed in their contest with those evil spirits who, by attacking the sun, were threatening the whole of human existence. This extraordinary panic of sounds, combined with the 'evening' twitter of bewildered birds and the unique, greenish half-light, evidently aroused within me some deep racial memory, and for an instant, at the precise moment of total eclipse and estrangement from our whole source of life, I felt as my own that primitive fear which was then dominating the whole of Nepal.

Epilogue

The last days are always sad. One's return is uncertain, but it is wretchedly certain that should one ever return 'all will be changed, changed utterly' in such places as Kathmandu and Pokhara.

Some changes would of course be welcome, especially in relation to the refugees. Their numbers are comparatively few in Nepal and, perhaps because of the scale of the problem, it is easier there than elsewhere to see clearly the fundamental problems inherent in every refugee situation. A consideration of these problems during my time in Pokhara led me to certain unpopular conclusions which have been reinforced, since my return to Europe, by discussions with other fieldworkers on leave from Asia and Africa. To the many generous and sympathetic supporters of Western charitable organisations our views may seem unfeeling, or even shocking. Yet they are based on observations made while sharing the daily life of the refugees – an experience which we hope does not impair our sensibility, though it may purge us of that dangerous sentimentality which so often bedevils the thinking of those who direct refugee aid operations by remote control.

The power of mass media to provoke emotional and ill-considered generosity was plainly shown by the public reaction to the Aberfan disaster, and one finds the same phenomenon, in a less extreme form, throughout the refugee world. Obviously the concern for refugees now felt in the West is stimulated partly by a sincere desire 'to help the less fortunate' and partly by an uneasy awareness that our own society is persistently over-indulging itself in a variety of ways. To give money to charitable organisations is one of the easiest possible methods of lulling one's social conscience, and as some of these organisations become more high-powered, and more ambitious to implement impressive projects abroad, situations can easily arise in which problems are aggravated because of the resources that have been accumulated to deal with them. Already, in certain areas, we are expiating our collective guilt at the expense of the refugees by absurdly prolonging the period during which a particular group is granted refugee status. Materially, and from a short-term point of view, this may be a positive achievement; yet if one looks far enough ahead it is seen to be entirely negative, since excessive cosseting cannot fail to breed a community of parasites.

It should be obvious that our first duty is to help the refugees to help themselves, rather than merely to feed, clothe and nurse them. Immediately after their arrival in a strange land they obviously do need considerable material support, as well as sensible guidance on how best to adjust to their new environment. Yet the essence of a refugee tragedy is not disease, hunger or cold. It is the loss of the emotional security of belonging to a stable community in a certain country, and therefore, in exile, the refugee's most valuable possession is his self-respect – which should be used by us as a tool to help him re-establish his identity as a responsible individual. However, this self-respect is not very highly developed among certain types of refugees and can soon be destroyed by indiscriminate 'aid'. Undoubtedly, less material support from charitable organisations would mean an initial period of greater hardship for most refugee groups; but – supposing the practical advice and reassuring affection of field-workers to be still available – a reduction in aid would also provide a valuable challenge which, if it were met successfully, could rapidly restore the refugees' self-confidence and sense of security. By leaving them in a position where, to survive, they must quickly integrate as productive units in their new environment we would be doing them a far better service than by singling them out for special treatment over an indefinite period – and thus increasing both their own and their neighbours' awareness of the refugee as an 'alien'.

In many cases there are of course innumerable political and economic obstacles to their employment; but these obstacles are not lessened when charitable organisations concentrate hundreds of people in one area. There is some evidence to support the theory that if refugees were to disperse in small groups throughout their host countries – perhaps having received, as aid, a small capital sum per family – they could earn a living much more easily than either they or their Western benefactors are now prepared to admit. In a world where millions are starving unobtrusively in their own countries the refugee 'Big Business' seems to be getting perilously out of proportion. If a million Indians migrated to Burma or Malaya this year, in order to qualify for Red Cross vitamin pills and WVS blankets and US Surplus Food, one could hardly blame them.

During my last week at Kathmandu I sent many frantic cables to New Delhi and Dublin on Tashi's behalf. Her entry-permit from the Irish Department of Agriculture should have been awaiting me at the British Embassy on 23 November; but it wasn't, and our flight home had been booked weeks ago for 3 December, and as time passed I began to detect a certain affinity between the relevant civil servants in Dublin and my friends in the Singha Durbar.

Every morning Tashi accompanied me to the new Indian Aid Telephone and Telegraph Office where, while I drafted progressively less polite messages to Dublin, the clerks eyed her critically and discussed the particular brand of lunacy revealed by a desire to bring any such object back to Ireland. Then, after four days of impoverishing communications, I ended the campaign with a defiant flourish and cabled that a black-and-tan bitch from Nepal would land at Dublin Airport at 3.20 p.m. on 3 December – with or without her visa, which had been applied for in September.

Early on the morning of 29 November Sigrid drove us to Gaucher Airport and soon we were flying parallel to one of the most magnificent sights in the world – the Himalayas seen from the air on a clear winter's day. To east and west they stretched as far as the eye could see, a wild symphony of remote whiteness, beautiful and terrible beyond all imagining. Yet, curiously, this was as imperfect an experience as seeing a tiger in a zoo. Better one glimpse of one peak from the top of a pass that has been struggled against than the whole of this facile, faintly sacrilegious survey from the artificial comfort of an aeroplane.

In Delhi we stayed with friends for a few days – while Tashi received and recovered from her inoculations – and this interlude was no bad thing before a return to Europe. Inevitably it is a shock to leave Nepal, whatever one's destination, and in India I now seemed to be encountering the acme of sophistication, luxury, convenience and reliability. It was a dull world – flat and predictable – for there is today rather less difference between Delhi and Dublin than between Delhi and Kathmandu.

Only after landing in India did I realise how efficiently Nepal insulates its guests against the twentieth century. Unless one belongs to Kathmandu's International Set (which most successfully evades the real Nepal) one unconsciously withdraws, within hours of crossing the frontier, from all the complications of our world. At first a bland fatalism diminishes their importance and then, as one succumbs to the natural isolation of the Kingdom – an isolation now less physical than mental – their reality comes to mean no more than that of Outer Space. Vietnam, war in Kashmir, famine in India, the pound doing odd things in Britain – all quickly recede into the realm of 'What-doesn't-matter-because-nothing-can-be-done-about-it'. Perhaps it is callous to recline comfortably on this indifference. But the fact that in our world millions of citizens are subjected daily to selected details of crises in sixteen different directions seems more likely to dement the citizens than to aid the crises. So now it felt strange indeed to be again Outside, where no mountains of indifference enclose valleys of calm.

In Delhi Tashi showed characteristic Tibetan adaptability, both to her new surroundings and her new friends – as she has continued to do in all her subsequent travels and social contacts. Since her migration to Europe she has been variously described as a 'stocking that was left too long on the needle' and 'something out of the Natural History Museum – perhaps a baby Dinosaur'. But though she will never make Crufts everybody loves her and she loves everybody, which is what matters.

Before leaving Delhi I had bought the statutory 'nose- and paw-proof' basket – but I had also cunningly taken Tashi to Air India's central office and introduced her to the Authorities. Nothing else was necessary; they completely agreed that it would be superfluous to imprison any such object in a basket between Delhi and London and, as there would be some empty seats on the plane, they arranged to have one beside me for the greater comfort of the object in question. So Tashi, born in a Tibetan nomad's tent in the heart of Nepal, now had the run of a Boeing 707.

At Beirut she expressed the need for a grassy spot – and promptly disappeared into the blackness of the night. However, we were already without hope of arriving punctually in London, having been delayed three hours in Bombay because of engine trouble, so the Captain asked the passengers if they would be good enough to forgive another slight delay while Miss Murphy pursued her dog. Fortunately the pursuit did not take long and I soon staggered into the cabin clutching a trembling Tashi, who apparently hadn't much liked what she'd seen of the Lebanon.

At Prague I kept her on her chain, lest she might have anti-Communist prejudices; and at London, feeling bleakly traitorous, I roped her in her basket and handed her over to the waiting RSPCA van which ferried her across to our Aer Lingus plane, where she was ruthlessly consigned to the terrors of the luggage-compartment, despite my pleas that she should be allowed to travel in her basket beside me.

At Dublin Airport I might have been a lion-tamer importing a troupe of man-eaters. Uniformed officials of obscure significance were falling over each other in their anxiety to ensure that the infinitesimal Tashi did not break loose and overnight turn the nation rabid. An absurdly large van stood waiting to transport the basket to the State Quarantine Kennels ten miles north of Dublin, and I was firmly refused permission to accompany Tashi on her journey into the unfamiliar cold wetness of an Irish winter night. However, the kennels are excellently run and, during her long imprisonment, Tashi remained in perfect condition, growing a little more and suffering none of the possible ill-effects of quarantine. On the day of her release she obeyed commands as promptly and took life as calmly as she had ever done – perhaps because I had visited her regularly, taking a book and sitting for a few hours on the straw in her kennel, while she untied my shoe-laces for

Auld Lang Syne. She always greeted my visits with joy, but accepted my departures with composure – and at last came the day when she departed too, into the breezy green fields and bright June sunshine. Nor can the joy she then showed at racing free have been any greater than my own on seeing that little black body again unfurling its ridiculous brown tail in the wind.

A seven months' visit is too brief for the development of a real understanding of any country as alien and complex as Nepal; but it is quite long enough for the visitor to come to love what has been experienced of both the virtues and the faults of this improbable little Kingdom. I am often asked, 'Did you like Nepal?' – to which I usually reply, 'Yes' and leave it at that. But no one merely 'likes' Nepal; Nepal weaves a net out of splendour and pettiness, squalor and colour, wisdom and innocence, tranquillity and gaiety, complacence and discontent, indolence and energy, generosity and cunning, freedom and bondage – and in this bewildering mesh foreign hearts are trapped, often to their own dismay.

There is much to be censured in the Kingdom, and there are many institutions that do need reforming; but to reform them in the image and likeness of the West would be a subtle genocide, for there is much, too, that should be cherished, rather than thrown to the Lions of Progress. However, it is of no avail to think or write thus. The West has arrived in Nepal, bubbling over with good intentions (though the fire that keeps them bubbling may be fed on expediency), and soon our insensitivity to simple elegance, to the proud work of individual craftsmen, and to all the fine strands that go to make up a traditional culture will have spread material ugliness and moral uncertainty like plagues through the land. Already our forward-looking, past-despising 'experts' are striving to help Nepal 'to make up for lost time' by discarding the sound values that lie, half-hidden but still active, beneath 'pagan superstition' – and that would provide a firmer foundation on which to build the new Nepal than our own mass-production code, which makes a virtue of unnecessary earning for the sake of unnecessary spending.

Perhaps nowhere in Asia is the contrast between a dignified, decaying past and a brash, effervescent present as violent as in Nepal; and one knows that here too, eventually, the present will have its shoddy triumph. Yet even when the Nepalese way of life has been annihilated the Himalayas will remain, occasionally being invaded by high-powered expeditions but preserving an inviolable beauty to the end of time.

Index